D1473940

Greece 1941

Greece 1941
The Death Throes of Blitzkrieg

Jeffrey Plowman

Pen & Sword
MILITARY

AN IMPRINT OF PEN & SWORD BOOKS LTD.
YORKSHIRE – PHILADELPHIA

First published in Great Britain in 2018 by
PEN & SWORD MILITARY
An imprint of
Pen & Sword Books Ltd
Yorkshire - Philadelphia

ISBN 9781526730251

A CIP catalogue record for this book is available from the British Library

Typeset in India by Vman Infotech Private Limited

Printed and bound by TJ International

Pen & Sword Books Ltd incorporates the Imprints of Aviation, Atlas, Family
History, Fiction, Maritime, Military, Discovery, Politics, History, Archaeology,
Select, Wharncliffe Local History, Wharncliffe True Crime, Military Classics,
Wharncliffe Transport, Leo Cooper, The Praetorian Press, Remember When,
White Owl, Seaforth Publishing and Frontline Publishing.

For a complete list of Pen & Sword titles please contact

PEN & SWORD BOOKS LTD
47 Church Street, Barnsley, South Yorkshire, S70 2AS, England
E-mail: enquiries@pen-and-sword.co.uk
Website: www.pen-and-sword.co.uk

Or

PEN & SWORD BOOKS
1950 Lawrence Rd, Havertown, PA 19083, USA
E-mail: Uspen-and-sword@casematepublishers.com
Website: www.penandswordbooks.com

Contents

Acknowledgements   vi

List of maps   viii

List of plates   ix

Introduction   xii

Chapter 1   The Road to War   1

Chapter 2   Political Machinations   7

Chapter 3   Operation Lustre   17

Chapter 4   The Fall of Yugoslavia   27

Chapter 5   Breakthrough at Vevi   34

Chapter 6   The Battle for Servia Pass   61

Chapter 7   Repulse at Olympus Pass   83

Chapter 8   A Near Run Thing at Pineios Gorge   97

Chapter 9   The Thermopylae Line   123

Chapter 10   Evacuation   141

Chapter 11   Operation Lustre in Retrospect   162

Appendix I   Composition of Opposing Forces   173

Appendix II   Commonwealth and Axis Commanders   176

Appendix III   Movement of W Force to Greece   186

Appendix IV   British Tank Losses in Greece   188

Appendix V   Embarkations from Greece   190

Appendix VI   Casualties   193

Glossary   194

Notes   196

Bibliography   215

Index   221

Acknowledgements

I am very grateful for the assistance I have received from the many people who have helped me during the preparation of this book, including those who have loaned me books, supplied me with photographs and made available personal stories. I am also grateful to the people who manage the Missing-Lynx website (http://www.missing-lynx.com/), in particular Tom Cockle who hosts the Axis WWII forum, to the people who manage the Axis History Forum (http://forum.axishistory.com/) and to all those who have contributed to discussions relevant to the Greek campaign over the years.

In New Zealand: the veterans Murray Loughnan and Harry Spence; Kate Foster and the late Jean Garner for allowing me to join their interviews with Frank White; Ian Collins, Charlie Grainger (via Phil Deed) Frank Horton and Frank Keyes for photographs; Douglas White for photographs from his father, the late Sir John White's collection; Peter Mossong for access to his photographs; Dr Aaron Fox for critiquing the manuscript and supplying additional materials from his own researches; Tony Ormandy and Peter Scott for German unit histories; Sam Robinson for Hugh Robinson's citation for the Military Cross; Perry Rowe for our many helpful discussions on the campaign; Susan Knight for German translations; Carolyn Carr and Katrina Willougby from the New Zealand Defence Library for the loan of Australian official histories; Heather Mathie from the Alexander Turnbull for photographs; Professor Glyn Harper of Massey University for his editorial assistance. I am particularly grateful to Terry Brown for sourcing material from Archives New Zealand in Wellington, for editorial assistance twice in the early stages of the preparation of the manuscript and for other helpful discussions.

I am also grateful to the help received from sources overseas. Australia: Shane Lovell for accessing files at the Australian War Memorial; Mark McKenzie, Michael Smythe, Larry te Keoti and Doug Sawyer for photographs; the Australian War Memorial for photographs and unit diaries. Greece: Aris Kosionidis for access to his photographs and helping to identify the location of others. England: Lee Archer for photographs; Peter Brown for providing files from the National Archives in England and sourcing material from Harold Charrinton's Archives; for help from the Liddell-Hart Military Archive, King's College, London; Richard Carstens, who made available Jack Elliott's accounts of his time in Greece, through his Our War project; James Payne of the 'Through Their Eyes' Military Photo Archives for Gunter Geuke's photos; Jonathon Holt of the Tank Museum Bovington for photocopies from the history of 5. Panzer-Division. The Netherlands: Karel Magry for locating photographs in the Bundesarchiv, for information on the correct names of German units and locating information on British officers who served in Greece. Germany: Bojan Dimitrijevic from Belgrade, Serbia for the photograph from the Croatia History Museum; Heiner F. Duske for information from Karl-Heinz Golla's book; the Bundesarchiv for photographs; Henning Koehn for German translations. USA: Bob Gregory for making available photographs from his collection.

I am also grateful to my family, Yvonne, Catie and Matthew for their support.

List of maps

1. 9 April 1941 – Initial moves by W Force to deal with the threat from the Monastir Gap
2. 10–14 April 1941 – The retreat of the ANZAC Corps to the new Aliákmon Line
3. 15–16 April 1941 – The German attack falls on the Aliákmon Line
4. 17 April 1941 – The start of the withdrawal of the Anzacs to the Thermopylae Line
5. 18 April 1941 – The critical day
6. 18 April 1941 – The Pineios Gorge attack
7. 24–29 April 1941 – The evacuations from Greece

List of plates

1. Italian infantry on the move into Epirus after their invasion on 28 October 1940.
2. A German light flak unit in Giurgui, Romania guards the pontoon bridge over the Danube.
3. On the evening of 10 April 14. Panzer-Division entered Zagreb to a warm welcome from its Croatian inhabitants.
4. New Zealand troops disembarking at Piræus..
5. A Fairey Fulmar aircraft flies over the British fleet in the Ionian sea off Matapan.
6. From left to right: General Sir Thomas Blamey, Lieutenant General Henry Maitland ('Jumbo') Wilson, General Sir Bernard Freyberg VC.
7. The carrier platoon from 25 NZ Battalion rode on railway flat cars on their way north to Katerini.
8. The SS *Clan Fraser*, which was carrying a load of explosives, is hit by a bomb, only to blow up later that night.
9. Locals look on as a PzKpfw III Ausf H passes the Hamza Bey mosque.
10. German troops inspect some Universal Carrier Mk Is and a Light Tank IIIB 'Dutchman' from 19 Greek Motorised Division at Stavros.
11. Greek civilians working on an anti-tank ditch along the Aliákmon Line.
12. German infantry on the move through a mountain pass in Greece.
13. Troops from 2/2 Australian Battalion crossing the Aliákmon River by ferry on 13 April after pulling out of the Veria Pass.
14. On 13 April the Australians in Servia found themselves having to contend with an endless procession of Greek soldiers and their carts carrying their equipment, which added greatly to the road congestion.
15. A German supply column crosses the Aliákmon River north-east of Lipsista over a bridge repaired by engineers from Leibstandarte SS Adolf Hitler.
16. B Squadron, 3 Royal Tanks were forced to abandon this and another tank in Kozani on the night of 13/14 April.
17. The railway bridge over the Aliákmon River after it was demolished by 2 New Zealand Divisional Cavalry Regiment.

18. A10 Cruiser tank under the command of Lieutenant Robert Crisp from 3 Royal Tanks.
19. A mixed patrol of SdKfz 231 8-rad armoured cars and motorcyclists from Leibstandarte SS Adolf Hitler on the road in Greece.
20. One of the highest 25-pounders in Olympus Pass.
21. New Zealand transport in the vicinity of Mount Olympus.
22. Transport carrying troops from 4 NZ Brigade withdrew from Servia Pass on the morning of 18 April.
23. Two of the victims of 2. Panzer–Division's attack on 21 NZ Battalion's positions at Platamon.
24. On 17 April I/3 Panzer-Regiment lost two tanks while fording the Pineios River and a further two the next day.
25. On 18 April I/3 Panzer-Regiment began to push more tanks across the river along the previously discovered route.
26. Tanks crossing the Pineios River.
27. The evacuation of 26 NZ Battalion from Larissa by train.
28. A Light Mk VIB from 4 Hussars abandoned in Larissa.
29. PzKpfw IIs from I/3 Panzer-Regiment motoring through Larissa at speed.
30. German infantry stop on the side of a road for a meal during their march south.
31. This platoon truck from 26 NZ Battalion took a direct hit from a Stuka.
32. A lone Anzac soldier rests forlornly among some Greek troops after his capture.
33. Robert Crisp and his crew abandoned this A10 cruiser after it threw a track on the road between Larissa and Lamia on 19 April.
34. Abandoned A13 from 1 Armoured Brigade Headquarters Squadron at the Sperchios River.
35. A Universal Carrier Mk I and Marmon-Herrington armoured car from 2 NZ Divisional Cavalry on the road from Volos to Lamia.
36. German troops in captured British vehicles pass a horse-drawn column outside Lamia.
37. PzKpfw III from I/Panzer-Regiment 31 knocked out on the road to Molos.
38. 2 NZ Divisional Cavalry take shelter among trees at Tatoi until dusk when they could make their way through to Athens.
39. On Anzac Day New Zealand troops were given a warm farewell on their way through Athens to their evacuation beaches.
40. Greek troops pass through the 4 NZ Brigade rearguard at Kriekouki.

41. Sturmgeschütze IIIs from StuG–Abt 191 make their way forward.
42. Athens became a trophy city, with rival columns seeking to get there first, eventually falling to the Germans on 27 April.
43. German troops guard both sides of the destroyed bridge over the Corinth Canal.
44. Troops from the Australian 16 and 17 Brigades entering Kalamata on 26 April.
45. After departing from Kalamata a stray bomb from a Stuka damaged the SS *Costa Rica*, causing it to start to sink.
46. RAF personnel were evacuated from Kalamata by Short Sunderland flying boat, this one from 228 Squadron.
47. Infantry from 26 NZ Battalion making their way down to Monemvasia on the evening of 28 April.
48. New Zealand troops rescued from Monemvasia on their way to Crete on HMS *Ajax*.
49. A group of Australian prisoners of war on their way back to Megara after their capture at Corinth.
50. A PzKpfw IV from 3. Panzer-Regiment, 2. Panzer-Division in the process of being loaded onto a freighter at Patras on 19 May.

Introduction

Blitzkrieg. Lightning war. First used in the German periodical *Deutsche Wehr* in 1935, this word was soon taken up by western media to describe the German campaigns in Poland and France. In blitzkrieg the attack, led by a strong force of armoured and motorised infantry backed up by close air support, is used to break into the enemy's line of resistance. While its use in Poland in 1939 and in France the following year are classic examples of it, could the German invasion of Greece be considered another? Certainly, on the face of it this appears to be have been the case: the campaign was over in three weeks after all. But is that a proper measure? What was so important about Greece anyway?

The root cause of the conflict between Greece and Italy in the Second World War lay with the breakup of the Ottoman Empire earlier in the twentieth century. In this Australian and New Zealand (Anzac) troops played a significant part, through their involvement in the ill-fated Dardanelles Campaign in 1915 and later in the thrusts into Ottoman-held Palestine and Mesopotamia between 1916 and 1918. Despite this, it seems unlikely that those soldiers, who came to fight from those far distant lands in the southern hemisphere, would have had any real knowledge of the geopolitics in this region of the eastern Mediterranean. Nor would any of those who arrived in Greece in 1941 have been better informed or have really understood the politics. To start to do so involves going back a little in time.

Around the turn of the nineteenth century the Ottoman Empire was in decline. In 1821 Greece declared their independence from the Ottomans, but it was not until 1827 that it managed to break away after a combined British, French and Russian naval force destroyed an Ottoman and Egyptian armada. The French took control of Algeria in 1830 after blockading Algiers for three years because of what they saw as an insult to their consul in that city. Between 1871 and 1878 Britain and France worked together to prevent Italy gaining control of Tunisia, in exchange for Britain taking over Cyprus. In 1882 they were forced to intervene militarily in Egypt to secure the Suez Canal, resulting in Britain assuming a measure of control over Egypt in conjunction with the Ottomans. However, it was not until 1911 that Italy became interested in another Ottoman possession, Libya, and set about planning an invasion. They eventually sought control over it by presenting an ultimatum to the Ottoman government. The Ottomans countered by offering to transfer control of Libya to Italy, while maintaining suzerainty over it as they had in Egypt. Unhappy with this, the Italians declared war on the Ottomans in September that year, invading and securing Tripoli the following month. From there they extended their control into Cyrenaica, defeating the Ottoman naval forces in the process. In the summer of 1912 Italy took over the Dodecanese islands from the Ottomans, returning control of them to the Ottomans by treaty in October 1912 in return for the Ottomans withdrawing all military personnel from Libya.

When war was declared in 1914 the Greeks were slow to join the effort against Germany and Austria-Hungary. While King Constantine wanted to remain neutral, Prime Minister Eleftherios Veneizelos preferred to fight; a situation that changed when Constantine was forced to abdicate. As a result of their joining the war, the Greeks were promised territorial gains at the expense of the Ottoman Empire by their western Allies. These included eastern Thrace and parts of western Anatolia around the city of Smyrna, even though the latter was part of the territory promised to Italy. After Italy walked out of the Paris Peace Conference in 1919 the British persuaded France and the United States to support Greece's interest in western Anatolia.

This did not guarantee Greece success in its territorial ambitions. In May 1919 the Greeks occupied Smyrna with the support of the French and British. Over the following summer they extended their control over all of Western and most of north-western Anatolia, concluding this by the signing of a treaty with the Ottomans. With British encouragement the Greeks advanced further into Anatolia. Meeting little resistance from the Turks, they continued to do so despite their own internal political ructions. In 1921 the tide began to turn against the Greeks. This prompted the French and Italians, who had been surreptitiously supporting the Turkish revolutionaries, to withdraw their troops at a crucial stage of the Greek advance, leaving them exposed. Taking advantage of this situation the Turks hit back, eventually retaking Smyrna in September. From there they launched an advance towards the Dardanelles and the Bosphorus. The British initially sought to resist this advance, but when the French and Italian troops abandoned their positions there the British had no choice but to seek armistice talks. At the conclusion of this Britain, France and Italy retained control of eastern Thrace and the Bosphorus, forcing the Greeks to evacuate their troops.

While this may have been a source of irritation between Greece and Italy, direct conflict between them can be traced back to 1914. Albania came into existence in 1913 at the end of the Balkan Wars. The following year the ethnic Greeks within it proclaimed the Autonomous Republic of Northern Epirus, which was recognised by the Albanian government through to the commencement of the First World War when Greek republics collapsed. The Greeks occupied this area until they were driven out by the Italians in 1917. They were then awarded it at the Paris Peace Conference in 1919, but it reverted to Albanian control at the end of their war with Turkey. In 1923 the League of Nations was forced to intercede over a boundary dispute in Albania by sending a commission headed by General Enrico Tellini. When Tellini and three of his assistants were murdered, the then new Italian prime minister, Fascist Benito Mussolini, sent an ultimatum to Greece demanding reparations and the execution of the killers. When Greece was unable to identify them, the Italians bombarded and occupied the island of Corfu. The Italians eventually withdrew after the Greeks agreed to the terms of settlement set out by the League of Nations. There followed a period of normalization between Italy and Greece that culminated in the signing of a friendship treaty between them in 1928.

There was a steady political shift towards Fascism in Italy over the following years. Moreover, in their relations with other members of the League of Nations and former allies, notably Britain, Italy had become somewhat resentful over its treatment after the First World War. In particular this related to a promise of control of land along the former Austro-Hungarian border, a central protectorate in Albania and parts of the former Ottoman Empire. Britain and France had reason to regret those promises. This was because of their view that during the war Italy had botched attacks on Austro-Hungary, had failed to honor naval promises and repeatedly asked for resources which they never used in the war. Instead all Italy received was the territories of the Trentino and Tyrol, a permanent seat at the League of Nations and a share of the German reparations, with which they were bitterly disappointed. All they did manage to do was to take over and hold the port of Fiume in Croatia for a short while. This national resentment continued to simmer and was later most effectively exploited by Mussolini.

As late as 1935, when Italian forces in Eritrea and Somalia invaded Ethiopia in an effort to further expand their empire, Italy was still regarded as friendly by Britain. This action prompted the League of Nations to impose limited economic sanctions on Italy, though nothing was ever done about it. The outbreak of the Spanish Civil War in 1937 saw a further shift in relations with Italy. This resulted from an offer of direct support from Mussolini to General Francisco Franco and, later, recognition of his regime. The formation of the Rome–Berlin axis in 1936 was also cause for concern. Fears were temporarily eased the next year by the signing of the Anglo-Italian Joint Declaration in January. Nevertheless, relations continued to deteriorate, with hostile references to the British in the Italian press. At the same time there were signs of an Italian naval build up in the Mediterranean and in their armed forces in Libya. To this the British responded by strengthening their defences in the Mediterranean and the Red Sea. The final straw came at the end of 1937 when Italy joined Germany and Japan in their Anti-Comintern Pact and withdrew from the League of Nations.

Italy's next act in the Mediterranean followed on from Germany's annexation of Austria in March 1938. Jealous of this, and in a move not predicted by British Intelligence, Italy sent troops into Albania on 7 April 1939. Within two days they had occupied the capital, Tirana, forced the king to flee to Greece and taken control of Albania's external affairs. The British response, while not wanting to provoke Italy, was to begin moving its fleet as unostentatiously as possible to Alexandria. Within a week of this they announced their promise to the Greeks and Romanians to do all they could to help maintain their independence. Five days later Britain reached an agreement with Turkey to cooperate in the event that the latter was threatened in any way. A similar agreement was reached between France and Turkey a month later.

Chapter 1

The Road to War

At the start of the Second World War Britain and France offered to support Greece against the Axis powers. At the time Britsh concern over the increasing level of rhetoric directed against them from Italy was tempered by the hope that they would not be forced into war against Italy so long as they were not openly antagonistic. Intelligence sources also told them that, at this stage, Italy was quite unprepared for war and would prefer neutrality. It was, in fact, favourable neutrality that Mussolini offered to the chancellor of Germany, Adolf Hitler, on the eve of its invasion of Poland.[1] Thus, the strategy of Britain and France was one of non-provocation by containing Italy in the Mediterranean through command of the Suez Canal, the Straits of Gibraltar and their joint naval control of the Mediterranean. By this means they could deny Italy access to its territories in East Africa and potentially its sources of raw materials in the Black Sea, particularly oil. They also saw the need to provide some guarantees to Yugoslavia, as failing to do so could lead to a collapse of their influence in the Balkans. Worse still, Yugoslavia, and even Turkey, might come to an understanding with Germany. Turkey's position was also crucial because of its command of the Dardanelles and the Bosphorus. This, along with the Corinth Canal in Greece, was the principal supply route for Italy's source of raw materials. If Turkey could be brought alongside the Allied cause, it would place a further stranglehold on the Italians. The strategic importance of Crete was also recognised by the British, but they realised that sending a small force there would compromise Greek neutrality and provoke Mussolini into declaring war.[2]

The reality, however, was that Britain, in particular, lacked the men and materiel to back up its guarantees of support to these countries, something which was readily apparent to Greece, Yugoslavia and Turkey. The Royal Air Force, equipped mostly with antiquated aircraft, was barely strong enough to carry out its primary role in the Mediterranean.[3] The British army was weak and badly dispersed, with troops in Gibraltar, Malta, Aden, British Somaliland, Kenya, Palestine and Egypt. Britain was also facing an increase of hostility within Iraq. At least in Egypt they had 7 Armoured

Division, fourteen battalions of British infantry and two artillery regiments.[4] Additional troops were on offer from Australia, New Zealand, India and South Africa.[5]

In May 1940 the British ambassador in Rome reported that, though Italy's armed forces were fully prepared for war, it was losing strength month by month, with stocks of all raw materials, except oil, low.[6] Not that this was enough to deter Mussolini from joining the war on Hitler's side. It was only after Germany had overrun the Low Countries, much of northern France and had turned its attention to Paris that the Italians played their hand, declaring war on France on 10 June.[7] As it turned out, this was very much an attempted territorial grab. Not a great deal happened until after the signing of the Armistice between France and Germany on 21 June. Then, when Italy launched its offensive, it quickly stalled after penetrating only a few kilometres into France.

With France out of the picture Britain found itself in a decidedly difficult situation. The Royal Navy could no longer blockade the German and Italian fleets, while the balance of naval power in the Mediterranean had shifted in Italy's favour.[8] Not only that, but they now faced potentially hostile forces in France's territories in the Mediterranean. Britain had also lost a sizeable quantity of men and equipment in France, which they had to make good, particularly as they were now facing a possible invasion by Germany. Nevertheless, the Middle East Command was starting to benefit considerably from the influx of Commonwealth troops. These included 4 Indian Division, which had been formed in Egypt in 1939, 6 and 7 Australian Divisions of the Australian Imperial Force (AIF) and 2 New Zealand Expeditionary Force, the first echelon of which arrived in Egypt in February 1940.[9]

The Middle East Command was also not slow in taking action after the Italians entered the war, though their Mediterranean Fleet had mixed results initially. Working with the French navy until France capitulated, they had some successes and were able to take a heavy toll on Italian merchant shipping.[10] By the end of July, after a series of running battles with elements of the Italian fleet, the British had also obtained a measure of ascendancy over them.[11] They had even more success in the Red Sea, clearing it of Italian submarines in short order. The one downside of this was the diversion to England of 5 NZ Brigade and 18 and 25 Australian Brigades. The RAF also became active from their airstrips in Egypt, targeting Italian-controlled subsidiary ports within range, such as Tobruk, Italian forts and troop concentrations. The Italians were slower to respond and when they did it became apparent that the RAF Gladiators were too slow to intercept the Italian bombers. A measure of how poorly equipped the RAF was can be seen in the fact that of the four Hawker Hurricanes in Egypt, the RAF only had access to one of them. However, by operating it out of different airstrips the Italians became totally confused as to how many the British had.[12] General Archibald Wavell, General Officer Commander-in-Chief, Middle East Command, also ordered the Western Desert Force into the desert. On 12 June his main striking force, 7 Armoured Division, set about dominating the Libyan side of the frontier with Egypt with lightning raids against Italian forts or units in the open desert.[13]

Unfortunately, Wavell's efforts to goad the Italians in Libya into a running fight fell a little flat. In fact, in July, the Italians seemed more interested in their east African protectorate and, having settled the situation in French Somaliland in their favour, began to attack border posts in British Somaliland. At the beginning of August this turned into a full invasion that saw it fall to the Italians on 19 August. One immediate consequence of this was the diversion of the leading brigade of 5 Indian Division, en route to Egypt, to Port Sudan and the dispatch of an artillery regiment and two anti-tank guns from Egypt.[14]

After the fall of France, Mussolini started to give serious thought to invading Yugoslavia or Greece as a way of improving Italy's strategic position in the Mediterranean. However, when Hitler made it clear that he did not wish to see the war spread to the Balkans, Mussolini turned his attention to Libya. This was despite the fact that Hitler was in the process of forcing Romania to cede territories claimed by Hungary and Bulgaria in order to curry their favour, because of a desire to maintain peace in the Balkans at any cost. Ultimately he wanted to bring the Balkans in under the Axis umbrella. The first stage of this he achieved in August with the cessation of southern Dobruja to Bulgaria on 21 August and one-third of Transylvania to Hungary nine days later.[15]

It had been Mussolini's intention to launch his assault on Egypt after the Germans landed in England, but when this did not happen he ordered Marshall Rodolfo Graziani to attack on 9 September. The start was hardly auspicious, as one unit lost its way on the approach to its assembly point. Graziani was disturbed by reports of a massive British concentration of armour to the south and in the end confined his movement to the coast road. In fact the British, having previously withdrawn the bulk of their armour to Mersa Matruh, were employing only the support group of 7 Armoured Division, backed up by part of a cruiser tank battalion. In the end it was a somewhat lacklustre offensive and, after reaching Sidi Barrani, the Italians halted and dug in. There they chose to wait until their engineers could extend a road and a water pipeline from Cyrenaica.[16]

Despite this shift of emphasis Mussolini had not given up on Greece. There were several reasons for this. On a number of occasions Hitler had agreed that the Mediterranean and Adriatic were exclusively Italian spheres of influence. As a result Mussolini took umbrage at Hitler's occupation of Romania at the beginning of October. After consulting with both the governor and military commander of Albania, Mussolini received assurances from them that they saw no problem in securing Corfu and the coastal sector of Epirus in a surprise attack. An additional advantage was that the Italians would not require German help. As a prerequisite Mussolini required that Graziani take Mersa Matruh, in the hope that this would prevent the British sending troops to help the Greeks. So when Graziani showed no inclination to comply, Mussolini stepped up his invasion plans, reinforcing the five divisions in Albania with three more.[17]

Though it was late in the season to start a war, Italy sent an ultimatum to the Greek government at 3am on 28 October, demanding that they be allowed to occupy certain facilities in Greece. This the Greek prime minister General Ioannis Metaxas rejected, and at 6am Italian troops crossed the frontier into Epirus. The immediate response of the British was to occupy Crete, dispatching a naval force with a battalion of infantry on board, with the view to securing Suda Bay for their own use. By 3 November they had set up anti-submarine defences, begun upgrading the airfield at Heraklion for Blenheims and commenced work on a new airfield at Maleme.[18] With the British taking over the defence of Crete, Metaxas withdrew the Crete Division from the island and sent it to Epirus.[19]

The Germans had never been entirely happy with the Italian plan, believing that the strategically important regions of the Balkans needed to be secured by a blitzkrieg-type operation. As the Germans saw it these did not lie in Albania, but in southern Greece and on Crete. They considered the Italian failure to take Crete to be a strategic blunder, as the British defences on the island threatened the Italian lines of communication to North Africa and strengthened the British lines of communication to Greece. As Hitler said to Mussolini in a letter written on 20 November 1940:

> I wanted, above all, to ask you to postpone the operation until a more
> secure favourable season, in any case until after the presidential
> election in America. In any event I wanted to ask you not to

undertake this action without previously carrying out a blitzkrieg operation on Crete. For this purpose I intended to make practical suggestions regarding the employment of a parachute and of an airborne operation.[20]

Hitler had another reason for being upset with Mussolini's attack on Greece. The British bombers dispatched to Crete were now within range of the Romanian airfields that Hitler had coveted for so long. Thus, four days after the British occupation of Crete, he ordered the *Oberkommando der Wehrmacht* (OKW) to prepare plans for the invasion of northern Greece from Romania via Bulgaria.

On 16 December the British Middle East Command dispatched Barbarity Force to Greece. Among the units sent over was a squadron of Bristol Blenheim light bombers and a squadron of Hurricanes, which were dispersed to airfields around Athens. The Army provided some troops who were entrusted with the job of establishing a base near Athens that could be expanded to accommodate two divisions, a fact that was to be kept from the Greeks.[21] Eventually the British War Cabinet authorized the dispatch of a squadron of antiquated Gladiator biplane fighter and three bomber squadrons. These were to be followed by a Hurricane squadron once anti-aircraft defences had been installed at the airfields, the latter at the expense of Britain's own air defences.[22]

Meanwhile, in Epirus the Italians, having met with some success initially, soon found their dreams of pushing south to Athens tempered by the strong resistance put up by the Greeks. In part this was because the Italians' success in securing a bridgehead over the Kalamas River was not exploited by Centauro Division's armour. It also did not help that in the Pindus Range their alpine troops got to within 12 miles of the Metsovon Pass only to be sent back in full retreat when the Greeks counter-attacked. The Greeks then launched a counter-offensive of their own, driving the Italians out of Epirus and carrying the fight into Albania.[23]

Worse still, with the Italian fleet concentrated at Taranto, the British chose this moment to launch an assault on it. Thus, on the night of 11 November, while some bombers launched a diversionary raid on an oil-storage depot, two waves of Swordfish torpedo-bombers from the carrier HMS *Illustrious* swept in on the main anchorage of the Italian fleet. Though two Swordfish were lost, half of the Italian fleet was put out of action, including three battleships, two of them rendered unusable for six months, while one battleship never saw service again.[24]

In October the British found out through Ultra decrypts of Italian army signals that a German army delegation had visited Graziani at his headquarters.[25] Led by General Wilhelm von Thoma, this had been sent with the express purpose of determining whether, with suitable reinforcements, the Italians could reach the Suez Canal. At the same time Hitler met with Mussolini at the Brenner Pass, where he made an offer of mechanized and specialist troops, which the latter politely refused on the basis that they were not needed until after the capture of Mersa Matruh, something that was in fact supported by von Thoma in his final report.[26]

In the end the Italians never had the chance to pursue their aims in Egypt as Wavell had no intention of leaving the initiative with them. So on 9 December 4 Indian Division, supported by 7 Royal Tank Regiment, under Lieutenant General Richard O'Connor, overran a series of fortified camps the Italians had built to the east of Sidi Barrani. Caught on the back foot, the Italians fell back and under renewed pressure from O'Connor's forces were soon in full retreat along the coast. By 15 December Sollum and Halfaya Pass had been captured, followed by Bardia on 6 January 1941 to 6 Australian Division under Major General Iven MacKay. Tobruk fell on 22 January.[27] Then, while thrusting westwards along the coast towards Derna, the British learned from an Ultra Sigint that the Italians were planning to abandon Benghazi. This prompted O'Connor to launch a second thrust inland,[28] which brought 4 Armoured Brigade to Beda Fomm on 5 February, where in a two-day running battle they overcame the retreating Italians.[29]

Chapter 2

Political Machinations

The British occupation of the area around Mersa Brega in February 1941 marked the high tide of O'Connor's desert offensive. A week after the fighting had died away at Beda Fomm the first elements of Deutsches Afrikakorps under Generalleutnant Erwin Rommel arrived in Tripoli as part of Operation Sonnenblume.[1] This was a result of a decision made a month earlier by Hitler to dispatch 5. Leichte-Division to Tripoli to act as a blocking force to shore up the Italian defence of Libya. Though the British did not find out about their actual presence in Libya until 20 February, they had been aware that the Germans had been planning something like this for some time, thanks to Ultra and other intelligence sources. By the middle of November there was evidence of the arrival of German units, including armour, in Italy. In January 1941 the Poles had sent information via the Security Intelligence Service, listing the movement of German stores and equipment suitable for African conditions on Italian railways. On top of this air reconnaissance had reported the concentration of half a million tons of shipping in Naples.[2] The fact that the British chose to dismiss this intelligence was possibly because the shipping, at least, could be there for the evacuation of Italian forces from Tripolitania. Nevertheless, the simple fact remains that British attention had shifted towards the Balkans.

German attention had shifted to the Balkans as well. As early as November 1940 Hitler had started to lay down plans for the invasion of Greece, with the view to securing his southern flank before his projected invasion of Russia. He also had some concerns about Russia's intentions in the Balkans, with good reason. While Germany was overrunning the Low Countries and France, Russia had forced Romania to hand over Bessarabia and northern Bukovina. More recently the Russians had moved some troops to the mouth of the Danube River. At this stage, though, German plans for Greece were limited to taking over its northern Aegean littoral region, the occupation of Romania being the first stage of that. For this the *OKW* had initially allocated three or four divisions, a figure that Hitler raised to ten divisions on 12 November.[3] In order to pursue his aims in Greece Hitler also needed free passage of his troops through Hungary. He achieved the first stage of this on 20 November when the Hungarian premier signed the Tripartite Pact in Berchtesgaden. Hitler also used this occasion to let the Hungarians know that he intended to assist the Italians against the Greeks.[4]

This subtle change in German interest in Greece soon became apparent to the British from Enigma decrypts to and from the Luftwaffe mission in Romania in the last week in December 1940. This intelligence revealed a shift from straight air defence of oil installations to something more serious, such as the transfer of a number of 12. Armee cooperation staff to southern Romania, three specifically trained for working with panzer formations. This was also accompanied by the build-up of Fliegerkorps VIII there. What was significant was that the British chose to take more notice of these activities in Romania than those in North Africa, reading more into German plans than their intelligence had determined. The thinking of the British chiefs of staff was that this represented a strategic threat, ultimately, to their forces in the Middle East, while Wavell merely saw it as a feint designed to draw their attention away from Libya.[5] There was also the first reference in the Enigma decrypts to something known as Operation Marita, Hitler's plan for the invasion of Greek Macedonia.[6]

At the end of December the British minister in Budapest reported an increase in German rail movement, sufficient for the movement of twenty divisions. Among the first loads being transported was the heavy bridging equipment needed for crossing the Danube. Work on the bridges was supposed to start early in January by engineers who had been sent to Romania, but snowdrifts delayed the arrival of the bridging equipment and as a result work did not start for another month.[7] Unbeknown to the British, Hitler was bringing pressure to bear on Bulgaria to join the Tripartite Pact, something that the Bulgarians continued to resist strongly because of their fears about Russia and Turkey. They were, however, willing to allow the passage of German troops through their country if the Germans chose to attack Greece.[8]

With winter now at its height, the Greek forces were struggling in Albania, frostbite being prominent among their problems, but there were also growing shortages of materiel, particularly clothing and ammunition.[9] These shortcomings were still evident to the New Zealanders who arrived in Greece in April 1941, as Jack Elworthy later recalled from an encounter with some Greek soldiers:

> we talked with the soldiers and exchanged cigarettes. They showed
> us their rifles and ammunition. The bullets were marked on the

base of the cartridge case with the year of manufacture and that year was 1881. It was now 1941. We asked ourselves what chance these poor devils had against Hitler's modern army, with its fast moving Panzer corps and front-line troops with tommy guns.[10]

The receipt of Enigma decrypts on 9 January 1940 revealed the arrival of more Luftwaffe personnel in Romania. This led the British chiefs of staff to conclude that the Germans intended to attack Greece on the 20th of that month. As a result Wavell and Air Chief Marshall Arthur Longmore flew to Athens on 13 January. In their subsequent meetings with Metaxas and the Greek Commander-in-Chief, General Alexander Papagos, the British delegation said they would divert a shipment of trucks to Greece and, later, to supply as many captured Italian vehicles as soon as they could. Unfortunately, there was little the British could do about ammunition for the French weaponry with which the Greeks were equipped; they did send over what clothing and blankets they could make available from their reserve stocks. Longmore offered to dispatch one squadron of Blenheims and two more fighter squadrons. This was all he considered Greece could support until more airfields were completed south of Mount Olympus. When it came to ground forces all the British could offer was a tank regiment, along with some anti-tank, artillery and anti-aircraft units.

The Greeks were not happy with this. While they were prepared to welcome British assistance, it had to be in sufficient numbers to act offensively. In their view what the British were offering would just provoke a German attack. In reality the Greeks were more interested in clearing up the situation in Albania, as this would allow them to release troops for the Bulgarian front. Wavell was clearly displeased with this, particularly the Greek desire to base British forces around Salonika. Nor was he much impressed by the British government's request for him to secure the Dodecanese Islands, particularly Rhodes, to prevent their use by the Luftwaffe. This was because the resources for this would have to come from the already thinly-spread forces in the Middle East and he had precious little to spare. Wavell was instructed that Greece was to take priority over the Middle East after the capture of Tobruk. Fortunately for Wavell, and something that he exploited to its fullest extent, this was not to stand in the way of an advance to Benghazi should this prove feasible. Nevertheless, in preparation for a possible Greek venture Wavell was to assemble a reserve of specialized mechanized and air force units out of his existing forces.[11]

The matter would have ended there had Metaxas not died suddenly on 29 January. His successor, Alexander Koryzis, was also adamant that no British troops should be sent to Macedonia until such time as the Germans crossed the Romanian frontier into Bulgaria. However, on 8 February he indicated that he was willing to reopen negotiations with the British; he also wanted to encourage Yugoslavian and Turkish participation.[12] Thus began another round of talks, around the time that it was becoming apparent that the Italian threat in East Africa would have to be dealt with, particularly if Britain wanted to secure its supply route through the Red Sea. The start of that operation was eventually fixed for 11 February, but on the basis of Wavell's force only occupying Eritrea. At this stage there was still the likelihood that two or three of the brigade groups he proposed to send would have to be withdrawn once that had been achieved.[13]

On 14 February the Defence Committee in London informed Wavell that he was to hold Cyrenaica as a secure flank with minimum forces, while he put together the force for Greece. For this he settled on Brigadier Harold Charrington's 1 Armoured Brigade, Major General Bernard Freyberg's 2 NZ Division, 6 Australian Division in Cyrenaica and Lieutenant General John Lavarack's 7 Australian Division in Palestine. On the Cyrenaican front he proposed to withdraw 7 Armoured Division to Egypt to refit, replacing it with 2 Armoured Division, while 9 Australian Division in Palestine was to replace 6 Australian Division. The Defence Council did offer Wavell 50 Infantry Division, but at the expense of 15,000 corps and administration units. This Wavell refused because of his need for lines of communication and transportation units to maintain his forces in Cyrenaica.[14]

As it so happened, all this coincided with a visit to the Middle East by the Australian prime minister, Robert Menzies. He was on a mission to London to seek more reinforcements for Australia in the event that Japan proved hostile.[15] On 10 February he met with Wavell, and talked about the need to keep the AIF together. Wavell's response to this was that it might not always be possible; instead he talked about having a certain amount of latitude with the deployment of Australian troops. After the meeting Wavell reported to Winston Churchill, the British prime minister, that Menzies was 'very ready to agree' to the Greece venture. Afterwards Menzies flew to Tobruk, and the next day to Benghazi, where he discussed Wavell's comments with Lieutenant General Thomas Blamey, commander of the AIF. Blamey expressed the view that the Australian forces need to be treated as under national command. Menzies returned to Cairo and two days later Wavell told him of their plans for supporting Greece. While it is not known what transpired at the meeting, it appears that Menzies did not say anything to block Wavell's plans to deploy Australian troops there. He did, however, write to Wavell later to remind him that Blamey would have to agree to any plan to break up the AIF.[16]

Blamey found out about British plans for Greece from his Australian liaison officer at GHQ on his return on 17 February. This was the same day that Wavell informed Freyberg that his division was to be sent to Greece.[17] When Freyberg raised objections he was told that the New Zealand government had agreed to the proposal. This was a lie, as no such approach had been made.[18] Freyberg was also told not to discuss it with anyone else except Blamey and, despite his doubts about the venture, made no attempt to contact the New Zealand prime minister, Peter Fraser.[19] As Freyberg was to say later:

> The decision to go to Greece was taken on a level we could not touch. ...I was never in a position to make a well informed and responsible judgment. ...Wavell told me our Government agreed. ...Wavell had established the right to deal with the New Zealand Government, without letting me know what was happening. ...We should have cabled them.[20]

Though this was partly a result of Wavell's warning, it was also because the charter Freyberg had signed with the New Zealand government limited his direct access to them to communicating matters of training, administration and policy. In truth it was a complicated arrangement. Freyberg was to take his orders from his commanding officer, in this case Wavell, but his actions were subject to the wishes of the New Zealand government. The New Zealand government, in turn, had the right to discuss with the British government matters of policy and, if necessary, consult with Freyberg.[21] Unfortunately, at this stage of the war Freyberg was still feeling his way with this arrangement.

Blamey was no more impressed than Freyberg with the Greek operation when he met with Wavell the following day.[22] When Blamey suggested that the matter should be referred to the Australian government, Wavell told him that it had already been discussed with Menzies.[23] Curiously, though Blamey had reservations about the whole operation, he did not attempt to contact Menzies at this time. (Instead he waited until 5 March to send a letter to Menzies expressing his disquiet about the operation, a letter that did not reach Menzies until 18 April, the day the British began planning the evacuation of troops from Greece.[24]) Menzies and his party flew on to London, arriving on 20 February. That same day the British decided to cable Australia regarding their negotiations with the Greek and Turkish governments over future support.[25] Apparently, though, there was no attempt to contact the New Zealand government at this stage.[26]

While Menzies was on his way to London, Churchill's foreign secretary, Anthony Eden, and Chief of Imperial General Staff, General Sir John Dill were on their way to Cairo. From there they flew onto Athens with Wavell on the 22nd where, before negotiations had even begun, Koryzis handed two documents to Eden, both of which reiterated the Greek view of the danger of sending an inadequate force. Of particular note was their view that unless insufficient forces were sent the Yugoslavs and Turks could not be persuaded to become involved and would instead remain neutral.[27] The Greeks considered that nothing less than ten divisions would be adequate, knowing full well that the British did not have them available. However, in the end they accepted the British offer of three divisions and an armoured brigade, as well as their choice of commander of the new force, General Henry 'Jumbo' Maitland Wilson. That was probably the first and only thing both really agreed on. While the Greeks were willing to admit that Macedonia and Eastern Thrace would be difficult to defend, even more so after the transfer of troops from there to the Albanian front, they still saw some value in holding it, if only to supply the Yugoslavs through Salonika. In fact they had started work on a defensive line along the line of the Struma River, near the Metaxas Line. What the British favoured was a line that ran further back, along the northern slopes of Mount Olympus through the Vermion Range and then north-westwards to the Yugoslav border, the so-called Aliákmon Line. This was because it would allow them to unload their troops at Pireaus and Volos and use their mobile forces in front to delay the advance of the Germans. Ultimately, both the Greeks and British agreed that the Aliákmon Line was the only one that met both political and military considerations. For this the Greeks maintained that they needed a minimum of eight divisions, with one in reserve. Despite this Papagos was still not happy with this new defensive line, desiring a line further forward that included Salonika.[28] An unfortunate consequence of this was that the British delegation left Greece on the 23rd under the impression that the Greeks were going to withdraw from their forward positions to the line the British favoured. The Greeks, however, did not see it this way. Instead they considered that this was dependent on the outcome of negotiations with the Yugoslavs and Turks, something Eden and Dill were tasked to investigate after their return to Cairo.[29]

One thing that had particularly upset Blamey was the news that Wilson had been named as head of the expeditionary force to Greece. He argued with Wavell that, as the bulk of the fighting troops were from Australia and New Zealand, he should have been considered for command. Wavell countered by saying that the Australian contribution to the force was only one-third of the total, though where he obtained the total figure of 126,000 is not clear.[30] Blamey was of the view that this was basically an estimate, and that some of the British units included did not exist at this point in time.[31] Not that it made a lot of difference: Wavell could not be moved on that point.

The same day that Eden, Dill and Wavell returned to Cairo, Churchill outlined the plan for Greece with Menzies. This he reiterated the following day when Menzies attended the War Cabinet meeting. When asked for Australian support, Menzies replied that he would have to consult with his own War Cabinet.[32] It was at this point that the decision was made to send formal cables seeking permission from both the Australian and New Zealand governments, both being dispatched on the 25th. The New Zealand government responded that they were in favour so long as the division was fully equipped and accompanied by the armoured brigade.[33] The Australian War Cabinet, however, decided that they needed to consult with Menzies. Frederick Shedden, the Secretary for the Department of Defence, who had accompanied Menzies, felt that Blamey should be consulted. This was after the vice chief of naval staff had expressed the opinion that the Greek expedition would end in an evacuation. With this in mind he prepared a cable to send to Blamey. That same day Menzies received a cable from Blamey raising his concerns over the command of what was then being referred to as Lustreforce, listing the units allocated to the Greek venture. Menzies took it from this cable that it was obvious Blamey was being consulted, and so Sheddon's cable was not sent. Thus, thanks to a series of misunderstandings between Menzies, Blamey and the Australian government of what was going on, Churchill obtained approval from them for the Greek venture.[34]

Eden and Dill's mission to Turkey was less successful. After hearing of British plans to assist the Greeks militarily, the Turkish government were adamant that they intended to remain loyal to their alliance with Britain and would defend themselves if attacked. They felt that their best option was to stay out of the war as long as possible. They also expressed the view that they would only enter it once their deficiencies in armour and aircraft had been made good.[35] At least this was something the British commanders-in-chief agreed with, as they felt that Turkey within their alliance could even be a military liability.[36] While Eden and Dill were in Ankara the Yugoslav ambassador delivered a message from his government that effectively ruled out any involvement by them. On Eden and Dill's return to Athens on 2 March they learned that Papagos had not withdrawn from the Albanian and Bulgarian fronts. This was what they had assumed would happen once the movement of British troops to Greece had begun. It turned out that Papagos's understanding was that this was dependent on whether Yugoslavia would agree to enter the war on their side. Certainly the failure to get Turkey on their side was a factor in Papagos's decision, but it soon became apparent that there were other things at work here. It transpired that Papagos was not willing to authorize this withdrawal because of the effect it could have on the people in Macedonia and Thrace, and on the morale of their troops in Albania. There was also the fear that they could be caught by the Germans as they were withdrawing, particularly now that the Germans had started to enter Bulgaria.[37] When the British refused to defend a position north of the Aliákmon Line he suggested a compromise, offering to divert some troops that were on their way to the Nestos Line. Eventually, on 4 March and with some misgivings, the British agreed to this plan.[38]

Nevertheless, the British were still keen to obtain the support of the Yugoslavs. The question was how to approach them. Eden considered that going to Belgrade would be regarded as provocative by the Germans.[39] Instead, while in Athens, he made a further attempt to contact their government via the British ambassador in Belgrade, without any success. At that stage the Yugoslavs were under pressure from Germany to join their Tripartite Pact. The trouble was that with the Serbians in the south favouring the Allies, and the Croatians in the north more sympathetic to the Axis, they could not reach a unified position. A meeting was arranged between Eden and a member of the Yugoslav general staff on 8 March in Athens, but this was inconclusive, as he had no authority to discuss Yugoslavian plans. In fact, the only reason he was there was to ascertain what materiel support the British could provide. Among them was the question of whether Salonika could be used as a southern base for their armies and what naval support the British could give them for evacuating their troops. This was something that the British were not in a position to do.[40]

These disturbing changes, coupled with evidence of the landing of German armour in Tripoli, necessitated a re-evaluation of the venture. Admiral Cunningham was confident that he could protect the convoys going to Greece, so long as they were subject to air attacks. Air Marshall Longmore, on the other hand, was now expressing grave doubts about his ability to deal with the German air force. At least the CIGS and the Middle

East commanders-in-chief were in agreement that it would be possible to extricate the bulk of the force should things go wrong.[41] Churchill even wondered whether emphasis should be shifted back to Libya. This led to more cables being sent to the Australian and New Zealand governments seeking their approval. Now, however, the British position had shifted their argument from one of establishing a front in the Balkans to that of the 'overwhelming moral and political repercussions of abandoning Greece'. In spite of this, both governments reaffirmed their support for the operation. In a parting shot Blamey further muddied the waters by cabling the Australian Minister for the Army on 9 March setting out his concerns and expressing his view that: 'Military operation extremely hazardous in view of the disparity between opposing forces in number and training'.[42] Though this cable was the cause of considerable concern to the Australian government, nothing was done about it. Blamey's actions did not go down well with Wavell either. At a subsequent meeting with Blamey, Wavell made it clear that his views would not be further sought on the operation.[43] By then it was too late anyway: the first troops were on their way to Greece.

Thus, by a convoluted process the British achieved what they had always wanted to do – provide troops for the defence of Greece – even though there was quite some fluidity in their reasons for doing so. Unfortunately it appeared that they had turned a blind eye to the true nature of Greek capabilities. While it was probably easy for the British to see the war in Albania as a heroic struggle between the Greeks and their Italian aggressors, the information provided by the various British intelligence agencies ought to have shown their government and chiefs of staff the deficiencies of the Greek military forces. Likewise, the first encounter Wavell's troops had with the Italians in North Africa during Operation Compass should have given them a measure of the military competencies of their opponents, at a time when British memories of their own bruising encounter with the Germans in France were still strong. However noble the British efforts were to support the Greeks (or the Turks for that matter), they occurred at a time when Britain was struggling to rebuild its army after its losses in France and support its wider strategic aims. So it is hard to understand why the British persisted in their efforts to provide military support for the Greeks, given this and the full knowledge they had of the level of military materiel and formations flowing into the Balkan region from Germany. The problem for the Middle East Command was that they were being called upon to face several different threats almost simultaneously with inadequate resources. For this reason Wavell took a dim view of the Greek venture, particularly when the opportunity to throw the Italians out of Libya appeared to be so tantalisingly close. Nevertheless, when finally forced to accept the reality of the poisoned chalice he had been handed, he was somewhat mendacious in his dealings with the Anzac commanders, leading them to believe that their respective governments were in agreement with their taking part in the Greek campaign in order to assemble the force he needed. In that he was aided by Blamey's odd preoccupation with the issue of the command of W Force, and the muddied lines of communication resulting from Menzies's mission to the Middle East and later England. The result of all this was that the Australian and New Zealand governments agreed to a deployment of their forces despite the distinct reservations of their commanders. The venture was decidedly shaky before it had even left for Greece. It was a case of a perfect storm waiting to happen, one from which no one would emerge unscathed.

Chapter 3

Operation Lustre

The decision to proceed with Operation Lustre, the British name for their Greek endeavour, occurred just hours before the armoured component of what was now known as W Force was about to embark (see Appendix I). By this stage of the war 1 Armoured Brigade had only two tank regiments: 4 Queen's Own Hussars, equipped with Light Mark VI tanks, and 3 Royal Tank Regiment, with A10 Cruiser tanks. Their other unit, 5 Royal Tank Regiment, had been detached from the brigade shortly after reaching Egypt in January 1941 and then, to the dismay of them all:

> On the first day of February 3 Royal Tanks reluctantly handed over their two squadrons of A13 tanks to 5 Royal Tanks and equally reluctantly received in return a motley collection of A10s. These had badly worn tracks, which became later a source of much trouble – even disaster.[1]

Brigadier Charrington described the situation to his daughter in a letter on 29 April 1941, written on his way back to Alexandria after the campaign:

> the quite useless tanks we had described as quite unsuitable before we left England. They did have some new ones ready for us when we arrived in Egypt, which came from Australia but they were quite hopeless rotten metal and not up to the specification in any way.[2]

On 8 March 4 Hussars departed from Alexandria,[3] followed by 3 Royal Tanks two days later.[4] When they arrived at Piraeus the following day the presence of the German Embassy staff writing down details of the new arrivals did not go unnoticed. They were still there three weeks later.[5] It was as a direct result of this that Hitler changed his plans, deciding on 17 April to occupy the whole of Greece, the start date being set to 1 April. Unfortunately, this was one time when Ultra failed to alert the British of German intentions, though it did fit in with their estimations of the likely start date for the German invasion. This view was reinforced by Enigma messages on the 23rd announcing that Fliegerkorps VIII was ready for action on the 25th.[6]

As it so happened, the troops of 1 Armoured Brigade were not the first elements of W Force to arrive in Greece. Wilson himself had preceded his advance guard by about four days, taking up residence in the British Legation. Somewhat bizarrely, the Greek government had requested that the giant general dress in civilian clothes and remain incognito; officially he was to be known as 'Mr Watt'. He was not allowed to contact W Force headquarters either, and was forbidden to conduct a thorough reconnaissance of the ground over which his force was to fight.[7]

The movement of 2 New Zealand Division to Greece began before 5 Brigade could rejoin it in Egypt from England. First to leave was 18 NZ Battalion on 7 March and thereafter there was a steady progression of units from the rest of 4 NZ Brigade and the whole of 6 NZ Brigade, plus the Divisional Cavalry Regiment, 27 NZ Machine Gun Battalion and one artillery regiment. During the crossings of the third and fourth convoys some dive bombers put in an appearance, hitting and damaging a tanker on 21 March. The vehicles and drivers of 27 NZ Machine Gun Battalion had gone with this convoy on the *Queen Adelaide*. Equipped with only an old Hotchkiss machine gun for anti-aircraft defence, the battalion had augmented its defences with ten Bren guns from their anti-aircraft platoon. Their battalion armourer, Staff Sergeant George Weeds, had gone one stage further and put together a 'Chicago piano': four Vickers machine guns on a multiple mounting. When the plane that bombed the tanker turned on the *Queen Adelaide*:

> It met a hail of fire from the Chicago piano, fired by Weeds, and went away smoking: it plummeted into the sea some distance from the convoy. The *Queen Adelaide*'s officers and men were delighted. Weeds was given two bottles of 'Black and White' and 1,000 yellow cigarettes to divide among the AA gun crews for saving his ship.[8]

Wavell's original plan had called for 7 Australian Division to follow 2 NZ Division to Greece, after which the Polish Brigade was to be shipped over. Once these movements had been accomplished 9 Australian Division was to replace 6 Australian Division in Cyrenaica, the latter then going to Greece.[9] Blamey, however, wanted 6 Australian Division to go first; his rationale for this was that its casualties from the fighting in Cyrenaica were minor and it had more battle experience than 7 Australian Division. Blamey asked for the order of movement to be reversed, but it was not until 5 March that he discovered that Wavell had refused to do so; he eventually got his way. This meant, however, that 6 Australian Division first had to be brought back from Cyrenaica[10], but not in its entirety – its divisional cavalry regiment was left behind.[11] The first to depart was 16 Australian Brigade. Lieutenant Colonel Henry Chilton's 2/2 Australian Battalion handed over to 2/4 Australian Battalion and left for Buq Buq on 7 March. At Mersa Matruh they were held up for three days by a severe dust storm, and as a result did not reach their staging camp until eight days later. Like the rest of 16 Australian Brigade their leave in Alexandria was cut short and they embarked for Greece on 19 March.

The transport of W Force over to Greece had all been smooth sailing till now, but that was to change. The departure of the first elements of 5 NZ Brigade from Alexandria on 25 March happened to coincide with a renewal of Italian naval activity. The following day they sent six *barchini* explosives from their *Regia Marina* assault flotilla into Suda Bay, hitting the 8-inch cruiser HMS *York* and the tanker M/T *Pericles. York* was so badly damaged that it had to be beached. To follow this up the Italian navy planned to attack the next Lustre convoy out of Alexandria. On the evening of 26 March Admiral Angelo Iachino put to sea in command of the main battle fleet of the *Regia Marina*, consisting of the battleship *Vittorio Veneto* and four destroyers from 3 Cruiser Division. Shortly after leaving port this force was joined by the cruisers *Trieste, Trento* and *Bolzano*, accompanied by three destroyers of 12 Flotilla under Vice Admiral Luigi Sansonnetti. Also called up were 1 Cruiser Division (*Zara, Fiume* and *Pola*) of Vice Admiral Carlo Cattaneo and 8 Cruiser Division (*Garibaldi* and *Abruzzi*) of Vice Admiral Legani and another six destroyers.[12]

While the British Middle East Command had received no intelligence of the attack on Suda Bay, the Ultra decrypts provided an inkling of another operation. The first decrypt, which was received on 24 March, indicated that German twin-engined fighters in Libya had been ordered to fly to Palermo in preparation for special operations. This was followed the following day by a decrypt of an Italian signal that announced 25 March was D-3 for an operation involving the Rhodes command. Further messages called for air reconnaissance and attacks on airfields in the Aegean two days before a particular operation, together with requests for information on British convoys travelling between Alexandria and Greece. Confirmation that this signals traffic all referred to the same operation prompted Admiral Sir John Cunningham to cancel the departure of a convoy from Piraeus. He also ordered another, to the south of Crete, to hold its position and reverse its course the next day.[13]

Nevertheless, there remained some uncertainty as to whether or not this operation was directed against British convoys to Greece. Then a brief sighting at 12.30pm on the 27th by a flying boat from Malta of three Italian cruisers 75 miles to the east of Sicily heading towards Crete confirmed that this was the case. Without delay Cunningham ordered Rear Admiral Henry Pridham-Wippell's 7 Cruiser Squadron (the light cruisers HMS *Ajax*, *Gloucester* and *Orion*, and HMAS *Perth*) to make to a position 30 miles to the south of Crete. This left the main battlefleet, consisting of the battleships HMS *Warspite*, *Barnham* and *Valiant*, the aircraft carrier HMS *Formidable* and nine destroyers still in Alexandria. Cunningham was anxious not to arouse suspicions when they did depart. Knowing that the Japanese consul regularly reported on the movements of his fleet, and that he was frequently on the greens of the Alexandria golf club, Cunningham visited the clubhouse with his clubs and an overnight bag, staying long enough to make sure he was noticed. That night the main fleet, with Cunningham on board, slipped anchor unnoticed and made for Crete.[14]

The following morning at around 7.30am, aircraft from the *Formidable* located the two Italian cruiser divisions. This sighting confirmed that both Italian divisions were steering to the south-west, some 35 miles to the north-east of Pridham-Wippell's force, now to the south of Crete. Shortly afterwards Pridham-Wippell's squadron found Sansonnetti's ships another 25 miles from the those ships, unfortunately at the same time as the Italians located Pridham-Wippell's squadron. When *Orion* eventually sighted Sansonnetti's ships and realized they were faster 8-inch cruisers, able to outrange them, they swung around in an attempt to draw them on to Cunningham's main fleet. The Italians initially took up the pursuit, opening fire at 13 miles range, but at 8.55am were recalled by Iachino. In the meantime Cunningham, having received *Orion*'s sighting report, altered course to meet up with Pridham-Wippell. At the same time he launched both Albacore squadrons in an air torpedo strike from the *Formidable*.

When Pridham-Wippell finally sighted the main Italian battlefleet at 10.58am, 16 miles away to the north, he responded by swinging around to the south to avoid getting sandwiched between them and the two Italian cruiser divisions. Nevertheless the next thirty minutes were harrowing as they endured a bombardment of 15-inch Italian shells. To their relief, at that very moment, *Formidable's* aircraft swooped in and launched their torpedoes, all six passing astern of the *Vittorio Veneto*. Caught off guard, the Italians broke off their attack and swung away to the north-west. The torpedoes launched against Sansonnetti's force also missed, as did those from the three Swordfish from Maleme airfield on Crete.

Cunningham set off in hot pursuit of Iachino's ships, meeting up with Pridham-Wippell an hour later. Another air torpedo strike was ordered and at 3.10pm three Albacores and two Swordfish from the *Formidable* sighted the Italian battleships and swung into action. Four of the torpedoes missed their target, but the fifth, fired by Lieutenant Commander J. Dalyell-Stead's Albacore, hit the *Vittorio Veneto*, only for his aircraft to be shot down with no survivors. The ship took on water and suffered damage to a propeller and had to stop for repairs before the fleet set off an hour later, its speed reduced by a third.

Though Iachino's fleet was still travelling too fast for Cunningham, he continued in pursuit. After *Warspite's* reconnaissance aircraft sighted the fleet again some 50 miles to the north, he ordered another air attack, with six Albacores and two Swordfish from the *Formidable* and two Swordfish from Maleme:

> The aircraft sighted their target just as the sun was sinking, and waited for the light to fade. At 7.25, skimming low over the surface of the sea they swept into the attack in single line ahead, and were at once met with a smoke screen and a tremendous barrage of anti-aircraft fire. Dazzled by searchlights and in danger of collision, the aircraft had to break formation and turn away before they could position themselves to aim their torpedoes at the Italian battleship.[15]

Nevertheless, other ships in the fleet were attacked and one of them, the *Pola*, was hit, losing its electrical power and, thus, all its turrets.

Unsure what to do next, Cunningham eventually ordered Captain Philip Mack's destroyers to continue the pursuit. At 8.15pm *Ajax* and *Orion* picked up a vessel on their radar, the *Pola*. Continuing their sweep over the next eighteen minutes and determining that it was stationary, Cunningham decided to investigate further. At 10.25pm he picked up the outlines of the *Zara* and *Fiume* and some other ships on their way to help the stricken *Pola*. With this he swung the *Warspite* towards them and shortly after opened fire, their aim being aided by the destroyer *Greyhound* illuminating the ships with its searchlights. *Barnham* and *Valiant* also joined in. When the first shells hit they saw:

Whole turrets and masses of heavy debris whirling through the air and splashing into the sea and in a short time the ships themselves were nothing but glowing torches and on fire from stem to stern.[16]

When three Italian destroyers turned to fire torpedoes *Warspite* swung away, leaving Cunningham's own destroyers to finish off the Italians. *Fiume* blew up and sank at around 11pm.

In the meantime *Havock*, in the process of finishing off the Italian ships, reported contact with another ship, which turned out to be the stricken *Pola*. Mack's destroyers, continuing on their course, ran into the *Zara*, which they sank with torpedoes as they passed by. The *Jervis* and *Nubian* eventually reached *Pola*, taking on the ship's crew before sinking it with torpedoes. The other ships then proceeded to pick up what other survivors they could from the water, a total of 805 being rescued. Before they departed they radioed the position of other survivors to the Italians and another 160 were taken on board an Italian hospital ship.

For the British the battle that had occurred off Cape Matapan in Greece had been an outstanding success. Even though they had failed to take out the *Vittorio Veneto*, they had sunk three fast heavy cruisers and two large destroyers. More importantly, the Italian navy made no further attempt to intercept convoys going to Greece or the evacuation of troops at the end of April.[17] One downside of this, though, was that the Battle of Matapan, along with a storm at sea, interrupted the timetable of troop movements, the next convoy not reaching Greece until 3 April. Worse still, it delayed the shipment of the rest of 6 Australian Division to Greece and its ultimate deployment. Blamey certainly had not helped the situation either, particularly in his insistence on sending 6 Australian Division before 7 Australian Division. Blamey had not taken into account the need to replace 6 Australian Division in the field before extracting it, and this would explain why it took so long to get the first elements of it to Greece.

Meanwhile, after their arrival at the Aliákmon Line, the New Zealanders discovered that there were disquieting shortcomings in the defences the Greeks were in the process of building. The intention was for them to consist of an anti-tank ditch, coupled with a line of pillboxes, minefields and demolitions that would eventually link up with a natural gorge. Chas Wheeler from 6 NZ Field Company discovered this first-hand after being ordered by Brigadier Harold Barrowclough, commander of 6 NZ Brigade, to find out when they could expect it to be completed. What he found was less than encouraging. One of the first things he started with was the anti-tank ditch:

Hundreds of labourers worked steadily excavating the tank trap. Their methods were crude. Baskets and buckets, sacks to carry spoil. No barrows. The big steam excavator, which could have competed with the whole gang, lay idle; the driver sat gazing hopelessly at its disabled vitals. A couple of Kiwi mechanics set it running in two hours and kept it working twenty-four hours a day until it had done all that could be done.

Wheeler had issues with the construction of their pillboxes too:

> At the first pillbox site we visited, the Greek carpenters were setting up framework for the concrete. It was beautiful work – like cabinet making. Dressed timber in cramped up panels, inside and out. A completed box across the gulley gleamed whitely in the sun.

Wheeler then asked to speak to the foreman and found him 'setting up a beautifully intricate piece of jigsaw carpentry for the firing loophole'. In response to the foreman's description of his workmanship, Wheeler went on to say:

> 'That,' I told him, 'is the worst example of a pillbox I ever saw in my life. See that road?' I pointed out across the plain to the north. 'When the German army comes down that road in a few days not a soldier will dare be withiin 100 yards of your beautiful pillbox, because it will stand out like a boil and be shelled to pieces at once.'

They eventually managed to convince them to lower their standards, but it would ultimately be of no avail:

> We might as well have saved our energy. Concrete takes a month to gain anything near its full strength, ten days before it's really worth anything. And you have to get the stuff mixed and placed first. Sunday, 6th April, wasn't even ten days away.[18]

To these problems was added another, that of the Greek units assigned to support the British expeditionary force along the Aliákmon Line. This defensive position ran from the mouth of the Aliákmon River along the front of the mountains to the Yugoslav border, and was only passable to vehicles at four locations: the coastal plain to the east of Mount Olympus; Olympus

Pass, between Katerini and Elasson; Veria Pass, connecting Salonika with Kozani; and Edessa Pass, linking Edessa with Florina.[19] Prior to the arrival of the New Zealanders the Greeks had deployed their 19 Motorised Division along the coastal sector, 12 Division in the Veria Pass and 20 Division in the Edessa Pass. The proposal was then for 12 and 20 Divisions to shift to the left when W Force arrived, while the 19 Motorised would occupy the coastal sector to the right of 2 NZ Division.[20] The reality, however, was somewhat more disturbing. 19 Motorised Division, which had only recently taken delivery of 100 Universal Carriers and a handful of Light Mk IIIBs, consisted of little more than 2,000 men, mostly untrained. It was supposed to occupy 12,000 yards of front north of Katerini, with the New Zealanders taking responsibility for the remaining 15,000.

On learning this Wilson ordered Freyberg to take over the entire line and move 19 Motorised Division forward into the Axios Valley and Dorian Gap, with the task of dealing with paratroop landings.[21] In turn Freyberg deployed 2 NZ Divisional Cavalry along the south bank of the Aliákmon River, with 6 NZ Brigade further south on the coastal sector and 4 NZ Brigade on its left. When the first elements of 5 NZ Brigade finally arrived they were kept back in reserve at Olympus Pass.[22] Unfortunately, the division's artillery units, which arrived around the same time, found themselves with little time to prepare their positions.[23]

Blamey and his chief of staff, Brigadier Sydney Rowell, arrived in Greece on 19 March and began a tour of the front-line positions. He met first with the Greek corps commander at Kozani, noting while there the vulnerability of this position from an attack through the Monastir Gap. On the 23rd he drove over to visit 2 NZ Division, where he learned of Freyberg's concern over the length of the line he had to hold, especially if the attack was supported by tanks. Freyberg was of the view that it made more sense to pull back to the mouths of the Olympus passes. Blamey, in agreement, promised to take the matter up with Wilson when he returned to Athens. Unfortunately, Wilson was of the view that the New Zealand section of the line was less likely to be attacked and so the matter was dropped.[24] In fact Wilson was more concerned about Papagos's reaction if Freyberg's troops were to abandon the Aliákmon River line. Clearly unhappy about this, Blamey made an unscheduled visit to the Peloponnese. While there he inspected and marked off several beaches on his road map, before returning to his corps headquarters at Gerania.[25]

There were also issues with 1 Armoured Brigade and its deployment. After landing at Piraeus it had moved up to the area around Florina where it was tasked with acting as a delaying force. However, shortly afterwards 4 Hussars, 1 Rangers Kings Royal Rifle Corps and 2 Royal Horse Artillery were moved to a position west of the Axios River with orders to fight a delaying action.[26] This left the rest of the brigade exposed to a possible outflanking movement by a German thrust through the Monastir Gap. The hope remained that the Germans would respect Yugoslav neutrality, or that the Yugoslavs would be able to prevent that from happening.[27] Nevertheless, recognizing the possibility that the Germans might use this route, Charrington was ordered to prepare a withdrawal route through the Edessa Pass into the Florina Valley.[28] With the brigade thus committed, 3 Royal Tanks back at Amyntaio was to be the blocking force.[29] Given the parlous mechanical state of its A10 Cruiser tanks, this may have also reflected a reluctance to move them unnecessarily. The lack of sufficient spares for the tanks had been of particular concern to the unit before it left Egypt, and this was exacerbated by the discovery that a shipment of spares received while at Amyntaio turned out to be for A13 Cruiser and A15 Crusader tanks. During a visit by Eden the issue of state of their tracks was raised but, perversely, in the course of a tank demonstration before him 'every possible manoeuvre failed to cause any of the known track faults'. No tracks were ever received while the unit was there, but during the retreat some were seen lying at Larissa station, by which time the regiment had virtually no tanks left.[30]

The Australians had been given responsibility for defending the Veria Pass, Servia Pass and Kozani,[31] though on 27 March only 16 Australian Brigade was in position at Veria Pass.[32] The first two battalions from 19 Australian Brigade that arrived on 3 April had been hurried back from Cyrenaica to Egypt. From there the brigade had been sent on to Greece with little time for proper rest or food, or for retraining, particularly the elementary training of its reinforcements.[33] Along with the brigade came two of 6 Australian Division's field regiments and its anti-tank regiment.[34] Three days later they had reached Larissa. On 5 April the Greeks urged the Australians to take over Veria Pass so they could use the Greek 12 Division to strengthen the defence in the Edessa area.[35] The rest of 6 Australian Division was either on the water or still to depart from Egypt.

All this was hardly an auspicious start for W Force. Having promised three divisions, the Middle East High Command had failed to deliver two complete divisions prior to the opening of the German attack on Greece, while their armoured brigade was crippled with sub-standard equipment. In fact it was hard to see how they could have shipped over the third division in time. Not so the Germans. For the invasion of Greece the

Germans had assembled three corps, two of which the Anzacs would come in direct contact with during the course of the campaign. Of these, XL. Panzer-Korps was composed of one armoured division, one motorized brigade and one infantry Division, while XVIII. Gebirgs-Korps fielded one panzer division, two mountain divisions and two infantry divisions. On paper it looked as though the Anzacs were facing an overwhelming force. However, only the two panzer divisions and the motorised brigade had equivalent mobility to the Anzac infantry divisions and British armour, while the other divisions literally marched on their feet to battle. In terms of armour the number of tanks fielded by one panzer division was roughly equivalent to that of the sole British armoured unit in Greece, except that the German light tanks were superior to the light tanks fielded by the British, and the German tanks were more reliable. Where the Germans had overwhelming superiority was in the air. The British could only field eighty serviceable aircraft, four Blenheim bomber squadrons, one Blenheim fighter squadron and three single-seater fighter squadrons, of which only one was fully equipped with Hurricanes. In contrast, in direct support of the German effort in Greece was Fliegerkorps VIII with 414 aircraft, while on call were another 168 from Fliegerkorps X.[36] Of the German aircraft fielded, the Messerschmitt Bf 109 and Bf 110 were far superior to their nearest British equivalents, the Hurricane and Blenheim respectively. The Italians could field another 150 in Albania. It hardly represented an equal fight.

Chapter 4

The Fall of Yugoslavia

The wild card in the defence of Greece was Yugoslavia. Though this nation had no desire to become embroiled in the impending conflict in the Balkans, Hitler regarded their involvement, in one form or other, as essential for his strategic aims. As such he had been actively seeking Yugoslav support, largely because there was no direct rail link between Bulgaria and Greece. Thus control of the Belgrade-Nis-Salonika railway line was critical for the rapid implementation of Operation Marita, and for the redeployment of their forces for the invasion of Russia afterwards. During a meeting on 28 November 1940 with the Yugoslav foreign minister, Lazar Cincar-Marković, Hitler made an offer to sign a non-aggression pact as part of the Tripartite Pact. As further inducement the Yugoslavs were offered an outlet to the Aegean Sea through Salonika. However, Hitler's overtures did little to impress Cincar-Marković.

A further meeting was held between Hitler, his Foreign Minister, Joachim von Ribbentrop, the Yugoslav Premier, Dragisha Cvetković, and Cincar-Marković on 14 February 1941. No further progress was made on this occasion either, but now time was running out for Operation Marita. In order to pursue this further Hitler invited Yugoslavia's Prince Regent Paul to Germany, the meeting taking place on 4 March. Not that this achieved much. Prince Paul, though more favourably disposed towards German plans, could not offer the Germans any military support given Yugoslavia's strict policy of neutrality. Underlying this was Yugoslavian concern over Mussolini's interference in the Balkans, something outside Hitler's control. Hitler's duplicitous guarantee that Yugoslavia would not be required to permit passage of German forces across its territory – something in fact that his military commanders specifically wanted – did not help sway Prince Paul.[1]

This occurred over the same period that Anthony Eden was pressing the Yugoslavs for their support, not that the British foreign secretary had any better luck with the Yugoslavs or Turkey. The Turkish government was not willing to do anything other than reiterate their determination to resist any attack by Germany.[2]

This impasse continued until Mussolini was on the point of reinforcing his garrisons along the Albanian-Yugoslav border, when the situation changed dramatically. On 18 March the Yugoslav government announced their intention to join the Tripartite Pact, with Cvetković and Cincar-Marković signing the protocol in Vienna a week later. On this occasion the Axis Powers handed two notes to the Yugoslavs guaranteeing their sovereignty and territorial integrity and promising that for the duration of the war Yugoslavia would not be required to permit the transit of Axis troops across its territory; the latter was a lie.

The development was not well received within Yugoslavia; three Serbian cabinet ministers resigned almost immediately, and there was worse to come. On the night of 26/27 March General Dušan Simović seized power in a military coup d'état.[3] Prince Paul was overthrown and King Peter II crowned regent in his stead and the borders were closed.[4] The British made a further approach to Simović, who eventually agreed to meet Dill in Belgrade, but this proved fruitless. The new ministers, preoccupied with taking over the reins of government and with their armed forces unready for war, were reluctant to do anything that would further provoke the Germans.[5] On 27 March they passed their assurances on to the German minister that they wanted to maintain their friendly status. Not that this convinced Hitler, who was firmly of the belief that the new government was anti-German and would sooner or later join the Western powers. As if to prove his point, shortly after this the Yugoslav government flew a delegation to Moscow on 3 April to sign a treaty of friendship and non-aggression.[6]

As if to further inflame the situation, on 29 March the Yugoslavs began to mobilise their army, not that the Germans had much to fear.[7] Though the Yugoslav air force was equipped with some 700 aircraft, most of them were obsolete. The French had supplied the Yugoslav army with some modern tanks, but the other half of their armour dated back to the First World War. Much of the remainder of the Yugoslav military equipment was of foreign manufacture, most coming from Czechoslovakia, and deliveries ceased when Germany annexed that nation. The Yugoslav army was also beset by internal friction between the different ethnic groups in the country, particularly between the Croatians and Serbians.[8] Just how serious this division was could be seen when Simović invited representatives of the Croatians to join his new government. They finally did so on 3 April, when they made an appeal to their people to put their support behind the new regime. Instead, five days later, Croatia proclaimed itself an independent state.

Unfortunately it was already too late for Simović's government. Angered by what he saw as Yugoslav treachery, and despite Simović's assurances, Hitler declared at a conference on the day of the coup that:

> Politically it is especially important that the blow against Yugoslavia is carried out with unmerciful harshness and that the military destruction is done in a lightning-like undertaking.[9]

Planning for the invasion, which was to take place simultaneously with the invasion of Greece, began immediately. While the original intention had been to launch Marita on either the second or third day of April, Yugoslavia was now to be attacked first, and this was to be preceded by a massive aerial bombardment of Belgrade on 1 April. This eventually had to be put back to 6 April,[10] with the ground attack on Yugoslavia to commence two days later.[11] Ultimately this delayed the launch of Marita by a few days as well, though it did open up a new option for Germany's invasion of Greece, of launching a drive through the Monastir Gap.

German plans for the forthcoming ground offensive in Yugoslavia, codenamed *Unternehmen Strafgericht* (Operation Punishment), called for a two-pronged assault on Belgrade. One arm of the assault was to be launched by II. Armee from the Austrian province of Styria, driving southwards between the Sava and Drava rivers, with the intention of destroying the Yugoslav armies in Croatia. At the same time 1. Panzer-Gruppe was to attack from the direction of Sofia in western Bulgaria. Unbeknown to the *Oberkommando der Wehrmacht* Hitler had also ordered 2. SS Motorised-Division Das Reich to launch a separate advance on Belgrade from Timisoara. While this was proceeding, a third force was to thrust from south-western Bulgaria towards Skopje with the aim of preventing any Yugoslav troops from joining up with the British and Greek troops further south. Simultaneously, part of XXII. Armee was to cut across the base of Yugoslavia from Bulgaria and drive down the Vardar Valley with a view to outflanking the Metaxas Line.

On the day of the air offensive, 6 April, the morning started out peacefully enough for Ruth Mitchell, an American-born photographer living in Belgrade. Around 7am, as she was pouring herself a cup of tea while listening to the radio, she heard an announcement from the German foreign minister von Ribbentrop announcing Hitler's decision to punish the 'clique of conspirators in Belgrade and to restore peace and security in Yugoslavia by force of arms'. Ribbentrop also announced that bombs were already falling in the city, and though Mitchell did not initially hear anything, she soon noted the first dull explosions in the distance and the sound of approaching bombers. Taking shelter under the stairs she endured blast after blast, some within 30 yards of her home. As she said later:

> The effect was almost inconceivable. It wasn't the noise or even so much the concussion; it was the perfectly appalling wind that was most terrifying. It drove like something solid through the house. Every door that was latched simply burst off its hinges, every pane of glass flew into splinters. The curtains stood straight out into the room and fell back in ribbons.[12]

Mitchell survived, but many others perished in the bombing. In this, the first, wave, some 74 Stukas and 160 medium bombers, protected by 100 Messerschmitt Bf 109s from Luftflotte 4, attacked in 15-minute intervals to commence their saturation bombing raid on the capital. Though some Yugoslav fighter planes flew up to meet them, many others did not make it off the ground. German attacks on airstrips across the country had put most out of action. Over the next hour and a half the Germans destroyed government buildings, communications facilities and army headquarters. In the case of the latter not only was there a great loss of life among members of the Yugoslav high command, but all communication with their field armies also ceased. By the end of the attack some 4,000 people lay dead, but the Germans did not stop there. In the afternoon they dropped incendiaries and followed up with a series of bombing attacks over the next two days. In the end a total of around 17,000 people in Belgrade were killed.[13]

Many of the ground units of the Wehrmacht assigned to the invasion of Yugoslavia were still a few days away from their staging areas when XXII. Armee launched Operation Marita. The attack on Yugoslavia was not supposed to start until 8 April, but a week earlier, in the north, XLVI. Panzer-Corps of II. Armee, while still assembling along the frontier, seized an important bridge at Barcs and a railroad bridge at Koprivnica to prevent their destruction. Other units took the opportunity to seize bridges over the Mur River before they could be destroyed by the Yugoslavs. Among them was one of the special *Feuerzauber* assault units under the command of Hauptmann Palten, who went one stage further. On the evening of 5 April, having taken their bridge, they began to attack bunkers across the river. Then, before dawn the following morning, they struck south towards the high ground beyond that, securing it with ease. Two days later they crossed a stream north of the town of Maribor on inflated rafts and captured the town. Not far away a bicycle detachment from 183. Infanterie-Regiment cycled into the town of Murska Sabota and took it without firing a shot. This appeared to be aided by the hostility of the local Croatians towards the Yugoslav army troops in the area. When advance elements of XLVI. Panzer-Corps seized bridgeheads over the Drav and Mur rivers, Croatian soldiers mutinied along the line. Finally, at dawn on 10 April, when II. Armee crossed the border, they discovered that the bulk of the Yugoslav army had withdrawn towards Zagreb, leaving only a few troops to cover the retreat. On discovering this the commander of LI. Corps sent 14. Panzer-Division forward. Despite the snow-covered roads, they managed to cover 100 miles and, by the end of the day, had reached the outskirts of Zagreb itself. On entering the city they were warmly welcomed by its pro-German population. The following day the newly-formed Croatian government called on its citizens to cease fighting and requested that they be released immediately from the Yugoslav army.

To the east, 8. Panzer-Division, accompanied by 16. Motorisiert-Infanterie-Division, struck out for Belgrade. Good progress was made initially against no significant resistance and by the end of the day they had reached Slatina. Their progress the following day, as they journeyed south, was less spectacular, as the deteriorating condition of the roads, coupled with Yugoslav army demolitions, made the going difficult. Nevertheless on 12 April, after capturing two bridges over the Sava River intact, they entered the town of Mitrovica. From there, however, they were diverted south in the direction of Sarajevo.

To the south XIV. Panzer-Korps crossed the border with Bulgaria on 8 April near the town of Pirot. After breaking through a strong line of bunkers, 11. Panzer-Division, in the lead, struck out for Nis, entering the town the following day. Less progress was made to the south, where the advance of 5. Panzer-Division soon ground to a halt on the poor roads near Pirot. By the time they did get going, with signs of collapse of the Yugoslav troops around Nis, they were ordered south to join up with XL. Panzer-Korps in their attack on Greece. On 10 April XIV. Panzer-Korps continued their drive up the Morava Valley, encountering strong resistance from the southern wing of 6 Yugoslav Army, overruning it two days later. By that evening they were within striking distance of the capital.[14]

Belgrade, however, was not captured by them but by XLI. Panzer-Korps, which had crossed the border at Vrsac and by 11 April had entered the town of Pancevo on the Danube River, some 12 miles from Belgrade. The honour of taking Belgrade fell to a motorcycle assault company from Das Reich, under the command of SS Hauptsturmführer Fritz Kingenberg. On the morning of 12 April, as they drove up along the northern bank of the Danube River, the company was disappointed to note that the Prinz Eugen Bruke over the Sava River had been destroyed by the Yugoslavs. Lacking bridging equipment, the Germans set about a thorough investigation of the riverbank and eventually found a motorboat, in which Kingenberg set off early that afternoon with one of his platoon leaders, two sergeants and five privates. On the way over they collided with a pier of the bridge, but eventually reached the far bank, from where they they made their way into the town, leaving two men to fetch the rest of the company. Kingenberg's detachment soon bumped into a party of Yugoslavs, whom they took prisoner without a fight, shortly afterwards capturing some Yugoslav-manned trucks. In these they drove to the Yugoslavian war ministry, with an ethnic German for their guide, but on discovering that this had been abandoned they continued to the German Legation, where they raised a swastika flag. Two hours later the mayor of Belgrade and some other local officials reached the legation and formally surrendered the city. Thus the entire city was held by this small body of men until Panzer-Regiment 'Hermann Göring' arrived the following morning.[15]

With the fall of Belgrade the Germans were free to pursue the remaining troops of the Yugoslav army who were now falling back towards Sarajevo. The western arm of the German pincer consisted of four infantry divisions and 14. Panzer-Division from XLIX. and LI. Korps, while to the east 8. Panzer-Division led the attack by XLI. Panzer-Korps. Both attacks kicked off on 13 April and made good progress, as by this stage of the offensive Yugoslav resistance had all but ceased to exist. Instead reports were received of fighting having broken out between Serbian and Croatian troops in Mostar and by the following morning the fighting between them had spread throughout Dalmatia. On 15 April the arms of the pincers finally closed on Sarajevo, 14. Panzer-Division and 8. Panzer-Division entering the city simultaneously from the west and east respectively. But their stay there was short. Leaving the city shortly afterwards they continued their drive south in pursuit of whatever elements of the Yugoslavian army remained.

Even as these troops were driving south towards Sarajevo, the first attempts to negotiate an armistice were being made. On 14 April what was left of the Yugoslav high command authorized the various army commands still fighting to negotiate separate ceasefires. The Germans would have none of this, wanting instead the unconditional surrender of the entire Yugoslav army. Later that evening a representative of the Yugoslav government made another approach and the following day in Belgrade the Germans drew up their conditions for surrender. These they handed to an emissary of the Yugoslav government on 16 April, but as he lacked the authority to sign it arrangements were made to fly Cincar-Marcović and General Milojko Yankovic to Belgrade. There the armistice was finally concluded on the following day.[16]

Thus in just over two weeks Germany had seized control of Yugoslavia. By all accounts it had been another classic example of blitzkrieg in action, but a number of things had worked in Germany's favour. The Yugoslav army was hardly prepared for war, having only just started mobilizing their armed forces, plus much of their equipment was obsolete or was of foreign manufacture, now under German control. The Germans were also able to take advantage of internal dissention between the Serbians and Croatians. What they would encounter in Greece was quite different.

Chapter 5

Breakthrough at Vevi

German plans for the invasion of Greece were based on the premise that the Greeks would have insufficient forces to defend their borders with Yugoslavia and Bulgaria because of their heavy commitments in Albania. The German invasion was assigned to XII. Armee under Generalfeldmarshall Wilhelm List. His orders called for a rapid thrust through southern Yugoslavia to Skopje by the mobile elements of XL. Panzer-Korps, under Generaleutnant Georg Stumme, with the aim of cutting rail and road communications with Greece. From there the Korps was to drive south to Monastir and attack the forces around Florina, after which part of his force was to be detached to link up with the Italians in Albania. At the same time the two mountain divisions of Generalleutnant Franz Böhme's XVIII. Gebirgs-Korps were to attack the Metaxas Line with the view to forcing the Rupel Gorge. Concurrent with this 2. Panzer-Division was to drive through southern Yugoslavia and then turn south towards Greece in a wide outflanking movement and take Salonika. The parts of the Metaxas Line behind the Nestos River were also to be attacked by XXX. Infanterie-Korps. All three corps were then to converge on Salonika and after the capture of that city three panzer divisions and two mountain divisions were to drive on to Athens.[1]

Although the British were unaware of exactly what the Germans were planning, they had been monitoring the build-up of the German invasion forces in Bulgaria in February and March through Ultra decrypts of both German ground and air force communications. By 30 March these decrypts were starting to reveal concentrations of German army and air troops on the Romanian border with Yugoslavia. In addition Secret Intelligence Service reports pointed to the assembly of other troops in Austria and Hungary for a move into Yugoslavia. By 2 April an Ultra decrypt of a message from the Italian minister in Sofia revealed that on 5 April the Gemans were planning to attack Greece and Yugoslavia simultaneously. The date for the attack was revised three days later to 6 April. These decrypts also revealed that six or seven divisions would be available for the attack on W Force.[2]

On 5 April, just before the German attack was about to begin, Operation Lustre suffered another setback when Wavell announced that 7 Australian Division would not be coming to Greece.[3] Just four days previously, on 1 April, in Libya the newly arrived Deutsches Afrika-Korps had struck a blow with a vengeance against the weak British forces in Cyrenaica, quickly overrunning their troops at Mersa Brega. The withdrawal of the Western Desert Force soon turned into a rout and, with the Germans on the rampage, Wavell had ordered 18 Brigade of 7 Australian Division to Tobruk.

Operation Marita was eventually launched on schedule on 6 April. However, thanks to the serious opposition faced by XL. Panzer-Korps when they entered Yugoslavia from Bulgaria that morning, progress of 9. Panzer-Division and 73. Infanterie-Division was slower than expected. As a result they did not reach Skopje until the following afternoon. Further south, 2. Panzer-Division, of XVIII. Gebirgs-Korps, in their wide, outflanking movement behind the Metaxas Line, encountered no real opposition, their advance being delayed only by demolitions, mines and muddy roads. They reached Strumica that evening.

While 2. Panzer-Division was sweeping around towards Strumica, the mountain divisions of the XVIII Gebirgs-Korps launched their assault on the Metaxas Line. Though this assault was to be preceded by an artillery bombardment and a dive bombing attack, the Stuka pilots had trouble distinguishing the well-camouflaged bunkers from the surrounding terrain and their bombs did little damage. The Greeks had also cleared the slopes of timber to provide them with unobstructed fields of fire. Thus, when the assaulting troops of 5. Gebirgsjäger-Division finally broke cover from the woods, they came under intense fire. In a few areas some progress was made as the mountain troops broke into trenches and a few bunkers, but in other places they were simply forced to go to ground. Around midday the Greeks compounded the Germans' misery by calling down artillery fire onto their own positions, killing and wounding more mountain troops. The following morning, reinforced by more troops, 5. Gebirgsjäger-Division renewed their attack, tackling each bunker in turn with demolition charges and flamethrowers, finally breaking through that evening. More luck was had by 6. Gebirgsjäger-Division away to their right. Climbing to an altitude of 7,000 feet, through terrain the Greeks thought inaccessible, the mountain troops broke through a lightly held part of the Metaxas Line. By late 7 April they had reached the rail line to Salonika to the east of Lake Dojran.[4]

More seriously for W Force the Luftwaffe launched a raid on Piraeus that night. Curiously enough the British were aware of the impending raid, according to Wilson's senior administrative officer, Brigadier Bruno Brunskill:

> That evening, when I met my RAF opposite number in the Grande Bretagne Hotel he told me that the Germans were going to bomb the Piraeus [docks] that night. He suggested that we watch it together from the roof of the hotel; he added that there was plenty of time for us to finish our dinner.[5]

No warning was ever passed down to the docks though, presumably so as not to reveal that the British could read German Enigma traffic. Around 8.35pm 7 Staffel, Kampfgeschwader 30, arrived over the target and swung into their bombing runs. Though the port only suffered minor damage, worse was to come. Around 10pm one of the ships in port, the SS *Clan Fraser*, carrying a load of explosives, was hit and set on fire. Efforts were made to continue offloading the ammunition, but four hours later the ship blew up in a spectacular fashion. In the resulting conflagration seven other merchant ships were destroyed, including two others carrying ammunition, plus sixty lighters, twenty-five caiques, an ammunition train, an ammunition barge and quays, offices and shops.[6] The damage put the port out of action for two days, forcing the diversion of some of ships to Khalkis and Volos, among them 2/1 Australian Machine Gun Battalion, which reached Greece the following morning.[7] With only five of the twelve berths usable, the ability of the port facilities at Piraeus to maintain and reinforce W Force was severely restricted. Nevertheless, the British did manage to get some revenge, in a limited way, that same night, when No.37 Squadron wrecked an ammunition train and railway installations at Sofia, while No.84 Squadron severely damaged another railway station further south.[8]

Continued progress over the next two days saw XL. Panzer-Korps, in the north, finally severing the Belgrade-Salonika rail link, while 2. Panzer-Division broke through in the mountains and overran 19 Greek Motorised Division south of Lake Dorian. The following morning an advanced element from the division entered Salonika itself, effectively cutting off the troops on the Metaxas Line.[9] Worse still was the loss of four out of the six Greek divisions needed to hold the line on this side of Greece. This was the price of General Papagos's determination to hold the Metaxas Line.[10]

On 8 April the British learned, through Enigma decrypts, of the German intention to push through the Monastir Gap and from there outflank the

Aliákmon Line. This route had previously been thought of as being extremely difficult for tanks and hence unlikely for them to use.[11] Armed with this new knowledge, Wilson ordered an adjustment to his defences. W Force's main effort was now to be along the line of the Aliákmon River and thence westwards along the Venetikos River. The area around Kleidi Pass at Vevi and Florina was to be held as long as possible to allow 16 Australian Brigade in the Vermion Range and the Greeks in Albania to retire. Kleidi Pass was entrusted to the Australians, specifically the two recently-arrived battalions of Brigadier George Vasey's 19 Australian Brigade.[12] At that stage all that was around the Kleidi Pass was the Amyntaio Detachment, consisting of 3 Royal Tanks, 64 Medium Regiment (less one troop) and 2/1 Anti-Tank Regiment (less one battery).[13] Fortunately reinforcements were on their way, but typical of the confused state of affairs was the experience of 27 NZ MG Battalion, which had been asked to send two companies to Amyntaio. On 24 March Lieutenant Colonel Frederick Gwilliam and a recce party from the battalion reported to the acting commander of 3 Royal Tanks, only to discover he had not been told that any machine gunners were expected. Nor was the British officer aware of the presence of an Australian brigadier in the area, not that one was there at that time.[14]

On 6 April Blamey sent a senior staff officer to press Wilson into withdrawing the rest of 2 New Zealand Division to the mountain passes, but Wilson was not prepared to do so until he had more information on the fighting further north. Fortunately, Wilson finally agreed to the withdrawal that afternoon but did so with such haste that he forgot to consult with Papagos until the evening of the 8th.[15] Blamey was now given command of 12 Greek Division, 16 Australian Brigade and 2 NZ Division, though the latter was to be split up.[16] This involved moving 4 NZ Brigade from Katerini to Servia Pass, and once the New Zealanders were in place 16 Australian Brigade was to withdraw from Veria Pass. At the same time 6 NZ Brigade was to abandon its positions around the anti-tank ditch north of Katerini and pull back through 5 Brigade, leaving the latter holding Olympus Pass.[17] Meanwhile 21 NZ Battalion was to proceed to Platamon from Athens.[18] An exchange of troops was also arranged between 1 Armoured Brigade and 2 NZ Division, the latter sending two troops of armoured cars from their Divisional Cavalry Regiment in return for the seven A13 Cruiser tanks of the Brigade Headquarters Squadron, the latter under the command of Captain Richard Dale.[19] This came about at the request of 1 Armoured Brigade, who felt they were lacking an armoured car equipped recce element. Just what 2 NZ Division got out of this arrangement is not clear.

Having spent a month preparing their defences along the Aliákmon River, the troops of 4 and 6 NZ Brigades now found themselves having to abandon a large proportion of their precious barbed wire and mines, as well as their wasted effort on a defensive position that had been of dubious value from the outset. One unit had already gone, 26 NZ Battalion having marched out in the pouring rain on the afternoon of 7 April to Servia Pass, their sector being taken over by two platoons of 24 NZ Battalion and one from 25 NZ Battalion. Orders for 4 NZ Brigade to withdraw were not received until the following day. Their supporting artillery, 6 NZ Field Regiment, pulled out that evening, followed by the battalions of 4 NZ Brigade in the early hours of 9 April, which picked up their transport just to the north of Katerini and set off for Servia Pass.[20]

The rest of 6 NZ Brigade pulled out on the night of 9/10 April, as Jack Elliott from 25 NZ Battalion later recalled:

at about 2am on the 10th, [a] runner came around with a message 'We are pulling out. Be up on the road in 10 minutes.' The night was quite dark. Luckily the drizzle had stopped but D Company, who had the furthest to go to the road, found the rest of the battalion had already gone. We set off with Captain Andy H in the lead, with a lantern on a forced march. On a forced march the troops kept marching rather than the standard 50-minutes march, 10 minutes rest. During the march we carried full packs plus a few extras: ammunition etc. Part way through the night march I tripped on something on the road and came down on both knees. They hurt at the time but I managed to finish the march.[21]

After an arduous 17-mile march the battalion eventually reached Katerini around 8.40am, where they lay up till their transport arrived some five hours later.[22]

Meanwhile, on the western flank of W Force, the commander of 6 Australian Division, Major General Mackay, received orders to assume command of the Amyntaio Detachment, which was now to be known as Mackay Force, and reinforce it any way he could: no mean task. Around midnight on 8/9 April Mackay reached Sotir only to find he had no infantry.[23] This was not the case for long, as early in the morning of 9 April 1 Armoured Brigade joined them from its positions along the Axios River, having destroyed all the bridges in the Vardar Valley before departing. In that they were successful with all but one, according to Brigadier Charrington of 1 Armoured Brigade:

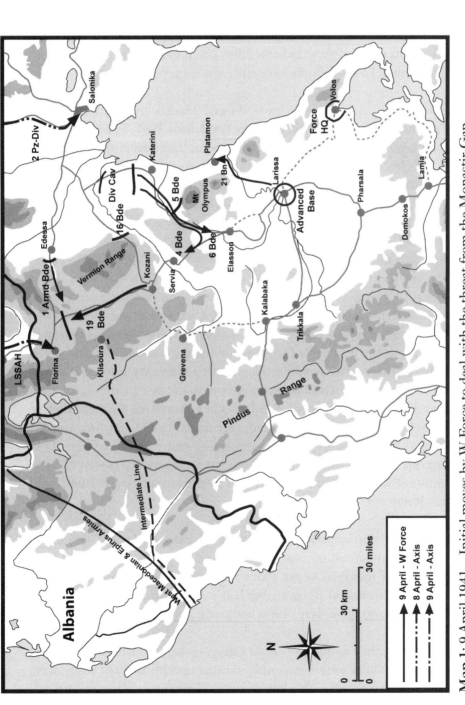

Map 1: 9 April 1941 – Initial moves by W Force to deal with the threat from the Monastir Gap.

The actual engineer detachment on the bridge responsible for blowing with one scout car were surprised by an English lorry driving up to them with a very dirty windscreen disguising the two men in front out of the tail of which jumped a dozen active Germans who did them in before they could quite realise what was happening. Four of the six have since got back.[24]

The arrival of 1 Armoured Brigade allowed Mackay to assign 1 Rangers to a position astride the road through the Kleidi Pass. The Dodecanese Regiment, when they arrived, he placed around lakes Vegorritis and Petron, while the Greek Cavalry Regiment went to Florina. By all accounts it was a perilous situation, but Mackay could take comfort in one thing: a patrol that day by armoured cars from the NZ Divisional Cavalry five miles north of Monastir had revealed the Germans (most probably Aufklärungsabteilung-LAH from Leibstandarte SS Adolf Hitler) to be held up by a blown bridge on the north side of the River Crna.[25]

The next unit to reach Mackay was 2/4 Australian Battalion under Lieutenant Colonel Ivan Dougherty. The battalion had been assigned to guard duties in Larissa on 5 April, with A Company at the airfield. The battalion was not complete, however, as C Company had been sent down to Volos to act as the protective company for Force Headquarters, and it was not until two days after reaching Kliedi that Dougherty learned it would not be coming at all.[26] A and B Companies were the first to arrive, reaching Mackay Force around 5am on 9 April. They moved up to their allotted positions to the left of 1 Rangers and were joined by D Company, less one platoon, that afternoon, the company taking the extreme left position. Setting up signals proved to be somewhat problematic, however; there was only sufficient cable to link all but A Company at first. As Lieutenant Claude Raymond recalled:

I hounded the brigade signal master for extra cable, but it was at a high premium because all units were experiencing the same problem. I managed to get about 2 miles of Don VI single cable from the Sherwood Rangers. We laid this in a straight line to 'B' Company and there were only a few yards to spare.

Unfortunately, the two platoons of D Company had to manage with Lucas signal lamps, which were notoriously slow to operate and not easily seen. The last to arrive were the battalion carriers, which came in later that night.[27]

For Lieutenant Colonel John Mitchell's 2/8 Battalion the journey north from Athens to Larissa had proved to be less than pleasant. They had set off from Athens late on 6 April, travelling by train, forty-two men and equipment crammed into each cattle truck, with little time for sleep. After disembarking at Larissa they had to march to the outskirts of town in the pouring rain, only to find that their transport had been delayed and would not arrive till the next day. With no other option they had to march, totally drenched, another 16 miles to their bivouac site. On 8 April trucks took them to Veria, a journey made more difficult by much of the unsealed road in a marshy area being under water. Some trucks became completely bogged down while trying to get through. At midnight the battalion was ordered forward again, with the section of the trip to Ptolemais taking six hours. The exhausted soldiers were eventually dropped off later that afternoon above the village of Xinon Neron.

On 9 April Aufklärungsabteilung-LAH occupied the town of Bitolj and, on probing further south, found the town of Florina unoccupied, but beyond there fire from the Australians at Vevi forced them to pull back to Florina. On 10 April, while advancing south, their Kampfgruppe Witt ran into British sappers trying to demolish a bridge.[28] Sent forward to protect the sappers was a troop of Marmon-Herrington armoured cars under the command of Lieutenant Darcy Cole from the NZ Divisional Cavalry:

> The detachment arrived about 9am and Cole placed Corporal Jeffrey King's car about a quarter of a mile up the road, with his own and Sergeant Sutherland's cars closer to the bridge at either side of the road, while the sappers began to prepare the demolition. It was going to be quite a lengthy task as the bridge was very solidly built of large hewn stones. But the enemy came into sight within twenty minutes. In the lead were several motor-cycle combinations, which were first engaged by King and then by Sutherland when he had backed off a little to gain a better fire position. Cole also backed down a little to observe his troop better. Then the sappers themselves, not unwillingly, as they became available, grabbed rifles and joined in. Presently some enemy vehicles moved up through the motorcycles, bringing more troops, some mortars and heavy machine guns. The chances of completing the demolition were rapidly fading. The enemy was using explosive bullets and the outsides of the cars were rapidly getting stripped of such things as bedding and tools. Cole noticed that he had even lost some of his

wheel-nuts; and his turret had become half jammed. With every hit on the cars the crews were being temporarily blinded by flying asbestos from inside the walls. When Cole saw infantry deploying to both sides he realised that there was obviously going to be no demolition and he radioed King to draw back, fearing that he would be surrounded. King's reaction was to move forward and engage the enemy even more vigorously, replying that to pull back to the bridge would only concentrate all the fire there of all places, just when Cole had to get the explosives truck turned round in almost full view of the enemy. Cole pulled back close by it to make some cover and then recalled Sutherland to where he could give supporting fire to King, who was almost surrounded. King finally consented to return and everyone moved under cover. Suspecting a trap, the enemy did not advance immediately and thus gave the detachment time to pull out.[29]

On the way back the Coles men set fire to a couple of wooden bridges, which was the cause of a minor headache for the Germans following up, as Karl Pfeffer from 1. Kompanie, LSSAH, recalled:

Our assault engineers received orders to prevent the Tommies from setting a wooden bridge near Nici on fire or blowing it up. We roared off in two trucks and parked the vehicles under lone trees to the left of the bridge. We immediately began taking enemy fire, which we answered with aimed fire. The Tommies subsequently pulled back. ...We had loaded into our vehicles pipe charges and hand grenade clusters, as well as two anti-tank mines and two boxes of explosives. One half of the squad went up to the burning bridge to extinguish the fire and look for explosives, while the rest provided covering fire. Suddenly we were attacked by low-flying British fighters, which strafed us several times. Five of our comrades took cover under one of the vehicles, which took a direct hit and exploded together with its cargo. I, myself, was lying about thirty metres from the vehicle and was thrown across the road by the blast wave of the explosion. ...We tried to put out the fire, but were ourselves threatened by the exploding ammunition. ...Our pioneer squad had lost almost half its men in its first day in action [30]

Just short of the village of Sitaria Cole's troop ran into a column of German vehicles, their crews all out and standing around.[31] Harry Spencer in one of the Marmon-Herrington armoured cars recalled what happened next: 'There were about 26 vehicles that cut us off at a culvert. Anyway Lofty King he went in with his Bren gun and had a bit of a pop at this and they all cleared out.'[32]

That afternoon 2/4 Australian Battalion first caught sight of vehicles from LSSAH approaching along the Itia-Vevi road. They tried to engage the column, but the Germans were well out of range of battalion fire. Instead their column was strafed and bombed by a flight of RAF Hurricanes and Blenheims. One Hurricane was brought down by anti-aircraft fire, but its pilot was later rescued by the Australians.[33] Towards evening LSSAH sent an assault detachment along the road towards the pass:

> A Beiwagen-Krad assumed the spearhead position and the detachment leader's vehicle followed, with a 3.7 cm Flak on a self-propelled mount, the Zugtrupp and the first Zug vehicles behind. The B-Krad had to drop out after just one kilometer because of a flat tyre and the leader's [armoured] car drove on ahead. Suddenly, there was an explosion ahead of us. At the same time, heavy MG fire started up. We dashed like lightning from the cars and into the wet ditch beside the road. The drivers were hard put to turn on the road. We first kept our heads down until the 'gentlemen from the other field post number' calmed down. The medic crept forward and reported that the three occupants of the car, Untersturmführer Witt, Oberscharführer Koch and the driver Rottenführer Brandhoff were dead. ...The crew aboard the self-propelled mount had also jumped down; only the gunner had stayed aboard and wanted to defend his vehicle with a pistol. Finally, however, he took the breechblock and also made his escape.[34]

That same morning 2/8 Australian Battalion awoke from an uncomfortable night in the snow and made their way forward across 10 to 12 miles of open ploughed country to their positions to the right of the Rangers. By now their lack of sleep over the last five days was beginning to tell, but they still had to ascend another 500 feet to an altitude of 4,500 feet to the ridge they were to defend. Some 100 of them had difficulty keeping up because of altitude anoxaemia, and twenty had to be evacuated. As darkness fell they started to dig in, with some difficulty in the hard ground, and many resorted to building rock sangars. As they did so a patrol of twenty Germans appeared in front of a section from C Company asking for food, and before the Australians realized they were the enemy five of them were captured. A section of New Zealand machine gunners were also taken prisoner after the Germans marched their Australian captives over the New Zealand position. Behind the ridge the battalion continued to struggle in their efforts to bring supplies and other equipment forward. The appalling road conditions forced their battalion transport to drop off weapons and stores at battalion headquarters at Xinon Neron. Their carriers then tried to bring this up to the front line troops, but the mud built up between their track covers and the tracks themselves, jamming their running gear. In the end the troops were forced to carry up their additional supplies themselves.[35]

On 11 April the weather rapidly deteriorated, as Lieutenant Cec Crystal of B Company, 2/4 Battalion, recalled:

> We did a fair bit of scrapping all morning and about 11am it began to snow and continued on and off all that day and night. The snow was so thick it was just like a smoke screen and it allowed Jerry to come practically on to us. ...I could see a number of machine guns being dug in near the railway line and road junction, so I rang through and was put on to a British regiment of artillery for whom I directed their fire on to these guns. Eventually, after causing them to fire a great number of ranging shots they got their range and blew the whole box and dice to blazes. Shortly afterwards, Jerry opened up his artillery and gave us merry hell for a good many minutes.[36]

On A Company's front the Germans made their way forward under the cover of the falling snow, but the weather lifted just in time. The battalion called down mortar and artillery fire onto the Germans, blowing holes in their ranks and forcing them to retire. Two tanks supporting the attack ran onto the minefields and blew up.[37]

Around 8.30am the men from 2/8 Australian Battalion watched as LSSAH launched an assault on the Rangers to their left. At one point the Germans threatened to break through, but after some heavy fighting were driven off. To counter this 10 and 11 Platoons were sent over to the left flank with C Company to strengthen their link with the Rangers. A detachment of mortars was also put under C Company's command. The Germans then launched an attack on D Company in the centre, just as 18 Platoon, in reserve, were sitting down to a breakfast of cold sausages. Abandoning their food, one section took up positions on the forward slopes. This proved to be a wise move, as the Germans dropped some mortar fire on the pits they had just vacated, destroying their gear. Within minutes the Germans shortened their range, hitting their new position, and forced the Australians back over the ridge. The situation was saved when a blizzard sprung up, bringing a halt to any further fighting that day.[38]

Though this encounter had ended inconclusively for LSSAH, help was on its way to them. Early in the afternoon the advance guard of 9. Panzer-Division discovered that the road south of Resan was flooded and could make no further progress. As a result they were diverted south in the direction of Bitolj and Florina, the first elements reaching Bitolj later that day[39].

Later that evening two Sturmgeschütze III from LSSAH passed through Vevi and opened fire on positions around the Kleidi Pass. In conjunction with them, 7. Kompanie launched an assault on the Rangers, driving them off their forward positions. The attack quickly ground to a halt, however, when the Germans came under heavy and accurate artillery fire, forcing them to pull back to Vevi.[40] After dusk patrols LSSAH resumed their previous night's activities, but by now the Australians were wise to their ruse of calling out in English. This time they responded with rifle and light machine gun fire, to the detriment of their attackers, though it soon became obvious that SS had occupied the dead ground 200 yards in front of 2/8 Battalion.[41]

While the Australians were under attack news was received by Mackay Force of a flanking move being made on the Greeks between lakes Petron and Vegorritis. To counter this C Squadron, 3 Royal Tanks and a troop from 102 Anti-Tank Regiment were sent toward Panteleimon as Lieutenant Robert Crisp recalled:

> The squadron progressed slowly towards the foot of the gorge, leaving behind it a trail of broken-down A10s like some Olympian paper-chase with Mars as the forerunner. ...The cross-country run of about five miles had played havoc with the squadron strength. One A10 had failed to start owing to a cracked distributor. Six others had not reached their destination because of track breakages. By the time they had been patched up by the shepherding R.A.O.C. personnel every spare part in the squadron had been used up.

The following day, realizing it had been a false alarm, the squadron returned, losing more tanks on the way back, as Crisp lamented:

> Five A10s were left lying out in the vineyards with hopelessly broken tracks, their crews alongside dejectedly awaiting orders; two

more had fallen by the way with broken pistons. A brief wireless inquiry elicited the information from battalion headquarters that no more spares of any sort were available, and that in future any broken-down tanks which could not be repaired from squadron resources would have to be abandoned and destroyed after machine guns and breech blocks had been removed. Seven dense columns of black smoke spread their message of doom over the Macedonia countryside that evening as the tanks burned in a series of violent detonations from exploding ammunition.[42]

It was an inauspicious start to their time in Greece and one that did not bode well for the future.

That same day Papagos informed Wilson's rear headquarters at Athens that he would start to withdraw his forces in Albania so long as the British rearguard remained in the area around Florina to protect it. Somehow, though, word of this did not get through to Wilson. Instead, early the following morning, he ordered all formations to withdraw to the Aliákmon Line as soon as possible. This prompted Mackay to issue new orders to both 2/4 and 2/8 Australian Battalions. They were to hold on for the rest of the day, start thinning out after dark and then make their way back to their transport. He also ordered the Dodecanese Regiment to begin moving over to his left flank and offered them transport to move their sick and wounded.

This redeploymentsoon became academic when, on the morning of 12 April, LSSAH began to move forward again under intense mortar and machine gun fire. Their thrust initially fell onto the east of the road against the Rangers, while on 2/8 Australian Battalion's left flank, 11 Platoon started to come in for attention from the advancing Germans and then under light mortar fire as well. The Australians were also briefly shelled by their own 25-pounders, though fortunately to no effect. Shortly after this, 17 Platoon, in the centre, came under heavy mortar fire. An attempt to deal with the German mortars was made by bringing forward an artillery observer, but came to naught because of a breakdown in communication to the rear. Mitchell then ordered 18 Platoon forward, but on moving up they ran into some German troops pushing around to the rear of C Company. In the end there was little 18 Platoon could do to help and around mid-morning 14 Platoon was overrun. At this point communication was restored with their artillery, allowing accurate fire to be brought down on the Germans. Aided by this, and fire from some nearby infantry, the party of Germans, some 350 strong, was driven back, but only to the forward slope of the ridge.

Concentrated artillery fire from LSSAH then started to fall on the Rangers' positions. To add to the Rangers' problems a StuG III took up a position in the dead ground in front of C Company, 2/8 Australian Battalion, and started shelling the Rangers. This forced the Rangers out of their slit trenches, some of whom surrendered. Faced with this assault C Company and part of B Company pulled back further up the slope. In the process they managed to rescue two New Zealand machine-gun teams, loading their guns and ammunition onto some packhorses they had found.[43]

Later that morning advance elements of 9. Panzer-Division reached Vevi, but there was little the Australians could do other than watch as they began to move their troops forward.[44] A number of their tanks made for the dead ground below 2/8 Australian Battalion, while trucks started disgorging German infantry who formed up with the tanks. Further back the Germans began setting up artillery in a depression, but with the weather deteriorating no attack developed for several hours. Around 11am the Rangers began to pull out from the pass to another position astride the road two miles further back. This exposed six 2-pounders of 2/1 Australian Anti-Tank Regiment and all but one had to be abandoned. Meanwhile, 2/8 Australian Battalion found themselves in the unfortunate position of holding a rather exposed salient along the ridge, so a platoon from A Company, under supporting fire from D Company, put in a counter-attack and managed to regain some of the ground lost by C Company earlier in the day.

With LSSAH heavily committed along the Vevi road it was not until 2pm that 9. Panzer-Division was able to link up with them and launch a combined attack. By now the Rangers were well on their way back to their pre-arranged rearguard position at Rodona, resulting in the attack falling on 2/8 Australian Battalion. Some 200 infantrymen from LSSAH thrust up a gully towards C and D Company, and for the next hour the Australians managed to contain this, but only until the last of the Dodecanese Regiment had gone. Then 2/8 Australian Battalion found itself in the invidious position of being under attack from the left and under fire from the right. Some support did come in the form of the crews of the Rangers' carrier platoon, but six of their carriers had to be abandoned and destroyed when they became bogged down forward of Kliedi. To make matters worse, around 4.30pm a German tank drove up the re-entrant between the two companies and opened up on them. Shortly afterwards the tank was joined by three more, all of which set about destroying the Australian sangars and weapons pits. With fire from their Boyes anti-tank rifles ineffective, and with more

German infantry moving up, the Australians had no choice but to pull back to the reverse slope.

Around 4pm, with signs of the Australians pulling back, LSSAH began to take up the pursuit. Hauptsturmführer Schulze, the commander of 2. Kompanie, later reported:

> Abandoned or destroyed British trucks lay to the left and right of the road. As we ran past one, we saw a dead driver at the wheel. After we had run another 20 metres we saw the truck suddenly start driving, the driver had only pretended to be dead and was now trying to break through at high speed. About fifty metres in front of us there was a gigantic explosion as the road was blown up by remote control detonation. The escaping truck and its driver flew into the air and a deep crater blocked the road.[45]

At that point 3 Kompanie, LSSAH also took up the pursuit around 4.30pm:

> With our bayonets on our rifles we rushed forward. The Pioniere had taken advantage of the fog and cleared paths for us through the minefields. Two Sturmgeschützen rolled along with us, firing as they went. It was lively up above on the slopes of the hills, as well: Tommy was beginning to break camp. We made sure that his retreat became a rapid flight. After the minefield the road and railroad tracks ran toward each other at a steep arc. Along the pass, the tracks and the road traced a sharply curved S with ridges thrusting into bends. Our 3.7-centimetre Flak and Sturmgeschützen were firing on the enemy groups pulling back across these hills. Behind the first bend in the S, the train tracks went into a curved tunnel. About 250 Australians and New Zealanders, and Tommys had pulled back into the tunnel. A Sturmgeschütz ricocheted a shell into the opening and it had the desired effect. All men hiding there came running out with their hands in the air and more followed supporting the wounded and carrying the dead.[46]

Although Mitchell had received orders from Brigadier Vasey to start withdrawing around 7pm, the situation was now becoming desperate. With the Germans having broken through the Rangers' position and the lines cut by shellfire, he sent a Lieutenant Sheedy back to Vasey's headquarters with instructions to explain the situation to the brigadier. Crossing the open ground south of the ridge Sheedy came upon a German tank on the road outside Kleidi and not far away its victim, a wireless van, on fire. Skirting the village he eventually reached a Light Mk VI of 4 Hussars, which shot up some German infantrymen who had broken through the Rangers' position. Sheedy eventually reached the forward troop of 2/3 Field Regiment, who loaned him a carrier. This he drove back to Vasey at brigade headquarters, but by then it was too late.

Around 5pm, as Mitchell called his company commanders together, they came under fire from one of the German tanks at the top of the C Company wadi. Half an hour later, just after the company commanders returned to their men, German infantry supported by tanks broke through their battalion lines. At this point all attempts at an organized retreat came to naught. Instead the battalion broke up into small groups that set off across the valley to the next ridge.[47] Here they came under strong enfilading fire from German tanks and supporting infantry on the road to Kleidi. Fortunately the guns of 2 Royal Horse Artillery and two Australian anti-tank guns astride the road prevented the Germans from closing in.

For many of the men from 2/8 Australian Battalion this was all too much. Too tired to carry their weapons, many threw them away, some under orders from their officers. After a long march through waterlogged ground the leading companies reached the reserve position at Sotir around 9pm. Two hours later they reached Rodona, where they were picked up by their battalion transport and driven back to the Aliákmon River. Others less fortunate filtered in later on during the night, bringing the battalion up to a total strength of 250.[48]

Around 5pm 1. and 7. Kompanien took the village of Kleidi, taking eighty-two prisoners in the process. A couple of hours later they reached the top of the pass itself, where they had their first view of the western Macedonian plain. As Shulze later recounted: 'It was swimming with British troops. We could see the batteries that were still firing and the trains that were retreating.' In the meantime, 12. and 13. Kompanien to their left, having secured the high ground, struck off toward Petrais, while 14. Kompanie made their way down to the shore of Lake Petron. At 8.15pm III. Bataillon took Petrais, along with a further sixty Australian, English and Greek troops. From there they sent out a combat reconnaissance towards Amyntaio.

After the Germans had broken through the Rangers' position in the afternoon, the initial response of 2/4 Australian Battalion had been to send B Company forward in an attempt to fill that gap, but their infantrymen ran into strong opposition. By 3pm they were all but surrounded, so Lieutenant Colonel Dougherty contacted their second-in-command Lieutenant Chrystal and ordered them to withdraw to battalion headquarters. The company did so under heavy fire, as Chrystal later recalled:

> The enemy machine guns and mountain guns gave us a merry time and when all had gone Hal and I decided to try and get out. Talk about running a gauntlet of death! I've never been in anything like it. We had to dump most of our gear and run about 50 yards up the exposed side of the mountain. Snow covered the deep steep slope. We were slipping and sliding and burying our faces in the slush as bullets whipped the snow up around us. Then we would see the mountain gun and the machine guns belch our a long stream of flame and there would be a lovely explosion near us which would cover us with snow. Lucky they were rotten shots. Somehow or other we got to the top and raced over the other side where we found our company sergeant-major, Wym Keast, had been hit in the leg and arm. We were helping him along when they opened up from the other side where we thought we were safe. We went flat again. Wyn let out a yell and we found he'd been pretty badly hit a second time. Before I knew what had happened Hal jumped up and grabbed 'Keasty', threw him over his shoulder, and we dragged him to a small wadi where we were out of view. He was so badly wounded that we found it impossible to move him further, so we said goodbye and left him there till we could find help. A few hundred yards further on we found a stretcher bearer, so we took a party back, grabbed Wyn, and set off carrying him in relays, never daring to stop with Jerry hard on our heels. By the time we reached Battalion headquarters everyone had gone except one truck. We put Wyn into that and pushed on, absolutely exhausted, for another six miles to the battalion assembly area.[49]

Also withdrawn were two platoons from A Company. Under orders from Dougherty to thin out his company Captain McCarty had sent these down to the base of the rear slope of the ridge, leaving Lieutenant Copland's 8 Platoon on Hill 1001. These, along with the rest of 2/4 Australian Battalion, continued to hold their ground until around 5pm. By then the Germans had broken through on the right and were driving down the main road. To Vasey it was obvious that the front had lost all cohesion and that there was no chance of a coordinated withdrawal. He contacted Dougherty with the message: 'Tell him the roof is leaking. He had better come so we can cook up a plot.'[50]

Dougherty realised the only option was to hold on to the right until last light so the darkness would allow them to withdraw in smaller groups. These were then to make their way to their embussing point south of Rodona, keeping well to the west of Xinon Neron. This was easy for B Company as they were already just to the south of battalion headquarters. Lieutenant E.D. Wren's platoon of D Company and the carrier platoon were ordered to hold on to the right to cover the withdrawal of the forward companies. McCarty sent two runners up to contact Copland's 8 Platoon and then led the rest of his company out.

Back at battalion headquarters Dougherty had other problems:

> Shortly after 9pm I was south-west of Xinon Neron, between the railway and the main road, with my 15 cwt truck, our RAP truck, two battalion trucks and a carrier. We had come to boggy ground and it was not possible to move the vehicles further. Except for the carrier my party threw petrol over the vehicles and their contents, and set them on fire. An anti-tank battery, commanded by Captain Crawford, was with us, and Crawford decided to move back to the railway and then move south-east along it. He had not proceeded far along the line when his battery was surrounded by the Germans and captured. I then returned to Xinon Neron in the carrier, and moved round the village looking for any elements of the 2/4th who might have assembled at our earlier embossing point and who might not have received word of the change that had been made because of the German advance. By this time the enemy was well down the road and south of the railway.
>
> From Xinon Neron I moved towards the embussing point by the road leading south-east from the village. I arrived at the small culvert on the main road, where the road crossed the stream running south-west from Sotir, at about 9.45pm and found Major Montgomery waiting for me there. He told me that the 2/4th, except the company headquarters and two platoons of 'D' Company, and Lieutenant Copland's platoon of 'A' Company had passed the culvert by 9.30pm. He also told me that the units which were to have fought a rearguard action south-south-west of Sotir were completely disorganized and that the 2/4th, with the remnants of

the Rangers (one company), had been ordered to hold the rearguard position until 9am the following morning (Easter Sunday).[51]

Though the runners from McCarty had made contact with Copland, he had continued to hold his position in the mistaken belief that the rest of A Company was still in place below him. It was only when the runners returned around 8.30pm that Copeland finally relented and led his men out, just in time to avoid the Germans, who were climbing up the forward slopes of Hill 1001. Further to the left Major Barnham had delayed the withdrawal of 17 and 18 Platoons of D Company until two sections from 27 NZ MG Battalion had moved out. This was to prove costly, though not for the machine-gunners, who carried their weapons to the base of the hill and then drove off in their trucks. Barnham then set off for their rendezvous point, accompanied by some gunners from 2/1 Australian Anti-Tank Battalion who had destroyed their guns. On reaching Xinon Neron they were joined by Copland's platoon, but from there strayed too close to the road. Just past the road junction they ran into a small party of German motorcyclists, with whom they exchanged fire, several Germans being shot and Barnham killed. The Australians successfully disengaged from this party, but further on ran into a road block set up by the German motorcycle company and all seventy were captured.[52]

This may have been the roadblock described by the commander of 6. Batterie (8.8-cm Flak), Obersturmführer Fend, from LSSAH. He had been trying to contact the commander of 2. Kompanie and was in the process of making his way back to his unit:

> At the crossing point of the road and railroad tracks, I was surprised and taken prisoner by an Australian motorcycle reconnaissance force. I was brought back several hundred metres along the railway embankment and handed over to a captain. His company was already loaded into personnel carriers. There was considerable nervousness in the air, because they did not seem to know in what direction to move. In the course of my short questioning I got the impression that they wanted to move in the direction of Klisura Pass. When asked, I told the captain that the Klisura Pass was already in German hands. I was even more surprised when he asked me if I knew a passable road to Athens, but I said immediately that I did. After a short map consultation, I was loaded into the first vehicle, and we drove across the railway embankment (the terrain

was marshy from the melting snows) toward the road and toward our 2. Kompanie. After a short time there was the sound of the advancing motorcycles braking and falling. The first personnel vehicle, in which the captain and I sat, passed the motorcycles and attempted to break through the Kompanie Schulz from the rear. Suddenly there was a cry: 'The English!' The first gunshots rang out. Soon thereafter, a hand grenade exploded on the car, and the motor stopped. MG fire started up on both sides and rained down on the entire column. I could recognize the positions in the moonlight. My call of 'Cease fire!' was met with the answer 'One of the pigs speaks German there!' and renewed MG fire. They did not stop until I yelled 'You fools, stop that shooting once and for all!' I jumped from the car, and from the ditch in front of me rose the figure of Fritz Witt; I told him of my misadventure and also informed him that he was moving behind the British positions. He knew that already. In the early morning of 13 April I was able to return to my unit on a motorcycle. About 90 Australians spent the night with 2. Kompanie.[53]

At Sotir, between Lake Vegorritis on the right and marshy ground on the left, the remnants of 2/4 Battalion joined up with the hastily assembled rearguard. The Australians took up positions on the right, while the Rangers, now down to the strength of one company, were to their left. With them were B and C Squadron of 3 Royal Tanks, a squadron of 4 Hussars, 2 Royal Horse Artillery, a platoon of 27 NZ MG Battalion and a battery from 102 Anti-Tank Regiment.[54] Having only just arrived that evening, 2 Royal Horse Artillery began to unlimber their 25-pounders, while the tanks moved over the crest of the ridge to the forward slope to cover them as they prepared their defences. It was not until midnight that the last friendly troops, the Dodecanese Regiment, passed through along the road. The tanks held their positions until just before first light when they were ordered back over the ridge. Deciding not to risk turning around on his A10's suspect tracks, Crisp ordered his driver to reverse slowly back. His sergeant's tank on the left conformed to his movements, but the other made a sharp turn to the right before disappearing out of sight. Shortly afterwards he radioed back to say his tank had broken a track. As Crisp later wrote:

I went over to where the disabled tank lay, its crew grouped on one side staring alternately at the track and into the darkness towards

Amyntaio. They seemed to be in a pretty fine state of nerves. The near-side track was broken in two places, and one end was wrapped round the driving sprocket. I studied the marks on the ground. It was immediately clear to me that the tank commander had given his driver an order 'Driver advance; hard left', in circumstances in which even a complete novice would have seen the necessity for a gentle, wide-angled turn. The tank commander was no novice. He was a regular soldier of many years service. He knew exactly what that tank would or would not do. He knew, I was sure, exactly what was going to happen when he gave that order. And so did the driver.[55]

Whether it was deliberate sabotage or not, there was no way the track could be fixed, so under orders from Crisp, the crew set fire to it and made their way back to squadron headquarters. Crisp never saw them again.

Around dawn on 13 April the leading elements of 9. Panzer-Division made their appearance as they descended Kleidi Pass. Their arrival did not go unnoticed at Sotir when a column of German vehicles, preceeded by some motorcyclists, hove into view on the southern side of the pass shortly after sunrise. As it grew lighter Crisp, from his tank, was able to make out more details:

It was not until 7.30 that we were able to identify any armour moving down among the vehicles. ...I was a little surprised that nothing unfriendly had yet been thrown at our ridge. All the same I nearly jumped out of the turret when I heard the crash of explosions immediately behind me. I looked wildly round for the upheaval of earth and smoke, but could see nothing. Then the series of bangs came again, in quick succession, and this time I spotted the flashes from the muzzles of the 25-pounders in the lee of the hill behind us. I switched the binoculars quickly to the entrance of the pass, and there, straddling the brown and yellow gash of the road, the quick, black plumes puffed up and blew lazily away up the mountain side. I could see men jumping out of vehicles and diving for cover. It was very satisfying.[56]

Mixed up within the advancing German column were elements of LSSAH, including Kampfgruppe Witt, but they were still short of support weapons, so the battlegroup's commander stopped their advance until these were brought up. At approximately 6.30am they came under fire from some twelve tanks, supported by artillery:

> Because of the blasting of the road, which had not yet been cleared entirely, only one 3.7-centimetre Pak gun, belonging to 5. Kompanie was at the front; it had been able to move around the craters and had arrived about 07.30 hours. The tanks concentrated their fire on this artillery piece; its crew was already short two men who had been wounded during the uncoupling. The remaining crew was able, however, to bring the gun into position and open fire.[57]

One of those on the pass that day was the commander of the 8.8cm battery from LSSAH, Fend, who had recently been freed from captivity. Making his way back up to Kleidi Pass he was stopped by their corps commander, Generalleutnant Stumme, who happened to be in the area. Stumme told him he thought it was madness to try to bring the heavy flak weapons into action against the tanks, but this did not deter Fend, who continued to make his way back up the road:

> Just before the top of the pass, Untersturmführer Martin Stolze (Ordonnanz-Offizier) came racing towards me on his motorcycle; with a cry of 'Werner, tanks! English tanks!' he roared on past. I had only seconds to move the newly-arrived gun in the direction from which the motorcycle rider had just come. We saw coming toward us rapidly over the next hill a classic example of a tank attack just as it would appear in a manoeuvre picture. Assuming our position here was as exciting as it was unusual. With the gun barely 'in alignment' I was already sitting at the telescope of the good old 8.8 and drawing a bead on the nearest tank. Only my hand, shaking with excitement of the hunt, had difficulty with adjusting the sights. With just a few shots in the space of a minute, I had the situation cleared up. The first four tanks were standing in flames, the others stopped and a few turned back.[58]

The combat report for Fend's battery later claimed that eight tanks had been knocked out and set on fire by this one gun. The truth was probably more prosaic. During the night C Squadron 3 Royal Tanks lost four more tanks to track breakage and one to steering failure. Possibly B Squadron's only casualty in this action was that of Sergeant Macintosh's tank, as Trooper Jim Caswell in the spare driver's position later wrote:

At 500 yards Sergeant Mac said: 'Immediately to our front, German infantry, 500 yards, gunners open fire.' I and the turret gunner had a good shoot at the still exposed German infantry. In about an hour they called up their anti-tank guns and their tanks were beginning to arrive. Our RHA joined in and we were giving the Germans a very hot time. We were now firing our armour-piercing shells at the German tanks and nearly all our MG ammunition was fired. Some German shells were ranging on us after about two hours of battle one hit our front and shot off one of our tracks. So Mac ordered the breech-blocks to be removed from the guns and to bail out.[59]

In the case of another tank:

Captain George Witheridge's tank was hit by gunfire and momentarily caught fire. The crew found themselves in enemy territory with most of them wounded or unconscious. Witheridge was the first to return to consciousness, but the driver was violently sick and was relieved by the second driver. They were now alone. A drill was worked out for speed in starting and moving off. The tank moved forwards to the steepest part of the ridge, the only way to avoid anti-tank fire. It fell rather than ran over the ridge edge and roared, out of gear, to the plain below. Lieutenant-Colonel Keller, alerted by a wireless message, came back in his staff car through shellfire to help the tank and crew, which managed to join the tail end of the regiment shortly before Ptolemais was reached.[60]

After two hours it was the turn of 3 Royal Tanks to withdraw to their next rearguard position at Ptolemais, the rest having been pulled out unit by unit. B Squadron went first and then C Squadron. As Robert Crisp was approaching the road in his tank:

A number of our cruisers went hurtling past. One A10 of B Squadron, going flat out, had its gun traversed at right angles to its line of flight. As it thundered down the narrow roadway I stared fascinated as the 2-pounder muzzle connected with a telegraph pole with a terrific whack. The turret whirled dizzily in a full circle, just in time to hit the next pole. Then it hit a third one before the crew got their crazy world under control.

While 2/4 Battalion continued on to Kozani and then the Aliákmon River, Crisp and his troop sergeant joined A Squadron and the rearguard at a defile south of Ptolemais. By now, however, breakdowns had reduced C Squadron from its original complement of sixteen tanks to his two A10s, the squadron commander's tank and another from 12 Troop.[61] Along with 4 Hussars, a battery of anti-tank guns, some New Zealand machine-gunners and part of the Rangers, the job of this rearguard was to give the Greek 12 Division more time to complete its withdrawal.[62]

Pushing on towards Ptolemais, 9. Panzer-Division made good progress. By 2.30pm they had reached a position close enough to the British rearguard for an exchange of fire. South of the town the Germans' advance ground to a halt:

> The easterly direction was impassable, as a bridge had been blown and the stream well dammed up. The westerly road led through a swamp with several ditches full of water, but was passable, even though there was no trace of traffic having used it. Most of the road through the swamp was in view of the enemy. The regiment chose this route for attack, and tried to push through Navropighi to the main road to surround the enemy's commanding positions and take him in the rear. This plan was successful. The regiment's approach and the crossing of the swamp were very difficult and had to be done at a walking pace. The approach was made under heavy shellfire, and later under anti-tank fire from several enemy tanks. We opened fire, drove off the enemy tanks and knocked out two. Only after crossing the swamp could the regiment deploy. Seven tanks were stuck and followed later. A feature of the plan was to thrust through as fast as possible to get behind the enemy. This part of the plan was made most difficult by the terrain, which was rising and in places steep and broken and by the gradual increase in the enemy tank and anti-tank fire, supported by artillery. All the regiment's tanks opened fire. The enemy tanks could be seen trying to drive off backwards after having been surrounded. Four were probably knocked out trying to do this. The regiment was now approaching Navropighi, and dusk was beginning to set in. Here violent engagements developed with enemy tanks and self-propelled anti-tank guns. It was impossible to see accurately what success the regiment had.[63]

The tanks seen withdrawing were most probably those of A Squadron that had been ordered back to Kozani, while the tanks the Germans claimed they knocked out were more likely the four A Squadron tanks destroyed by their crews after suffering track or engine and transmission failure.

Here, in the falling light, Crisp noted a line of around twenty German tanks moving forward in single file. Working towards the column along a diagonal course, his tank and that of his sergeant managed to get ahead of them after pulling up sharply to avoid driving into some boggy ground:

> The range was about 800 yards, perhaps a little more. The gunner shouted up at me that he could barely see the target so I told him to get on the leading tank and I would correct him for elevation. Almost immediately my teeth and skull jarred to the crack from the muzzle of the 2-pounder and I watched the shell pitch about 50 yards short. 'Up one hundred!' The tracer of the next shot seemed to bore right into the brown shadow, which was the leading tank. I told my gunner to keep it there but after every second shot he was to go up 50 and move down the line of tanks. ...The sergeant's gun was barking fiercely alongside. The orange tracers of our two guns kept up an almost continuous stream of light in the gathering darkness. Once I saw some men running about and switched to the machine-gun. My sergeant spotted them too and soon the air was filled with the small glowing meteors of bullets mingling with the comets of our guns. I was not aware of anything being fired back at us and I do know that after a few minutes the column halted and two columns of smoke rose black against the afterglow.[64]

The anti-tank guns with them accounted for another two tanks, the Germans recording losses of one PanzerKampfwagen I, one PxKpfw II and two PzKpfw IVs.[65] The rearguard then pulled back to the Aliákmon River unhindered further by the Germans, who had been forced to halt at Pondokoni because their ammunition and petrol were running low.[66]

Ordered back to the road, Crisp and his sergeant came upon a sorry sight:

> We found [Major] Bimbo [Warren] standing on the edge of the metalled surface, woefully regarding his tank and cursing like mad. He had tried to come after us, but had struck a swampy patch in the bad light; the track had filled with mud, and snapped as it went over the driving sprocket.

Ordered back to Kozani, this sad remnant from C Squadron set off up the road, but on reaching the town Crisp and a troop of Hussars' tanks were ordered to set up a roadblock and hold it for another hour. When they finally decided to leave Crisp's tank refused to start, the cause a broken fuel pump. With no spares available the tank was set alight and Crisp and his crew made their way back to Kozani. There they hitched a ride with B Squadron, which itself had lost seven tanks to track, engine or transmission failure, two in Kozani itself.[67] Thus it was a somewhat subdued 3 Royal Tanks that lay that night south of the river, breakdown losses having reduced it to seventeen tanks from a complement of fifty-two.

Despite their narrow escape from Sotir, 1 Armoured Brigade was now in a difficult position, according to their Brigade Major Richard Hobson:

> We marched that night to a place called Grevená, south of River Aliákmon and right out on a flank from which Force HQ told us that it would take 10 days to make a road to get out of. Next day was misery; all of us very tired and not knowing quite what to do next. Greeks broke and poured through us. They fairly cluttered up the only road with their bullock carts and donkey carts and old lorries and buses, and had no idea of road discipline or movement. Bombing started too, which hitherto, owing to the wet, we had been free from. Grevená was bombed, our road was bombed, we were machine gunned ceaselessly and our headquarters had six different attacks on it. Hell it was, and I think it was our worst day. However, we survived somehow and then got orders to make a stand 20 miles further south-east, so off we trekked again that night.[68]

From Grevená 1 Armoured Brigade set off on 15 April over a rough mountain road rather than the main road, thanks to a faulty decision by W Force Group. This proved to be a disaster for 3 Royal Tanks. More A10s dropped out en route through mechanical failure and by the time they reached the Venetikos River they could only muster six operational A10s.[69]

Thus, at the end of the defence of the day Mackay Force had successfully delayed the Germans at Kliedi Pass, though very few of the units involved had come away unscathed. Of those 3 Royal Tanks had probably suffered the most, having had its tank strength reduced by two-thirds by the time they crossed the Aliákmon River, something that would have been entirely preventable had their pleas for tracks and spare parts had been properly answered. Next in line would have to be 2/8 Australian Battalion, who were hardly in a fit state to repel the German attack by the time they moved into the line. This was something that might have been avoided had Blamey not been so insistent on 6 Australian Division going first. It is a bit sad to think that this might have been all because of his dislike of the commander of 7 Australian Division. The behaviour of the Rangers also has to be called into question. Their sudden departure from the pass itself at a critical time unhinged the whole defensive line. Nevertheless, the careful siting of the two fall-back positions at Sotir and Ptolemais bought time for the retreating troops and for W Force further back, though German logistical failures helped as well.

Chapter 6

The Battle for Servia Pass

While the disengagement of the Australian and British troops from Kliedi Pass had been messy, it had served its purpose. Along with the subsequent rearguard action of 1 Armoured Brigade at Sotir and Ptolemais and the logistical problems of their panzer division, the German thrust through the Monastir Gap had been blunted long enough to help establish the next defensive line along the Aliákmon-Venetikos Line. Here the intention was for W Force to set up its main defensives at the Servia and Olympus Passes, with subsidiary blocking positions at Grevená and Platamon. As luck would have it 5 NZ Brigade was already in place at Olympus Pass, having originally been the reserve brigade behind 6 NZ Brigade, the latter on the plains south of the Aliákmon River. Under the revised plan 4 NZ Brigade was ordered to Servia Pass and once properly established 16 Australian Brigade was to be withdrawn from its blocking position on the Veria Pass. If this could be carried out in time the German spearheads would meet up with troops that had had time to prepare their defences and recover from their redeployment.

On the evening of 9 April 4 NZ Brigade reached Servia Pass. For 19 NZ Battalion it had been a difficult move over mountain roads deteriorating under a deluge of rain and a heavy flow of traffic, to which misery were added mechanical issues with the unit's new transport. Then rain, sleet and snow greeted them as they debussed and marched into their new positions. Most of them spent an uncomfortable night under groundsheets, only to discover on waking that there was little in the way of natural ground cover, apart from some coarse tussock-like grass. Positions were assigned that morning, 19 NZ Battalion taking over the road junction at the mouth of the pass, with six 2-pounders from 32 Anti-Tank Battery and a platoon of Vickers machine guns from 2/1 Australian MG Battalion thrown in for good measure. On their left was 18 NZ Battalion, while 20 NZ Battalion was to their right.

As a defensive position Servia Pass had much to commend it. The valley from Servia was almost eight miles long, closing to about 60 yards at the throat of the pass. The narrow and precipitous rocky ridge on the northern side was almost unscalable. The infantry of 19 NZ Battalion took up positions on the hills to the south, overlooking a stream that was crossed by a small concrete bridge, in front of which they dug three anti-tank ditches as well as laying mines in the road and streambed. They also found and occupied a system of trenches and posts, including a concrete pillbox that had been prepared by Metaxas' army during the Bulgar war in 1912.[1]

With 4 NZ Brigade in place, the next move was to extricate 16 Australian Brigade from their positions at the eastern end of Veria Pass and get them back across the Aliákmon River. The question was how to do this. Though routing them through Kozani using their battalion transport offered the quickest and most logical option, a sudden German breakthrough at Vevi would catch them on the back foot while withdrawing along the main road. Blamey was anxious to avoid a potential disaster and, with the additional concern over whether MacKay Force at Vevi could withstand a full-scale assault, ordered the brigade to retire on foot over the 6,000-foot Vermion range and thence to Servia. Orders were received on 10 April for the battalions to prepare for an immediate withdrawal. Some of their excess gear was loaded onto donkeys and taken to Veria village, where it was handed over to their battalion transport. Each man then sorted out a ground sheet and five days of rations and ammunition for himself. The rest of their equipment and weaponry they set about destroying before nightfall, including greatcoats, blankets and even spare gun barrels. Some men burnt their blankets; others urinated on them before burying them in the snow. To their dismay the order was countermanded a short time later and they were told that they were not to move out until the next day. The blankets were dug up and, as Jack McCarthy from 2/2 Battalion recalled:

> We slept in threes fully dressed and had our boots sticking out of the bottom of the blankets and they were covered in snow. I have been wet and almost frozen all day and no fires allowed, so meals were cold bully beef and biscuits.[2]

On 11 April 2/3 Australian Battalion withdrew to the foot of the pass and took up a blocking position near the junction of the main road and the track leading to the Aliákmon River. Thereafter two companies from each of 2/1 and 2/2 Australian battalions started to make their way back. The other companies of each battalion left the following night. Having made their way through the Veria Pass they had to cross another small range of hills to reach the Aliákmon River. What had become a trudge through ankle-deep mud soon turned into an exhausting trek through snow. Uncertain of the way, the leading troops of

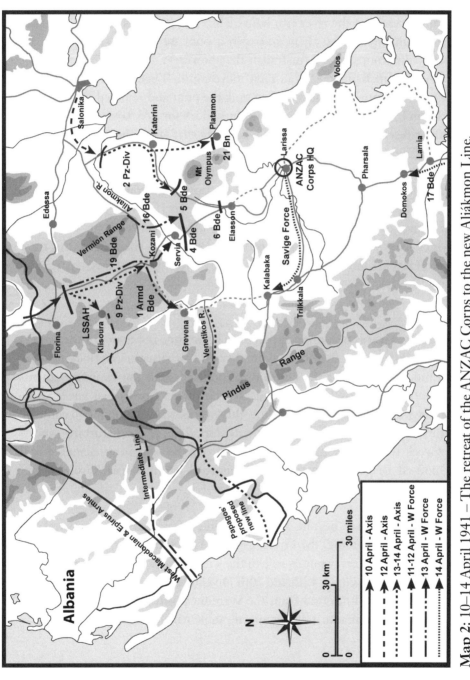

Map 2: 10–14 April 1941 – The retreat of the ANZAC Corps to the new Aliákmon Line.

2/1 Battalion sought help at the village of Avlianna, waking up a villager for information. They eventually gained the summit of the pass around 6am on 13 April, reaching the river two hours later. Here sappers of 2/1 Australian Field Company ferried them across in a punt guided by a wire rope. By midday the troops of 2/2 Australian Battalion were all across, at which time 2/3 Australian Battalion began their move south. Their last platoon crossed the river at 10pm. The sappers then sank the punt and rejoined the brigade.

From from the river it was an arduous climb for 2/3 Australian Battalion to their reserve position at Moskhokori. By that stage they were tired and short of food, having had to live on what rations they had carried with them since their departure. In the case of 2/1 Australian Battalion, after reaching Velvendos that night, they found they had another six-mile climb next day to their new positions above the village of Moskhokori. By now they were 5,500 feet above sea level, in two-foot deep snow and in an area cut by precipitous ravines. Nor was there any sign of 6 NZ Brigade to their right; the latter were in fact six miles away and separated by rugged mountains.[3]

*****

By now was it was becoming apparent that the stoic resistance of the Greeks was no substitute for their lack of mobility, and the situation was looking more and more perilous for the entire operation. Though the various elements of the Anzac Corps (redesignated as such on 12 April[4]) had successfully withdrawn to the new defensive line, the Greeks were struggling to conform to this. On the 13th Wilson and his staff started to receive disturbing reports of Greek troop movements. One came from the retreating elements of 1 Armoured Brigade, who reported their road jammed with Greek troops trudging south. Wilson was later to report:

> from the outset, in spite of every possible effort being made to avoid misunderstanding, the Greek Central Macedonian Army failed in every way to carry out its role in the withdrawal ...It may be said, in fact, that the Greek 12th and 20th Divisions never regained control after their withdrawal from the Vermion positions, but continued to disintegrate into a disorganized rabble whose main object was to reach Athens.

Nor had it helped that both divisions had been ordered to thin out of their positions too late. There were even reports that Greek troops on the Albanian front were not willing to take up positions along the new defence line. The only good news was that the Greek Cavalry Division was still holding the Pisoderion Pass.

The problem now facing Wilson was that, in the course of withdrawing to the new line, the Greek army had been left holding a salient bounded by the mountain range west of the Florina-Kozani Valley and the Albanian frontier. In fact Papagos had only just ordered the commanders of Western Macedonia and Epirus to commence their withdrawal to the Venetikos River Line on 13 April. For this they now faced a march of around 100 miles, but this would mean holding the Klisoura and Siatista passes and the Grevená road for several days more, assuming that the Germans did not get there first. In fact, Blamey received word the following day that the Germans had taken the Klisoura Pass, threatening the withdrawal of three divisions of the Western Macedonian Army.[5] Worse still, from the point of view of the whole of the Anzac Corps, if the Germans were to push south along the Grevená road they would be in a position to cut off troops north of Larissa. Wilson's concern about this threat led him to commit 17 Australian Brigade, 2/11 Australian Battalion, artillery and other supporting arms as Savige Force, under Brigadier Stanley Savige, to secure this open flank, the brigade having disembarked at Piraeus on 12 April. Wilson, in consultation with Blamey, also decided to withdraw to Thermopylae along a line encompassing the Thermopylae, Brallos and Delphi passes. The danger of this move was that it involved abandoning all prospect of further cooperation with the Greek army. In fact, Wilson went so far as to say:

> within the limits of responsibility, Anzac Corps will make every possible effort to ensure Greek forces do not withdraw along routes available to Imperial forces, and that they do not in any way whatsoever hinder the withdrawal.

This was to be carried out as quickly as possible, on the basis that Wilson's motorized troops could achieve in days what it would take the Greeks weeks to do.[6]

*****

On the morning of 13 April Major General Mackay had left 1 Armoured Brigade's rearguard position at Sotir to take command of the defences at Servia Pass. On reaching the Aliákmon River bridge he learned that 26 NZ

Battalion was on its way from the vicinity of Katerini to Rymnion to back up his badly depleted brigade. Later that afternoon, on his orders, the Aliákmon bridge was demolished by Australian and British sappers. They also broke up the pontoon bridge further downstream after six British trucks had shown up at the very last minute and crossed over. The remnants of 19 Australian Brigade arrived later that day and set off into the hills from the village of Kerasia. The following night 26 NZ Battalion crossed the river by way of a rope bridge and took up position alongside 2/4 Battalion, 2/8 Battalion being placed further back in reserve.[7]

Later that afternoon the weather finally started to clear, allowing the Luftwaffe, now operating out of hastily prepared airstrips at Prilep and Monastir, to make its first appearance over Servia.[8] This was something of a rude awakening for 19 NZ Battalion, the attack occurring just as their evening meal was being served:

> Suddenly across the sky, silhouetted by the evening sun, a flight of seventeen aircraft made its appearance. The men watched with disinterest and munched contentedly – ours no doubt, probably Blenheims. Then the leader banked and dived. In a moment all was pandemonium; up and down the line the aircraft flew, roaring and spitting like devils out of hell. The mess groups scattered, each man cowering in what cover he could find.[9]

The battalion responded with Bren guns and their fire was joined by some Yugoslav-manned 88mm anti-aircraft guns that had reached 20 NZ Battalion headquarters the previous day.[10] Though short of ammunition, the Yugoslavs stayed with them for two days, engaging enemy aircraft until they ran out of ammunition.[11] Eventually, their bombs exhausted, the dive-bombers flew off, but it was now apparent to the brigade that the front line was rapidly approaching. Large numbers of refugees had started to stream back the previous day and mixed in with them were Greek soldiers on foot, along with remnants of 19 Australian Brigade in their trucks, while that same day line signallers, working out in front of the battalion, were greeted with the sight of German armour from 9. Panzer-Division rolling into Kozani.[12]

The Germans' next objective was Servia and the pass south of the river. An air reconnaissance report at 12.25pm had noted the blown bridge, which was not good news, but another was more hopeful: '... the pilot had flown at a low level and discovered that there was not a single enemy soldier between the river and the heights SW of Servia.'[13] It was not long after that that the men of 19 NZ Battalion saw some troops approach the blown bridge over the Aliákmon and start to construct a temporary replacement. This activity soon attracted shellfire, and though the Germans continued to work on it they had not managed to launch it by nightfall.[14] In fact, when it became evident that this was not going to work, their engineers turned their attention to constructing a ford in the river and an approach to it. This was not a great success either; the ford proved to be impassable and an attempt that evening to drive a PzKpfw II across it failed when they lost the tank in the river. The current was too swift to even move artillery across.

That night, under orders from the commander of 11. Infanterie-Regiment, Colonel Graf von Sponeck, 6. and 8. Kompanien crossed the river and at 5.30am on 15 April passed through Servia.[15] Approaching the pass itself the Germans captured two Greeks on horseback, leading them to believe that the Allies were pulling out.[16] Two hours later sentries in section posts of Nos 7 and 8 Platoons of 19 Battalion heard the sound of footsteps approaching:

> The challenge was answered with cries of 'Greko! Greko!' And the listeners relaxed: more refugees. Private Jack Barley left the trench to go down to the tank trap, which spanned the road and which the party was evidently trying to negotiate. He dimly discerned just what he had expected to see, a straggling party of Greeks. A Greek soldier was leading – he signed for them to go on, and went back to his post.[17]

After crossing the first tank trap this party of Germans carried on until the next two anti-tank ditches, where they sought cover and opened up on the leading New Zealand outposts. The first to respond were elements of 7, 8 and 9 Platoons and they were soon joined by Hawkes Bay Company and the Australian machine-gunners, their combined fire pinning down the Germans. By now, a party of Germans had worked their way round behind 7 and 8 Platoons, while their comrades in the ditches below provided covering fire with their machine guns and mortars. A captain from this party then attacked 7 Platoon in the rear, killing two of them and fatally wounding another. At this point Lance Corporal Christopher Kelly returned fire, killing the German officer and two others. Private Jim Frain stopped another group of twenty attackers with his Tommy gun, while Corporal George Cooke forced another party to surrender with well-aimed rifle fire.

The party of Germans that got behind 8 Platoon were also stopped by a few well-aimed shots from a Tommy gun wielded by Private Ray Wellman forced them to surrender. Then, as it became lighter, 9 Platoon were able to direct Bren gun, rifle and 3-inch mortar fire into the area around one of the tank traps. Very soon those troops surrendered as well. On the left of 8 Platoon, and out of sight of 9 Platoon, the Germans set up a light mortar but a few rounds from privates Hugh Erskine and Vincent Salmon's 2-inch mortar took care of it.

Once the sun started to rise, the German positions in the anti-tank ditch became untenable. Overlooked and under harassing fire from above they started to give up. One group of seventy Germans surrendered at 7.15am. The rest tried to get away, but when several were cut down by the battalion's accurate fire, another fifty surrendered. In the final count, of the 300 or so who had attacked, only twenty or thirty escaped, while 150 were killed or wounded.[18]

Around 9am von Sponeck ordered I. Bataillon to cross the river on a wider front. Their 1. Kompanie attempted to make their way over it east of Kranizia, but came under heavy and accurate artillery fire. When a number of the pontoons of the bridge were destroyed, they were forced to abandon their light infantry guns and other equipment on a sandbank in the middle of the river.[19] Then 2. Kompanie tried to cross upstream of the blown bridge, but they too suffered under heavy shellfire and had to abandon their attempt.[20]

An attempt was made to reinforce the Germans over the river by sending in two companies from 59. Kradschutzen-Bataillon, but they fared no better. As they made their way through the trees towards Servia 18 NZ Battalion opened up once they got in range with their mortars. Around midday the first of the Germans managed to enter Servia itself. It was at this point that CSM Edmond McCormack of B Company 18 NZ Battalion gathered up a scratch patrol of men and led them down the hill to the outskirts of Servia, where they shot up the Germans at close range and then withdrew as fast as they could.[21] It was then the turn of 19 NZ Battalion to open up at point-blank range, forcing the Germans to seek shelter in the village.[22] Those that were further back were forced to find what cover they could around the northern edge of Servia and there they remained pinned by the intense small arms and mortar fire for the rest of the day. Those Germans who made it into Servia were no better off as they were unable to move around to any extent. The fire from the New Zealand positions also meant that it was impossible to bring up any of their support weapons. In the end the Germans were forced to hold until nightfall. Then the firing eased up and the survivors were finally able to withdraw.

Despite this setback, the commander of 9. Panzer-Division, Generalleutnant Alfred von Hubkicki, was keen to launch another attack on the Servia position the next day, but was dissuaded from this action by Stumme and instead decided to outflank it by way of the road from Grevená to Kalabaka, with the view to ultimately coming in behind Servia Pass. This task was assigned to 5. Panzer-Division, advance elements of which had driven into Kozani from Ptolemais on the afternoon of 16 April, but there was a problem. All the bridges over the Aliákmon River had been demolished by the retreating British troops, and the approach and egress routes to the river had become inundated with water. In the end the division was limited to pushing their troops over it on rafts until their bridging column came forward.[23]

*****

On 14 April, while 19 NZ Battalion was preparing to face the German onslaught, Brigadier Savige had been on a reconnaisance from Kalabaka to the Pindus Mountains. On his return from this he was recalled to Blamey's headquarters and given orders to hold both the road to Grevená and Pindus with 17 Australian Brigade and 2/11 Australian Battalion. These orders also required him to be prepared to move north from Trikkala to support 1 Armoured Brigade at the Venetikos River.[24] At that stage all he had were his carriers, but around 3pm they were joined by the seven A13 Cruiser tanks from the Headquarters Squadron of 1 Armoured Brigade. These he sent north to Kalabaka with orders to cover the bridges over the Mekanes River, on the understanding that some infantry would join them later that night. Unfortunately, on the way north one tank became a permanent casualty and was later destroyed. The first of his infantry, 2/11 Australian Battalion and the bulk of 2/5 Australian Battalion, arrived at 5pm. They were followed an hour later by a battery of 2/1 Australian Anti-Tank Regiment, though they only had eight guns. The rest of 2/5 Australian Battalion, D Company and its carrier platoon, had been sent on to provide additional support for 2/2 Australian Battalion near Tempe. Savige organised the 2-pounder anti-tank into three troops, attaching one to each of the battalions, keeping the third in reserve. This achieved the force set out for Kalabaka at 8pm.[25] There they found the town in a chaos, with Greek troops looting the shops for food. So on 15 April Savige moved his troops to a line two and half miles to the west of the town anchoring on the upper Pineios River to his left, with his front covered by a narrower stream. Around midday the following day 1 Armoured Brigade passed through Savige Force, but there was some doubt as to whether the brigade had demolished the bridge over the Venetikos River. A party of men from 292 Field Company was sent forward to investigate and they found the bridge still intact but with its demolition charges already in place. These they set off before returning.[26]

Though some artillery also arrived on 16 April to reinforce Savige Force, no other units were sent north. Instead, with the situation deteriorating rapidly, Wilson had decided to set up a further rearguard at Domokos utilising the rest of 17 Australian Brigade.[27] In the event 2/5 Australian Battalion's D Company, under Captain W.T. Tolstrup, and part of B Company, only made it by train as far as Larissa, as Major Henry Guinn, the battalion second-in-command, recalled:

> The engine crew was then ordered to proceed to Larissa. On arrival at Larissa it was just bedlam, the station was packed with retiring Greek Army personnel and civilians anxious to get away from the advancing enemy. The only official on duty was a very loyal Station Master who, fortunately for me spoke English and was most helpful. There was no representative from 17th Brigade to contact us or give us any information. My only plan was to contact British HQ in Athens per phone. The Station Master assisted by obtaining information by contacting the HQ through Greek Railway Authorities in Athens. In the meantime I informed Major Marshall of my intention and instructed him to move the troops back along the railway line to an open area await my arrival. Captain Tolstrup was advised of the happenings and was instructed to move his company with the 2/7th personnel. Within a short time a Staff Officer from Brigadier Lee's HQ arrived and escorted me to him. Lee did not mince words: 'The show is over and a defensive line is to be occupied at Domokos'. He suggested that we use the train we came in and get back to Domokos. I informed him that was impossible as the troops had detrained and were moving to open country along the railway line and that the train, crammed with Greek Army personnel and refugees was well on its way back to Athens. With a quiet smile he said: 'The problem is yours'.[28]

Fortunately, when Guinn got back to his men they found three railway engines and some trucks, the latter loaded with army stores. A call for volunteers

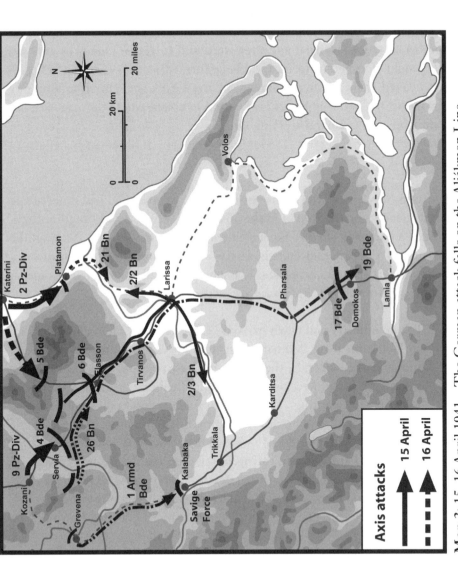

Map 3: 15–16 April 1941 – The German attack falls on the Aliákmon Line.

found some troops from 2/7 Australian Battalion to work the engines, while the rest of the troops emptied the wagons. As dawn broke they set off, detraining at Dermerli where the bulk of the soldiers were loaded onto trucks bound for Domokos. There was, however, no room for D Company 2/5th and C Company 2/7th. Later that afternoon a dispatch rider arrived to inform them that withdrawal by road was now impossible owing to the number of trucks using it and they were told to get to Domokos any way they could. Desperate to escape, they stormed a train carrying refugees and evicted them, taking command of the Greek crew at rifle point. By this means the two companies made it to Domokos, where they came under command of 2/6 Australian Battalion.[29]

*****

Just as at Servia Pass, the improvement in the weather had had unfortunate consequences for the RAF. On the 13th the Luftwaffe had caught a flight of six Blenheims from 211 Squadron and shot them all down. Now, on the morning of 15 April, they launched a dawn attack on 33 and 113 Squadron at their airfields around Larissa and Elasson, as Aircraftsman Marcel Comeau, a Bren gunner with 33 Squadron, recalled:

> They pounced upon newly arrived 113 Squadron's Blenheims over the hill from us at Niamata, roaring and blazing guns down the line of parked aircraft, then came back three more times, killing ground crews and wrecking every single Blenheim. At Larissa there had been no warning. Twenty Messerschmitts swept across the aerodrome as three Hurricanes, led by Flight Lieutenant Mackie, were taking off. The erks [lowest rank in the RAF], abandoning their starter trolleys and racing for shelter, turned in time to see Pilot Officer Cheetham's aircraft destroyed at once. Mackie, already hit by cannon fire from half a dozen fighters, suffered the same fate. As he became airborne he was killed, his aircraft crashing nearby.

One aircraft piloted by a Sergeant Genders got airborne:

> As his wheels came up, he skidded away from the strafing Messerschmitts ...held the nose down, gaining speed ...then climbed at full throttle towards the mass of Germans. The 109s, surprised, scattered – but not before Genders had sent a long burst

into one of them. The fighter fell out of the sky and disappeared from view. Now the solitary Hurricane was being hit from all directions. An aileron disintegrated with a burst of cannon fire. Undaunted Genders kept the machine flying with harsh kicks on the rudder-bar. Forced to make flat, clumsy turns, and by now out of ammunition, Genders was a dead duck. Flying through the smoke clouds rising from the bomb-straddled town, a fresh formation of fighters crossed the aerodrome, heading east. Ignoring his pursuers, Genders dragged the Hurricane's nose around and chased them in a dive. His audacity paid, for the Messerschmitts did not stay to fight[30]

That evening both squadrons began to pull out, destroying anything they could not take with them, before making their way south to Athens.

*****

A certain degree of urgency was inserted into the withdrawal to Thermopylae on 15 April when Wilson received an Enigma decrypt of German intentions to operate south of Olympus.[31] His orders, issued that morning, called for 4 NZ Brigade to hold Servia Pass during the first phase, while 6 NZ Brigade moved south to take up a position on the road between Tirnavos and Elasson. This was to allow 19 Australian Brigade to pull back to Domokos, where it was to be joined by most of Savige Force, while 16 Australian Brigade was to withdraw from Servia and take up a position astride the Larissa-Trikkala road at Zarkos. The commander of 2 NZ Division, Major-General Freyberg, was then to take responsibility for the second phase, withdrawing 4 NZ Brigade from Servia and 5 NZ Brigade through 6 NZ Brigade, starting on the night of 17/18 April. Savige Force, 16 Australian Brigade, 6 NZ Brigade and 21 NZ Battalion were then to withdraw on the night of 18/19 April, their movement across the plains of Thessaly on 19 April to be covered by 1 Armoured Brigade. Once south of Larissa 2 NZ Division was to follow the coast road to Volos, while 6 Australian Division used the main road to Phársala.[32]

The problem now for Brigadier Arthur Allen, with his 16 Australian Brigade having just taken up positions around Servia, was how to get through to them quickly when there were still no telephone links to Allen's headquarters. One of Allen's staff found a pony and rode up to 2/2 Battalion on Hill 1628, reaching them just after dark on the 15th. Finding their widely scattered companies that night proved difficult:

By the time the message reached company areas it was completely dark and their plight can well be imagined as they attempted to contact each other, withdraw patrols and locate and load their worn out donkeys. As a consequence it was 0315 hrs, 16 April before we were able to cross the start line. We were spurred on by the noise of the nearby guns as we rounded a knoll, which led into Servia Pass, on our track southwards. We were somewhat cheered as we watched the effects of a lone British bombing raid on the enemy positions, the first RAF activity we had witnessed since the Germans started their attack. Before dawn it commenced to rain and this kept on unerringly for the rest of the day. In spite of this the enemy reconnaissance planes were up early looking for us. The good discipline of the troops kept them from being detected. We made our way across the mountains by a devious route arriving on the main road at Elasson at 1200 hrs. Here a meal was prepared and we knew that we were at the end of our epic withdrawal on foot. The donkeys were unloaded and abandoned and we were driven by ASC troop carriers to Larissa in comparative comfort.[33]

Their sister unit, 2/3 Australian Battalion, had got out earlier. After a long march they reached the Servia-Elasson road and then had to march a further four miles to get to their transport, all the companies being there by 2am. After some food and whiskey the Battalion set off for Larissa in their trucks, eventually reaching their destination 10 miles west of Larissa. There they learned they had been ordered back to the Vale of Tempe.[34]

This was because the original intention had been for 16 Australian Brigade to support Savige Force at Kalabaka, but now events to the east had overtaken this plan. A little while earlier Brigadier Sydney Rowell at Corps headquarters had started to receive disturbing reports from 21 NZ Battalion at Platamon. Rowell contacted Blamey and suggested that Brigadier Cyril Clowes, commander Royal Artillery, Anzac Corps, should go there to investigate. Blamey disagreed; he wanted to send a New Zealand colonel attached to Corps headquarters, but Rowell insisted, saying he did not have faith in Blamey's choice, and eventually got Blamey's agreement with what Rowell later described as 'very ill grace'. Clowes left at 1am on 16 April. Sometime later Rowell was awakened to be told that the situation at Platamon had deteriorated further, and ordered the first troops of 16 Australian Brigade to Pineios Gorge. Blamey was angry when he found out what Rowell had done as he had planned to send the NZ Divisional Cavalry.

Rowell disagreed with this; in his opinion this unit was not only unsuitable, but it was also too dispersed and could not be concentrated in time. Once again Blamey was forced to agree with Rowell.[35]

*****

Last to go from 16 Australian Brigade at Servia was 2/1 Australian Battalion as the brigade liaison officer had been unable to find the unit, all the tracks being covered with snow. In fact it was left to the battalion to find out the situation for themselves:

> Soon after dawn Lieutenant Fairburn and the CO [Lieutenant Colonel Ian Campbell] set off with a small party and donkeys to try and find a way through the snowbound mountains behind them to procure rations as all supplies were exhausted. When the location of the pass was ascertained the CO returned to the battalion HQ, while Lieutenant Fairburn pushed on with the remainder of the party, finally finding the QM and supplies at Leviadon, also found there A and C Companies who had spent the night at Pheri on the right flank and had been withdrawn owing to the impossibility of taking up a defensive position. The QM informed Lieutenant Fairburn that we should have been withdrawn the night before but Brigade had been unable to locate the unit with orders, as tracks all covered. A small party was sent off with sufficient rations for one meal and instructions to withdraw at once, as troops on the right and left had withdraw the night before. Meanwhile, about 1200 hours, Lieutenant MacPherson at Brigade HQ had succeeded in reaching the remainder of the unit in the mountains and arrived with orders to withdraw immediately. [They] at once set off over the mountains to Leviadon, a difficult route owing to the weather conditions and several feet of snow. [The] Battalion reached Leviadon by companies, except Battalion HQ and HQ Company, which were taken by a very circuitous route by their liaison officer and after a most exhausting march did not arrive at the village until 0100 hours, 17 April. The heavy rain and snow made the motor road to the Katerini Pass impossible for MT [motorised transport] and the battalion was forced to continue the march that night to MT rendezvous for a further 12 miles. The unit was with the MT by dawn at which time it set off for Trikkala, firstly by a short cut

which proved to muddy for the MT and finally by the main road through Larissa, where we turned west towards our destination, about three miles short of Trikkala. The Divisional HQ was found, who, owing to a change of plan, ordered us to move back and defend Larissa aerodrome against paratroops.[36]

*****

Early on the afternoon of 15 April Brigadier George Vasey also received orders to pull 19 Australian Brigade back across the Aliákmon River. The intention had been to use a timber trestle bridge over the river that had been started the previous day by 2/1 Australian Field Company, but this was still not finished. The engineers redoubled their efforts and, with the assistance of some infantry from 26 NZ Battalion and British engineers, the work was eventually completed, albeit an hour later than ordered. Though the bulk of the Australians crossed over that night, the bridge proved incapable of carrying vehicles. One carrier was loaded onto a raft, but it overturned and was swept away. The rest were rendered useless by smashing their engines, while the gunners threw the breechblocks of their anti-tank guns into the river.[37] Assembling 2/4 Australian Battalion proved more difficult, because it was so spread out that one company had to be contacted by runner and as a result did not start to move out till 9.30pm. Vic Hill recalled what happened next:

> By 3.45am we had gone two or three miles towards the enemy and still hadn't found the guide. Knowing we must negotiate the river before daylight we swung right towards it in an attempt to find the bridge or a suitable alternative crossing. At first light we sighted the deep, swiftly, flowing river. There was no bridge or likely fording spot. However, after a time, a rowing boat was found and the slow process of getting 100 men across by sevens and eights at a time began. We had only paddles instead of oars, and so fast was the current that the boat used to drift downstream at least 150 yards each trip.

Nevertheless, by the time they had ferried everyone over and marched up to 2/3 Australian Field Regiment, the rest of their battalion had gone so they hitched a ride to Domokos with the gunners.[38]

The commander of 26 NZ Battalion, Lieutenant Colonel James Page, only learned of the withdrawal of 19 Australian Brigade after the latter had started crossing back over the river. Vasey informed Page that his battalion was to form the rearguard and he was not to start moving his men until all the Australians had gone. Page's men would also have to make the best use of their own transport as no additional vehicles could be provided. All equipment that could not be carried was to be destroyed. This done, the battalion started to move out at 11pm.

In the meantime, the rear battalion headquarters of 26 NZ Battalion, having received no word of what was happening, sent the battalion transport forward. The convoy had not gone very far when they encountered a column of trucks carrying the withdrawing Australian troops and were forced to turn back. Eventually, 26 NZ battalion rear headquarters made contact with Page at the river and arrangements were made to get the battalion transport to a nearby monastery. This the drivers were able to do, even managing to salvage some petrol from a nearby supply dump before the Australians spiked the tins.

While their transport was making its way to the monastery, the first infantry from the battalion were working their way up from the river. Having had little sleep and no proper meals for three nights it proved to be a tough climb and they were forced to discard more surplus materiel on the way. The leading troops eventually reached the monastery seven hours later. While they waited for their trucks, mostly 15cwts, they rummaged for personal possessions through the gear they had dumped only a few days earlier. Page decided that the trucks, when they arrived, should be used to run a shuttle service to Elasson. Thus, when the first company arrived at the monastery those that were present were loaded into the waiting trucks and set off toward the Diskata Pass. The rest set off on foot just as it started to rain and though it made the journey unpleasant, it did ground the Luftwaffe at their airfields.

As the day wore on the condition of the road got worse. The ferry service also started to slow down. Many of the trucks got stuck in the mud and all on board had to help extricate them. As they were now running low on fuel, a request for more transport and petrol was sent to Elasson. When nothing resulted those that were still running loaded up what men they could and set off in that direction, though many did not make it and ended up stuck or stalled along the Diskata Pass, along with some Australian transport. By 10pm that night word was finally received that additional transport was on its way, but by that time most of those on foot or in the trucks had passed through the NZ Divisional Cavalry and reached Diskata village. The transport eventually arrived around midnight and by 4am the first of the battalion had been deposited at the village of Domenikon.[39]

*****

Wilson was not able to discuss the plans to withdraw with Papagos until 16 April, but when he did Papagos endorsed the move and suggested that the British should consider withdrawing from Greece altogether. Wavell was not surprised to hear this news from Wilson, particularly after learning that the Germans had taken Belgrade. He advised Wilson to continue to work with the Greeks but to fall back as necessary, while he would stop the movement of further supplies to Greece. Wavell also told Wilson that he was developing a plan to evacuate the troops based on them holding a defensive line at the Thermopylae. Back in London Winston Churchill was happy for the evacuation to go ahead so long as the Greek government was in agreement with Papagos's suggestion of a total British withdrawal from Greece, although Churchill was adamant that Crete, with its vital harbour and airfields, should be held.[40] On the strength of this advice Wilson contacted Middle East Headquarters the following day and they, in turn, sent over Rear-Admiral Tom Baillie-Grohman to Athens to start planning the evacuation, codenamed Operation Demon.[41]

*****

At Servia, 4 NZ Brigade began to march out in the rain on the evening of 17 April, loaded down with what equipment and ammunition they could carry, 19 NZ Battalion being all out by midnight. However, only part of 18 NZ Battalion had appeared by that stage, leaving the commander of the rearguard, Lieutenant Colonel Howard Kippenberger of 20 NZ Battalion, with a dilemma:

> [Lieutentant Colonel] John Gray himself appeared about 2.30am, very exhausted. He said that two of his companies were still on the hill route and he thought they would have to be abandoned. I gave him some rum and he went on, but Lyons, then second-in-command of an Eighteenth company, promised to get hold of more transport and bring it back to where we were waiting. It seemed no use in leaving Washbourn any longer, and he came in and

passed nonchalantly on in good order. The German shelling and mortaring continued steadily. Ross, my faithful driver, continued as steadily to make cups of tea. The Brigadier had warned me to be out of the Pass by three, but two companies were worth waiting for. It was nearly four when another company of the Eighteenth came down the river-bed, climbed up the bank and into the trucks, and not long afterwards the other company appeared. This was better. When there was no response to our calls I ordered Kelsall to blow. This he did with a magnificent crash, but when the echoes had died away we heard a chorus of cries, very far away up the black hill-side, clear and faint, 'New Zealand here, wait for us.' I went to the edge of the bank and called out that I would wait, but to hurry. Kelsall very properly reminded me that I was endangering is sixty men, waiting in the wet night at their posts down the pass, but I replied that I was resolved to wait. I thinned out the rear-party and sent Teddy Dawson off in his carrier with instructions to go as far as Larissa and tell everyone he saw preparing demolitions that I was going to be late and not to blow till I arrived. We moved 500 yards to the next demolition point, the party, which had called out arrived, exhausted and grateful, were packed on to one of Lyon's trucks and went away. We waited a little longer. The shelling continued with some shells pitching very close, while far away we could hear the Germans heavily mortaring our empty positions. Then we blew again, and, maddeningly, there were more cries. I waited stubbornly and four stragglers arrived. At 5.30am, just before ordering another blow, I called to the hillside once more. Very faint and far off came one single voice, 'New Zealand here, wait for me.' Kelsall looked doubtfully at me but I was unable to leave. We shouted to hurry but it was another half-hour before our man slithered down the opposite bank into the stream. He was quite unable to climb the near bank and Sergeant Lawrence went down and dragged him up, a fully equipped, greatcoated private soldier, still carrying his Bren gun and nearly dead on his feet. We put him in the truck, and blew again. It was past 6am and there were signs of dawn. We went down the Pass at top speed, stopping at each demolition point, where there was a pair of patient sappers waiting. Kelsall would light the fuse – the rest of us waiting around the next corner – then he would and I would run back, see the result, in each case satisfactory, and on to the next. No time was wasted, but it was nearly eight when my little column – some sixty sappers, my three Bren carriers and my car – emerged from the Pass on to the plain.

Thus Kippenberger successfully managed to extract the stragglers; unfortunately this was to prove costly later.[42]

After being picked up by their transport 4 NZ Brigade made good progress as far as Larissa, but their passage through the town was impeded by damage caused by the recent German bombing. Once clear of that town they were diverted onto the road to Volos, only to discover that this was in poor condition, so instead they were re-routed back onto the main road to Lamia and into the mass of other transport moving south.[43]

*****

At 11am on 17 April the leading elements of 5. Panzer-Division finally reached Grevená after following the same route of narrow, unpaved, boggy and meandering roads that had caused the British 1 Armoured Brigade so much grief earlier. In fact things were so bad that almost everybody, except the pioneers, became involved in road building. The following morning there were further delays as the division had to wait until some pioneers from XL. Panzer-Korps reached them. In the end the division only covered 30km before nightfall brought their advance to a halt.[44]

*****

The traffic was no better for the retreating Anzacs on 18 April. Among the retreating forces south of Larissa on 18 April were the remnants of 1 Armoured Brigade, 3 Royal Tank losing a further A10 that day with steering failure, while the last tank was abandoned due to a broken track pin the following day, as Robert Crisp later recalled:[45]

Then the mountain and the precipice moved away from the edge of the road, and we came out onto a broad platform of earth, churned into a ploughed field by the passage of thousands of wheels. It was time for a rest, a brew and some maintenance before we began the descent. I said into the mike: 'Driver left'. We swung round through the mud and stones, heading for a cluster of bushes and a convenient ditch away from the roadway. Ten yards later there came a wrenching jerk and clatter, and I felt my heart come into my

Italian infantry on the move into Epirus after their invasion on 28 October 1940. (Plowman collection)

A German light flak unit in Giurgui, Romania guards the pontoon bridge over the Danube on 5 March 1941. (Zbigniew Lalak)

On the evening of 10 April 14. Panzer-Division entered Zagreb to a warm welcome from its Croatian inhabitants. (Croatia History Museum via Bojan Dimitrijevic)

New Zealand troops disembarking at Piræus, the first of them reaching Greece on 7 March 1941. (Sir John White Collection)

A Fairey Fulmar aircraft flies over the British fleet in the Ionian sea off Matapan in April. (Australian War Memorial)

From left to right: General Sir Thomas Blamey, Lieutenant General Henry Maitland ('Jumbo') Wilson, General Sir Bernard Freyberg VC. (Alexander Turnbull Library)

The carrier platoon from 25 NZ Battalion rode on railway flat cars on their way north to Katerini. (Alexander Turnbull Library)

During the night attack on 6 April by 7 Staffel, Kampfgeschwader 30 on Piræaus harbour, the SS *Clan Fraser*, which was carrying a load of explosives, was hit by one of their bombs, only to blow up later that night in a spectacular fashion. (Australian War Memorial)

On 9 April 1941, as 2. Panzer-Division enter Salonika, locals outside the Hamza Bey mosque look on as a PzKpfw III Ausf H passes by. (Bundesarchiv, 101I-161-0257-09A)

German troops inspect some Universal Carrier Mk Is and a Light Tank IIIB 'Dutchman' from 19 Greek Motorised Division at Stavros, when they were forced to surrender after the Germans took Salonika. (Gregory Collection)

Greek civilians working on an anti-tank ditch along the Aliákmon Line. This would soon be abandoned by 6 NZ Brigade during readjustments to the line. (Sir John White Collection)

German infantry on the move through a mountain pass in Greece. (Gregory Collection)

Troops from 2/2 Australian Battalion crossing the Aliákmon River by ferry on 13 April after pulling out of the Veria Pass. (Australian War Memorial)

On 13 April the Australians in Servia found themselves having to contend with an endless procession of Greek soldiers and their carts carrying their equipment, which added greatly to the road congestion. (Australian War Memorial)

A German supply column crosses the Aliákmon River north-east of Lipsista over a bridge repaired by engineers from Leibstandarte SS Adolf Hitler. (Gregory Collection)

B Squadron, 3 Royal Tanks were forced to abandon this and another tank in Kozani on the night of 13/14 April. (Gregory Collection)

The railway bridge over the Aliákmon River after it was demolished by 2 New Zealand Divisional Cavalry Regiment. (Stratton Morrin)

This A10 Cruiser tank under the command of Lieutenant Robert Crisp from 3 Royal Tanks threw a track after crossing the Venetikos River. (Mark MacKenzie)

A mixed patrol of SdKfz 231 8-rad armoured cars and motorcyclists from Leibstandarte SS Adolf Hitler on the road in Greece. (Bundesarchiv, 101I-158-0094-33)

One of the highest 25-pounders in Olympus Pass was this one from 5 Field Regiment. (Sir John White Collection)

New Zealand transport in the vicinity of Mount Olympus. (Peter Mossong)

Transport carrying troops from 4 NZ Brigade withdrew from Servia Pass on the morning of 18 April under a heavy shroud of mist. (Alexander Turnbull Library)

Two of the victims of 2. Panzer–Division's attack on 21 NZ Battalion's positions at Platamon were these PzKpfw IIIs.

On 17 April I/3 Panzer-Regiment lost two tanks while fording the Pineios River and a further two the next day, among them were a PzKpfw II and these two PzKpfw IIIs. (Plowman Collection)

On 18 April I/3 Panzer-Regiment began to push more tanks across the river along the previously discovered route, a number, like this PzKpfw III, carrying infantry. (Bundesarchiv, 101I-162-0294-03A)

Once Balck's men had established a safe route up the Pineios River they were able to send them upstream at a steady pace, with several in the river at one time. This PzKpfw III is followed by a PzKpfw II, while another tank is just about to enter the river. (Bundesarchiv, 101I-162-0294-10)

Shortage of transport on 18 April forced the evacuation of 26 NZ Battalion from Larissa by train, the troops seen here boarding cattle trucks that evening. (Frank Keys)

A Light Mk VIB from 4 Hussars abandoned in Larissa. (Gregory Collection)

PzKpfw IIs from I/3 Panzer-Regiment motoring through Larissa at speed; 40km south of here they would run out of fuel. (Plowman Collection)

German infantry stop on the side of a road for a meal during their march south. (Gregory Collection)

This platoon truck from 26 NZ Battalion took a direct hit from a Stuka during an attack on their convoy during the retreat south. (Frank Keys)

A lone Anzac soldier rests forlornly among some Greek troops after his capture. (Larry Te Koeti)

Robert Crisp and his crew abandoned this A10 cruiser after it threw a track on the road between Larissa and Lamia on 19 April. Later Germans daubed on it the words: 'Overtaking forbidden till Lamia' and 'England's last hope'. (Gregory Collection)

The crew of this A13 from 1 Armoured Brigade Headquarters Squadron were forced to abandon it at the Sperchios River after New Zealand engineers demolished the bridge. (Mark MacKenzie)

mouth. The track had snapped. We all climbed down and stood in a tight circle surveying the dangling plates – the most woebegone party in all Greece.[46]

Their efforts to repair the track came to naught. While they were searching for something to substitute for a track pin, the rest of the column on the road was subject to an attack by Stukas. One bomb damaged the front track and suspension beyond repair.

*****

Savige Force finally received its orders to pull out on 18 April, the rearguard to be commanded by Lieutenant Colonel Roy King of 2/5 Australian Battalion.[47] Just after dawn 2/11 Australian Battalion marched back to Kalabaka, to waiting transport. From there the convoy made good progress until later in the afternoon when they discovered that the main bridge over the Pineios River had been blown by their engineers. The convoy was diverted to a wooden bridge three miles to the north, but only nine trucks made it across the river before some Stukas appeared and destroyed it after only two bombing runs. Faced with no alternative, their trucks set off on a route that took the battalion through Tournavos and Larissa. The rest of the battalion was ferried across the river on a punt and by 8pm had been reunited with their transport and were mobile again.[48] According to Lieutenant Colonel Tom Louch:

> Two traffic police in Larissa guided us on to the Athens road and by daylight the column was through the defile of Phársala (the town had been heavily bombed and deviations were poor) and out on the long stretch of plain north of Domokos. At this stage there was a hold up, which lasted some hours on account of enemy bombing on the Domokos Pass. During the lull we were machine gunned until two Hurricanes appeared and shot down two enemy planes.[49]

Later that day the remaining troops left Kalabaka, the bulk of 2/5 Australian Battalion finally clearing Larissa around dawn on 19 April, while the rearguard was ferried across the Pineios by punt.[50]

Thus by early morning on 19 April the Anzac and British forces had all but abandoned the Aliákmon–Venetikos Line and were in full retreat to the next defensible position at Thermopylae. In this they had been aided by the difficulties the Germans were experiencing in trying to operate on the flanks, but also in the exemplary defence of Servia Pass by 4 NZ Brigade and 5 NZ Brigade at Olympus Pass. There is no doubt too that they were aided in this by natural advantages in the positions they occupied. The steep terrain around the pass certainly favoured defence, and the Allied destruction of the bridges over the Aliákmon River deprived the Germans of their one major advantage: armour. As a result they did not cope very well, their attack ultimately faltering. Contributing to this was an overall failure of their reconnaissance that led the Germans to believe there was no serious opposition in the area. Ultimately they decided that it was easier to try to bypass Servia Pass and so they chose to divert their armour through Grevená to Kalabaka. The trouble for them was that sending them down the same route that caused 1 Armoured Brigade so much trouble was hardly an ideal solution either, and ultimately proved costly in terms of time. The nead to clear and repair the route after numerous demolitions set off by the retreating British forces also did not help. It was this move, coupled with Ultra decrypts and the situation that the Greek army in Albania found itself in, that ultimately dictated what the Anzac Corps could do. Though their defensive line along the Vermion and Olympus ranges had natural adavantages, the rapidly changing situation along the fringes of the Allied front meant that the new proposed line at Thermopylae offered the prospect of being more easily defensible than their existing one, at least until they could finalise their evacuation plans.

Chapter 7

Repulse at Olympus Pass

On the same day that 4 NZ Brigade was fending off the Germans at Servia Pass, another German force ran up against Brigadier James Hargest's 5 NZ Brigade at Olympus and suffered a second setback to what had been, up until then, an easy advance. Fortunately for 5 NZ Brigade, both the 2 NZ Division commander, Major-General Freyberg, and Anzac Corps commander Lieutenant General Blamey, had been adamant that defence of the original Aliákmon Line was untenable, even before the redeployment of the Greek troops from it. Both had favoured pulling back to the Olympus mountain range, the passes of which were more easily defendable. With the dispatch of 26 NZ Battalion and 4 NZ Brigade to Servia Pass and the withdrawal of the rest of 6 NZ Brigade to Elasson this left 5 NZ Brigade responsible for the passes through the Olympus mountain range. In Olympus Pass itself Hargest had two units from his brigade, 22 and 23 NZ Battalions, to which the 28 (Maori) Battalion had been added to replace 21 NZ Battalion, which been ordered to defend the Platamon Ridge to the south. For additional support Hargest had 5 NZ Field Regiment and a battery of 2-pounders from 7 NZ Anti-Tank Regiment.

The initial German attack fell on the NZ Divisional Cavalry two days earlier along the Aliákmon River. The regiment had been there for some two weeks and had had time to prepare its defences, as well as to dig in and camouflage all its vehicles. A squadron was occupying a stretch of the river from the village of Aiynion to the main bridge, while upstream B Squadron covered another stretch of the riverbank. With the regiment were O Troop, 7 NZ Anti-Tank Regiment, E Troop, 5 NZ Field Regiment and 3 Section from 5 NZ Field Company. All but one of the bridges in the unit's sector had been destroyed, with the last one prepared for demolition, that being dependent on the arrival of the A13 tanks of Captain Dale's 1 Armoured Brigade's Headquarters Squadron. These finally reached them around daybreak on 9 April and were guided in by lieutenants Hugh Robinson and Frank Ward. With this the bridge was blown and a temporary wooden structure beside it dismantled.[1]

The orders for XVIII Gebirgs-Korps after the fall of Salonika were to swing to the south-west and secure the passes at Edessa and Veroia, but the collapse of the Australian and Greek forces around Vevi rendered this unnecessary. Their main objective was the town of Larissa, as this provided the most direct route to Athens and places south.

In the vanguard was 2. Panzer-Division, which had been switched south towards Katerini. In turn a battlegroup, based around II/3. Panzer-Regiment, was detached and sent on towards Olympus Pass, finally reaching the Aliákmon River early on the afternoon of 12 April.[2] First to appear were some motorcycle sidecar combinations and motorized infantry, who drove up to the bridge approaches. There they came under withering fire from the A Squadron troop to the right of the road, all being mown down, apart from one motorcyclist who escaped. Thus checked, the Germans contented themselves by sniping from the other side of the river.

The sun was well up the following day before the next attack was launched. Some trucks arrived, from which the Germans unloaded and set up mortars in the open. These soon began dropping rounds on the New Zealand troops dug in under the banks near the bridge. To add to their discomfort the Germans started directing machine-gun fire on to them as well. Under this covering fire German infantry came forward and launched assault boats above and below the bridge. Once on the water they came under intense fire at point-blank range from A Squadron and the 25-pounders further back, from which none survived; the same fate befell the subsequent waves when they tried to repeat the exercise. After these assaults had been beaten off 5 NZ Field Regiment turned their attention to the transport and mortars to the rear, destroying two halftracks.

As the morning wore on the Germans began to switch their attention from the road bridge to the destroyed railway bridge downstream. This necessitated the dispatch of the reserve troop from A Squadron, NZ Divisional Cavalry. As this new attack threatened their line of withdrawal, B Squadron was ordered to pull out and, when they were clear, around midday, the guns withdrew. Half an hour later A Squadron began to thin out, one troop at a time. By 4pm, with still no sign of the enemy across the river, A Squadron rallied along the road beside the ruins of the railway bridge and then made their way back to Aiyinon.

That night the NZ Divisional Cavalry pulled back to an anti-tank ditch to the south, B Squadron via Kolindros, blowing the route over it once they had crossed. On the morning of 14 April the Germans came into view, this time pushing tanks forward to cover their infantry. With Bren and rifle fire from C Squadron taking care of the infantry, E Troop, 5 NZ Field Regiment, dealt with the tanks and together they managed to hold the Germans for two hours. Eventually some German infantry started to work their way through the scrub between C and B Squadron. This forced C Squadron to withdraw to the next obstacle, a culvert, blowing that after crossing. There they remained until 10am, when, with the enemy approaching, the regiment received orders to pull back through 5 NZ Brigade in Olympus Pass.[3]

That same day the two remaining battalions of 6 NZ Brigade, in reserve behind 5 NZ Brigade, were sent back to Elasson to establish a rearguard position to cover the withdrawal of the troops from Servia and Olympus.[4] By this stage of the campaign Jack Elliott from 25 NZ Battalion was riding in an ambulance, having suffered injuries to his knees:[5]

> The Germans had by this time gained complete air control. RAF fighters had been shot down or destroyed on the ground, so any vehicles caught on the road in daylight were being strafed. Our first encounter was two Messerschmitts coming up the road in front of us. Luckily they respected the Red Cross on our ambulance and roared over with a slight waggle of their wings. About an hour later we could see smoke and planes bombing ahead of us and came to Elasson shortly after the raid. A Bofors AA gun sited on the edge of the town had been hit and overturned, with no sign of the crew. A bus was lying on its side and blazing furiously, again with no sight of casualties[6].

Late that evening the vanguard of 2. Panzer-Division announced their presence in Olympus Pass when some motorcycle sidecar combinations from 1/38. Panzejäger-Abteilung, their headlights blazing, hove into sight in front of a demolition at the head of the pass. Minutes later a short burst of Bren and rifle fire emanated from 11 Platoon, 22 NZ Battalion, astride the road above the demolition, and the Germans fled, leaving behind five wrecked motorcycles and weapons. That would have been it, as news came through the following morning that 5 NZ Brigade was to pull back to the southern end of the pass. What followed was a flurry of activity in preparation for the move that came to naught that evening when word was received that the withdrawal had been postponed by 24 hours. Instead German artillery started up later that afternoon and their patrols became active during the night. D Company of 22 NZ Battalion in particular had a hard time covering the wire and minefields on their front:

> Parties could be heard stumbling against bushes in the darkness. Sergeant Jerry Fowler fired his 2-inch mortar towards one party

and was annoyed at derisive cries in English of 'You'll have to do better than that!' D Company, thinking this a ruse to discover their positions, lay low, and in the morning found their wire cut and all their carefully laid mines by the little bridge removed.[7]

No serious attacks occurred on 15 April as the Germans took a while to assemble their forces for the assault, though this did not stop Luftwaffe activity. Jack Elworthy, from NZ 5 Field Regiment, noted the attention the New Zealanders in the Olympus Pass got from the German reconnaissance planes:

> The reconnaissance plane came over one morning around breakfast time, so low we could actually see a man photographing our positions. Then it turned and came back nearly as low again. The Browning was mounted and ready, so the bombardier in charge of the guns from regimental headquarters came leaping over and got a good long burst away. The bullets seemed to be going where they should but the plane just carried on. We heard later that it had crashed near our front lines and the infantry had claimed it as theirs.[8]

The main attack developed shortly after daybreak on 16 April, preceded by the usual artillery barrage. Chas Wheeler from 6 NZ Field Company had a grandstand view of the enemy attack as it began:

> The first enemy challengers were a group of those amazing motor cycle scouts whom we were to come to know as the suicide squads of all advances. Like a unit on parade, they swept disdainfully along, right up to the spot where the ruins of a small bridge barred their path. A dozen cycles and sidecars, a couple of dozen grey-clad figures armed with short sub-machine guns. They dismounted and gazed curiously at the obstruction before them, regardless of the astounded Kiwis only a few hundred yards away. A word of command and a few short bursts of fire accounted for them all.
>
> On vengeance bent came a group of light tanks and armoured cars. The first tank ran deliberately into the gap, filling it and providing a quite sufficient foothold for the next. The second struck a mine and disappeared in a cloud of black smoke. We saw the crew scramble madly out before the gunners gaily completed the destruction of the vehicle.

By this time the road beyond was filling up with vehicles. A squad of sappers marched rigidly forward and began a painstaking search for the mines. They lasted a matter of minutes under the murderous hail of fire but as they fell others took their places. The average life must have been about two minutes on that job. They gave it up. No troops will do that for long. British sappers wouldn't be asked to do it.

Meanwhile the road further north was not escaping attention. An armoured car had been hit in the petrol tank and was blazing merrily, blocking escape for many. A dozen more vehicles were destroyed before they could retire. The artillery boys were enjoying a gunners' paradise; trucks and trailers packed with German infantry suffered direct hits.[9]

Meanwhile, infantry from 11 Platoon of B Company, 22 NZ Battalion, sighted a few men and armoured vehicles sheltering under a cliff and directed 3-inch mortar fire on them, causing casualties and knocking out two of the vehicles. The Germans responded by sending up five tanks at 7am that closed to 400 yards range and started firing on 11 Platoon, three of them being killed and one wounded. Though their Boyes anti-tank rifle proved useless, they were able to direct some artillery fire onto the tanks forcing them back. By now the situation was starting to become more perilous for the battalion, as at least another forty armoured vehicles, including one medium tank, numerous light tanks and infantry half-tracks, could be seen below the battalion positions. Further down the pass a great mass of enemy tanks, half-tracks and other transport could be seen building up. To add to the battalion's discomfort some German mortars had managed to get the range, while some 25-pounder rounds were landing short because they could not clear a ridge: that is, until 5 NZ Field Regiment set up a special observation post:

At 8.40am a strong enemy tank attack was launched again up the road. These tanks had been hidden in trees and scrub not more than 600 yards from the front. Colonel Kenneth Fraser, seated in the open on a folding chair, ordered ten rounds' gunfire. The gunfire and tanks arrived at the same spot simultaneously in a cloud of dust and smoke. Infantrymen saw the attack splinter and smash. At least ten vehicles, including an ammunition truck and at least one tank, were knocked out. Then another tank and an ammunition truck went up, the truck being credited to hard-working Private Selwyn Whibley and his Boyes anti-tank rifle. The hard-pressed 11 Platoon was rushed by three tanks at 9.18am. One tank charged straight down into the hole left by the demolition. The platoon disposed of its crew. The two remaining tanks tried to cross the demolition, apparently attempting to use the first tank as some sort of bridge. Failing to do this they sprayed B Company's front[10]

These attacks having failed, 72. Infanterie-Division sent 9. and 11. Fahrrad Kompanien forward to infiltrate around either flank towards Ay Dhimitrios at the head of the pass. Capitalizing on the scrub and mist that had started to envelop the area, they overran one post from 13 Platoon, 23 NZ Battalion on the right flank. Though 13 Platoon counter-attacked immediately and retook the position, they could not rescue the men. A more serious attack by the Germans developed later in the afternoon on 16 Platoon, but a break in the mist allowed the New Zealand infantry to break up the attack with a short burst of automatic fire.

In contrast, 28 Maori Battalion, on the left flank, had a relatively quiet morning thanks to the mist and rain in their sector, until the afternoon when II/2. Infanterie-Regiment sent three companies round to the west. Around 3pm, when the mist cleared, their 8. Kompanie came under fire from the Maori and were soon pinned down. The Germans then sent 7. and 9. Kompanien up the Mavroneri stream, but their movement was observed by some scouts from D Company, one of whom personally dealt with three of them.[11] The Maori Battalion was preparing to pull out and B Company had already stacked their packs and tools at company headquarters when German troops were sighted moving down a bare ridge. At 1,200 yards the fire brought to bear on them was ineffective, but when the Germans had eventually worked their way up to the wire in front of B Company they opened fire at close range and called up fire from A Company's mortars. After losing six men the Germans withdrew, while both B and C companies continued to direct fire onto the opposite side of the gorge, pinning down one third of the Germans for the rest of the afternoon.[12]

Having held the Germans in check for the better part of the day, the various elements of the blocking force commenced their withdrawal that night. In the centre 22 NZ Battalion made their way down to the road and then up to Ay Dhimitrios where they were picked up by their battalion transport. Over on the right flank 23 NZ Battalion climbed across the range to Kokkinoplos. As they did so they came under fire from 3. Pioneer-Kompanie and 12.

Maschinengewehr-Kompanie of 72. Infanterie-Division, who appeared out of the mist and opened fire on A Company headquarters. At this point 10 Platoon, B Company, 23 NZ Battalion came forward to assist, later joined by elements from C and D companies. Nevertheless, under the cover of the mist they were able to successfully disengage, though in fact the Germans were really exhausted, frozen, wet and cold and suffering from a lack of food. Of the artillery three of the 2-pounders of E Troop, 7 NZ Anti-Tank Regiment were retrieved, but the other nine to the south of the highway had to be abandoned. This was also the case for the 2-pounders of F Troop that could not be manhandled across the Poros stream. They were stripped of their telescopes and pushed into the gorge, while three other guns south of the road were dismantled. Two other anti-tank guns with G Troop were wrecked on the spot. The remaining guns were withdrawn successfully. The Maori Battalion had to wait until the fighting died down, making their escape later that night. They climbed up through some heavily wooded slopes, making for the highway east of Ay Dhimitrios. The last company reached it just as the engineers were about to set off their demolition charges, though these proved less than successful. The explosions failed to blow away the cliff face and instead created a series of craters, none of which proved an effective barrier to the Germans.[13]

The original plan had been for 5 NZ Brigade to form another line along the crest of Olympus Pass and hold it on 17 April before pulling out the following evening. Freyberg decided otherwise when he came up to visit the forward troops and discovered that thick mists hung over both the mountains and the road. Now the brigade was to continue withdrawing that day. Thus, under the cover of a rearguard from the NZ Divisional Cavalry, with O and P troops of 24 Anti-Tank Battery and 3 Company 27 NZ MG Battalion, 5 NZ Brigade began to make their way back to their waiting transport. First to arrive at Pithion was 23 NZ Battalion, who received their first proper meal in over 24 hours before boarding their transport.

The rest of the brigade and their supporting artillery reached Pithion later on the afternoon of 17 April, the rearguard from the Maori Battalion and F Troop, 5 NZ Field Regiment, coming in around 6pm. This was all aided by the fact that the Germans had made no real effort to follow up, their armour and other vehicles not being able to start moving until that evening thanks to the time taken to repair the bridges and road in the pass.[14] The plan then was for 5 NZ Brigade to be taken south to Volos in their own transport, transfer to 4 NZ Brigade's transport and travel on to Thermopylae. This had to be revised when it was learned that stretches of the Larissa–Volos road had become impassable because of recent heavy rain. Instead the brigade was ordered onto the main road intended for the evacuation of the Australians. Their convoy was then optimistically instructed to halt halfway between Larissa and Lamia, unload and return for 6 NZ Brigade. However, they soon discovered that the road was already jam-packed with Australian transport moving south, and no one knew exactly where their convoy was supposed to stop. At times it did anyway, often during air attacks. On one such occasion the traffic refused to start moving again. In the end Jack Elworthy from 5 NZ Field Regiment, frustrated with this, took matters into his own hands:

> However, I was tired of being strafed for so long and I knew the Germans behind us were moving up fast. The driver of the next truck to mine felt the same way. His truck was big and solid-looking so I asked him if he would back it hard into a stone wall and knock it over. That way we could take a chance and drive over the fields to escape the shambles around us. He agreed to do this next time there was a lull. When the wall came down we drove as fast as we could along the fields parallel with the road. When I looked back there was a long stream of vehicles following us. We tried to get back on the road further on, but when the drivers of the vehicles that had been blocking the road ahead of us saw us moving they forgot their fears and started off, so there was another traffic jam.[15]

In the end 5 Brigade was driven all the way to Thermopylae.[16]

With the departure of 5 NZ Brigade on 17 April, 6 NZ Brigade now prepared to hold the approaches to Tirnavos, south of Elasson. To this end they deployed 24 NZ Battalion to the east astride the road, and 25 NZ Battalion to the west of it, while 26 NZ Battalion was held in reserve. For artillery support they had a battery of 25-pounders and a troop of 2-pounders but, with the situation at Tempe deteriorating, these were diverted there. Later 2/3 Australian Field Regiment and a troop of 64 Medium Regiment came up, and finally 5 NZ Field Regiment joined them from Olympus Pass. Demolition charges were also laid on the road to 24 NZ Battalion's position and on the western approaches on two bridges over the Xerias River, the withdrawal route of the rearguard. All other bridges were demolished. However, with the situation deteriorating almost hourly, there was grave danger of encirclement from either flank.[17]

On the morning of 18 April C Squadron of the NZ Divisional Cavalry at Elevtherokhorion caught sight of the leading elements of 5. Kompanie,

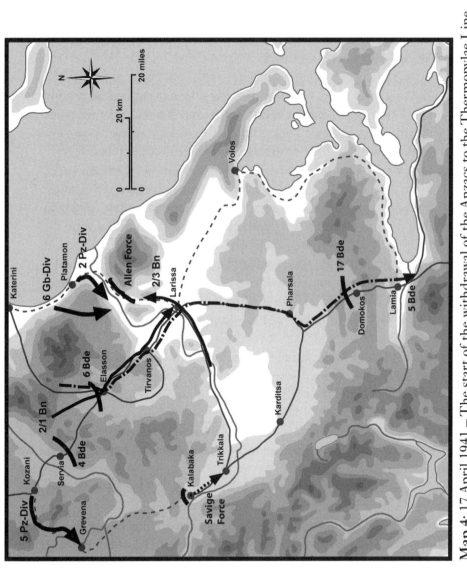

Map 4: 17 April 1941 – The start of the withdrawal of the Anzacs to the Thermopylae Line.

II/3. Panzer-Regiment moving down Olympus Pass from Ay Dhinitrios, intermingled with flocks of sheep and refugees. In a short space of time C Squadron came under fire and were then forced to withdraw when several German tanks appeared around the bend, but not before O Troop, 7 Anti-Tank Regiment knocked out two of them, losing one Portee in some swampy ground. C Squadron then withdrew through A Squadron and P Troop, who were holding the bridge itself.[18] At this point the rearguard from Servia Pass arrived, as Kippenberger recalled:

> Walking back to my car I saw that everyone had stopped again, and saw a truck, half a mile ahead, burst into flames. Another truck blazed up an instance later. The men were scrambling up the low bank right of the road or diving into the shallow ditch beside it. ... Half a mile ahead, fairly across the road, were two German tanks, firing fast down the road toward me. As I watched, with bitter disappointment, one swung its turret around and started firing in the opposite direction. I saw tracer from there lashing all around the tanks. ... A carrier from somewhere ahead in the column swung out from behind a truck and raced straight at the tanks. As I watched it suddenly slewed into a ditch and capsized. There were now three tanks, a hail of tracer round them and bouncing off. I beckoned to the carriers to hurry, and the leading one was moving off the road beside me and had opened fire, when I saw coming across the field truck after truck of lorried infantry, all sitting upright like tin soldiers. I counted seven, more in the distance, and rightly or wrongly decided the odds were too heavy and we must run.[19]

In the end only the leading truck from Kippenberger's rearguard got across the bridge. He and his party abandoned their vehicle and made their escape through the hills to the west.[20]

This put the NZ Divisional Cavalry at the bridge in an unenviable position. At this point the rest of A Squadron withdrew, leaving Lieutenant Hugh Robinson's troop and some engineers holding the bridge. One of the armoured cars was hit on the wheel but was still mobile, while another broke down but was repaired under fire. When the German tanks approached across some open ground, Bombardier Trevor Bellringer's 2-pounder disabled one tank before his gun was hit and he and another gunner were killed. Sergeant Arthur Fowler's gun was luckier, disabling four tanks, two armoured cars and one heavy truck before they successfully manhandled their gun out. Eventually, after two hours, the engineers blew the bridge and made their escape.[21] As it turned out the loss of the bridge did not prove a major impediment, as the Germans soon found a steep-sided ford just below it and started crossing there. Their luck ran out further on. After Robinson's force had withdrawn through 25 NZ Battalion's position, some New Zealand engineers demolished several sections of the road through the gorge north of Elasson. This held the German tanks up for several hours.[22]

From 10.30am, following the withdrawal of the NZ Divisional Cavalry, the artillery with 6 NZ Brigade were able to disrupt attempts by the Germans to cross the river, putting fire down on groups of German tanks up to 10,000 yards away, several being hit in the process. The artillery also fired on German vehicles in the hills to the north of Elasson. The guns of 64 Medium Regiment ran out of ammunition early in the afternoon and had to pull out. Not so the gunners of 2/3 Australian Field Regiment, who found themselves with a surfeit of ammunition thanks to a fortunate misunderstanding by 5 NZ Field Regiment. The latter had been ordered to bring back one load of ammunition from Servia Pass, but instead, working all night, had brought back considerably more in readiness for a longer stand. In the end the Australians expended something like 6,500 rounds.[23]

Undeterred, the Germans were not held up for long. Their leading troops swung eastwards across some rough country and by evening a force of some thirty German tanks, accompanied by infantry in half-tracks, started to build up in front of 24 NZ Battalion's position. This was brought to a temporary halt when the leading tanks ran onto some mines and then found themselves under fire from 2/3 Australian Field Regiment.[24] Fortunately for 6 NZ Brigade, preparations for the withdrawal were well underway. The main dressing station behind the brigade had been steadily thinning out all morning, while their B Echelon transport had already gone. At this point, though, it became apparent that there was insufficient transport to extricate the whole brigade. Instead arrangements were made for 26 NZ Battalion to travel by rail and at 4.30pm they departed for Larissa in trucks from a British transport unit.

Around 8pm, just as 24 NZ Battalion was beginning to pull out, the German armour began to advance, the tanks firing as they went. Fire from 2/3 Australian Field Regiment forced their accompanying infantry to go to ground, but did not deter the tanks. This initially created a problem for 13 and 15 Platoons, 24 NZ Battalion as the German tanks became intermingled with them, but on reaching the first demolitions, with the fading light, the tank commanders hesitated and the attack ground to a halt, allowing 24 NZ Battalion to slip away largely unmolested. Last to go was 25 NZ Battalion, who started to pull out at

8.30pm, their rearguard clearing Tirnavos around midnight, just as a German column was closing in from the east.[25] Jack Elliott from 25 NZ Battalion was still confined to his ambulance when they pulled out:

> The raids came about every hour with a clear period between each. Any traffic wanting to go through Larissa waited under some trees near the bridge and then made a dash for it until the bombing stopped. Luckily no near hits, the ambulance undamaged except for a few dents. The driver managed to turn around and proceed back through the town. We found an MP on duty at a corner in the middle of the town where we should have turned right, however two MPs had been hit in the previous raid – one killed and the other wounded who was back on duty again. We were very pleased to be clear of the town when the next raid started. The night was spent at a casualty clearing station (CCS) south of Larissa and next day we again travelled to Lamia.[26]

The train carrying 26 NZ Battalion did not depart from Larissa until 8pm that evening. Crewed by two sappers from 19 NZ Army Troops Company, it had taken them some three hours to assemble a motley collection of carriages and wagons. The engine itself was in bad shape, lacking a braking system, and could only be stopped by torch signals to the brake vans near the end of the train. It only had sufficient coal and water for 60 miles. With the whole battalion crowded into fourteen carriages the train set off, stopping first at Doxara to take on more water and coal and then stopping before each bridge and tunnel so the sappers could examine them. Unfortunately, at each stop Greek soldiers climbed onto the roof of the train or clung onto the outside. At Demerli Junction the train ran into a stationary engine and five carriages. Though it suffered little damage, it took half an hour to push this train into a siding before they could proceed. The train then faced a steep climb over the Domokos Pass, and as it slowed down it soon became evident that it would never reach the top. When it ground to a halt all the men from 26 NZ Battalion were crammed into the first nine carriages and the Greek troops were persuaded to occupy the rear five. Then, as the train set off, the rear carriages were uncoupled, leaving the Greeks behind, allowing the battalion to reach the pass. However, the loss of two braking carriages meant that there was insufficient braking capacity in those left, resulting in the train rapidly picking up speed as it descended. The sappers only managed to slow their progress by reversing the steam slowly through the engine.

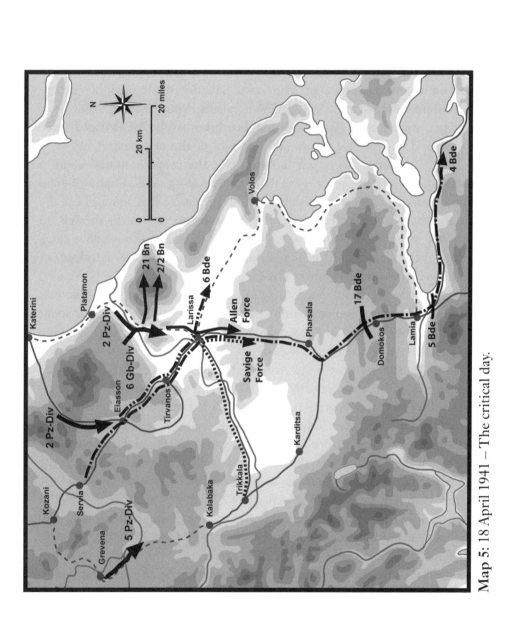

Map 5: 18 April 1941 – The critical day.

On reaching Lamia the battalion detrained while efforts were made to secure a new engine and brake vans. The officials on duty at the station added to their woes by insisting that it had to be crewed by Greeks. Eventually an agreement was reached to attach the Larissa wagons to another train carrying a battalion of Cypriots and some Australians. That achieved, they had only just entrained and the train started moving when the whole shunting yard came under attack from the air. The New Zealanders made good their escape and suffered no casualties, but some Australians, who remained inside their carriages, were killed. Worse still, the bombing had badly damaged three wagons and cut the line behind and in front of the new engine. So while the New Zealanders were sent a mile away, the sappers cleared another section of the line and began assembling more rolling stock. Finding a good engine proved to be the main problem, and they were just about to use the one that had brought them from Larissa when an Australian showed up with one in better condition. It was quickly coupled to the rolling stock and the Australians and Cypriots reboarded and then held off hundreds of Greek soldiers with rifle butts. The Greek crew then had to be persuaded at gunpoint to stop for New Zealanders further down the line. The rest of the journey was completed without incident, the troops detraining about two miles from Kephisokhori, where they spent a night in the open before transport arrived to take them to Molos.[27]

Thus, by the morning of 19 April all troops north of Larissa had been successfully withdrawn in the face of a serious threat on the right flank. Part of the success of this operation can be attributed to the solid defence by 5 Brigade at Olympus Pass. As at Servia Pass, the brigade had been in place in Olympus Pass well before the Germans arrived and had the opportunity to develop their defences in a natural bottleneck, which did not favour the use of armour. With the German armour unable to move off the road the New Zealanders were easily able to block any moves the German assault force made to break through. The one attempt the Germans made to bypass the position brought them hard up against the Maori Battalion. Though Olympus Pass could have been held for some time, the need to defend it was overtaken by the situation at Platamon, where by the afternoon of 16 April the situation had deteriorated so much that it was imperative that all troops along the Vermion–Olympus defensive line were withdrawn as soon as practicable. The one thing that stood in their favour was the fact that the terrain along the route south lent itself well to disruption of the efforts of the Germans to follow up by means of demolitions in appropriate locations.

Chapter 8

A Near Run Thing at Pineios Gorge

The defence of the other pass through the Olympus Mountain range to the ancient Vale of Tempe had been entrusted to 21 NZ Battalion, their orders being to deny German access to a railway tunnel at Platamon. Though this seemed an innocuous task, it was to sorely test the battalion and ultimately the whole of the Anzac Corps, throwing the entire withdrawal into jeopardy. Its high strategic value lay in the fact that a breakthrough here by the Germans could open up the route to the strategically important town of Larissa, via the Pineios Gorge (the Vale of Tempe). This route offered them an opportunity to execute a classic 'left hook' and unhinge the entire Allied defence line. A breakthrough here would also lead to the cutting off and capture of a great number of retreating Greek and Anzac troops, particularly as there were now moves afoot to pull back to the Thermopylae Line. To this task the Germans assigned 6. Gebirgs-Division and a combat group from 2. Panzer-Division, the latter under the command of Oberstleutnant Hermann Balck. The Anzacs were wrong-footed, though just why is not clear. One thing is clear: senior commanders of the Anzac Corps had not given serious consideration to such a move, certainly not by an armoured unit, regarding this sector as impregnable.

For their defensive task 21 NZ Battalion had been been transported north from Athens by train. On 9 April the battalion disembarked at Platamon station and made their way up to a saddle along a rough track that eventually joined the railway line at the northern entrance to the tunnel. Lieutenant Colonel Neil Macky placed A Company on the hill above the tunnel and B Company on Point 266 to the west of the saddle track, leaving other two companies in reserve. Later that day 19 Army Troops Company NZE arrived, armed with explosives and a depth charge. Their orders were to prepare the tunnel and saddle track for demolition and lay out an anti-tank minefield near the top of the ridge. A couple of hours later A Troop of 27 Battery, 5 NZ Field Regiment, arrived from Katerini and set up their guns behind A Company. Further reconnaissance of the area revealed that it would be possible for the Germans to cut off their retreat to Platamon station via other tracks in the area. To block this threat Macky placed

C Company at the junction of these to the east of the village of Panteleimonas and D Company on the reverse slope of Castle Hill, the site of the Turkish fort of Skotiniotika Manzarda. The carrier platoon was given responsibility for the area south of Platamon station.[1]

General Freyberg visited the battalion on 14 April to inform Macky of the plan to withdraw to Thermopylae. While there he was at pains to emphasize that the importance of their job was to deny the position to the enemy. Before he departed he left them with the assurance that they were only likely to encounter infantry because of the terrain. Thus it was with some trepidation, not long after he departed, that reflected light was sighted on moving windscreens some 5,000 yards to the north. These vehicles were engaged by the 25-pounders, and what was initially presumed to be a patrol was brought to a halt. However, a continuous stream of traffic could be seen another 7,000 yards behind them, including what looked like tanks. Captain Walter Tongue at Panteleimonas said he could see at least 100 tanks, at which point Macky asked him not to count any further as nobody would believe it, so their wireless message just said: '50 tanks and 150 other vehicles were parking in front of Platamon ridge'. That established, the engineers collapsed the tunnel roof with a depth charge and some gelignite. Not satisfied with that, they detonated a smaller charge in the hole in the roof. Craters were also blown in the saddle track, after which the sappers departed for Pineios Gorge to prepare further demolitions along the road and railway.[2]

The forward elements of 2. Panzer-Division completed their movements that night, headlights burning all the while. At dawn the following day they started shelling the position, the old Turkish castle coming in for some attention. On the Platamon ridge Macky noted that:

> Reconnaissance planes flew low, so low that the Bren gun armed anti-aircraft platoon was told to leave them alone. There were too many of them and they were obviously offering targets so that the infantry positions could be spotted (for the artillery).[3]

What followed was an hour-long artillery bombardment, after which the first attack was launched:

> The enemy infantry, supported by a line of tanks at a distance, began to search through the smoke and scrub for advanced posts of A and B Companies. The sustained fire of the forward platoons prevented any infiltration with one exception. A section blundered through

the smoke on to 7 Platoon but Second-Lieutenant Southworth had taken the precaution of saving some gelignite he had been using to blast holes for his weapons pits. The engineers tied them in pairs with a fuse and detonator attached and with one of the home grenades the patrol was completely liquidated. The attack lost its sting after half an hours fighting and the infantry withdrew. For the rest of the day the whole ridge was drenched with smoke and high explosive fire but the weapons pits hewn out of solid marble or rock gave excellent shelter and there were very few casualties. During the afternoon tanks were heard through the smoke crashing and thrashing about in the scrub endeavouring to force a way over the ridge.[4]

At 7pm 2. Kradschützen-Bataillon attempted to outflank the position by launching an assault on Panteleimonas. The brunt of the attack was born by 15 Platoon under Lieutenant Charles Mason. His forward troops were driven out of the village, the Germans filtering in behind them. Realising the seriousness of the situation, Mason organized a counter-attack and re-established his positions. Then, with support from 13 Platoon, Mason and his men drove the Germans off another spur.

The next attack was launched in the centre and right by tanks from I/3. Panzer-Regiment. As was later noted by Macky:

The infantry did not emerge from the scrub but tanks made a determined effort to climb the ridge. Small arms fire was poured into them from all angles to no avail and the anti-tank rifles only rained sparks on the armour. The artillery was unable to protect A Company owing to the steepness of the hill but only one tank succeeded in getting behind 8 Platoon. It was however not able to complete the climb and returned baffled. The main thrust as along the track between A and B Companies and on the left of B Company. Two were halted under 9 Platoon's positions and one got past 10 Platoon's post on the side of the track. They were engaged by every rifle that could be brought to bear and retired discomforted by the steepness of the ridge and the demolished track. Seven more tanks attempted to get up the ravine where the Lieutenants Yeoman's and Findlayson's platoons were dug in but this was one place where the guns and mortars could be enfiladed and the attempt was defeated.[5]

A platoon of light tanks did manage to get close to the New Zealand positions, only for all of them to shed their tracks.[6] With the attack a failure, the tanks laagered for the night at the base of the hill, while some German infantry continued to infiltrate around B and C Companies, forcing them to give up ground.

Though the German attack had been halted, A Company continued to come under intermittent shellfire, while enemy movement in front of B Company brought a strong response in return as the area was sprayed with fire. A more serious incursion occurred on C Company's front at Pantaleimonas around midnight:

> An enemy patrol, which had got up behind them, opened up with automatics, spraying tracer bullets at random. They lit up the position like a rocket and almost served their purpose for some 14 Platoon posts, under the impression that they had been surrounded, began to filter back on Company headquarters and were ordered back to their positions by Lieutenant O'Neil of 13 Platoon and the patrol, failing to dislodge the company with its stratagem, withdrew.[7]

On the morning of 16 April the Germans turned their attention to Panteleimonas:

> Shortly before first light the reconnaissance battalion of 3. Panzer-Regiment, which had got into position during the night, commenced an enveloping movement on C Company. The attack was preceded by artillery and mortar fire from below and by machine gun and rifle fire from the heights above Panteleimonas. Pinned down by the coordinated fire from the front and flank, 15 Platoon found itself surrounded and a German office demanded their surrender. Lieutenant C.T. Mason's reply was to order the section he was with to go in with the bayonet while the rest of the platoon extricated itself. Lieutenant Mason killed the German officer and the others withdrew hurredly into the scrub.[8]

At this point 14 Platoon was withdrawn behind 13 Platoon, but they soon found themselves surrounded on three sides. When attempts to contact 21 NZ Battalion headquarters failed, they started to withdraw down the hill towards the main battalion position. Over the next four hours they fought a delaying action, the platoons leapfrogging through each other before they became surrounded.

At the same time the Germans launched their main assault on A and B companies, putting down an artillery barrage before closing in on the New Zealanders. As Balck later reported:

> The right-hand company of tanks forced its way forward through scrub and over rocks, and in spite of the steepness of the hillsides got to the top of the ridge. The country was a mass of wire obstacles and swarming with the enemy. In the thick scrub visibility was scarcely a yard from the tanks, and hardly a trace was to be seen of the enemy except an occasional infantryman running back. The tanks pressed forward along a narrow path. Many of them shed their tracks on the boulders, or split their track assemblies, and finally the leading platoon ran onto mines. Every tank became a casualty and completely blocked the path. A detour was attempted. Two more tanks stuck in a swamp and another was blown up on a mine and completely burnt out.[9]

At the same time more German infantry tried to infiltrate between A and B companies, but were prevented from doing so by some heavy fire put up by the forward posts. Eventually, B Company had no choice but to withdraw 12 Platoon, but in the process this created a problem for 21 NZ Battalion. C Company's withdrawal and the enfilading fire from Panteleimonas had been brought to bear on D Company, which left the battalion with a tenuous hold on the position. If that was not enough their supporting 25-pounders, now almost out of ammunition, began to pull out. Around mid-morning Macky signalled corps headquarters that they were retiring, destroying their wireless and abandoning their signals lines before leaving. The companies then withdrew one by one, B Company covered by 18 Platoon, the latter being joined by C Company just before they withdrew.[10]

Luckily for 21 NZ Battalion, the Germans were reluctant to follow up. Instead, with many of their tanks disabled and their petrol supply some 4km away, they spent the rest of their day recovering tanks and clearing mines from the track and surrounding area. They did, however, take time out to hoist their flag on the castle.[11] In fact, while Balck was no doubt anxious to push on in pursuit, the recovery of his disabled tanks was more important and proved to be no simple task. There are indications from their report that twenty or more tanks were either disabled in the rough terrain or on mines during the attack. Their battle report lamented that the following day, when the regiment started down the track from Platamon Ridge towards the Pineios River, they had hardly any PzKpfw II tanks left, suggesting that they were still trying to recover and repair many of them.

With Platamon firmly in German hands, the commander of 6. Gebirgs-Division, Generalmajor Ferdinand Schörner, was keen to push on to support Balck's battlegroup. His original orders had called for him to secure the area south of Litohoro as part of the German drive on Larissa. At 2.45pm he decided to accelerate those plans and send an advance guard towards Kallipevki and Gonos with the intention of attacking the Tempe hills and opening up the road for the tanks. As he was later to state in his divisional orders:

> This flanking move by the whole division over the southern slopes of Olympus might have a decisive effect on the whole course of the battle for Larissa, as the enemy had so far been very successful in slowing up the tanks' advance. If we broke into the Larissa basin we would be on the Greeks' main withdrawal route from Albania, and this campaign would be brought to a decisive end.[12]

He might as well have added that this flanking move would also have posed serious problems for the withdrawal of Anzac troops to the north of Larissa.

Just after midday both Aufklärungs–Abteilung 112 and II/143 Gebirgsjäger-Regiment, along with two pioneer platoons, set off on a route that would take them through Leptokarya, Skotina, Kallipevki and Gonos, where they would be in a position to attack Itia. Several hours later this line of advance proved too much for Aufklärungs-Abteilung 112. According to its commander, the climb up to Skotina was difficult and the track passable only to infantry. With his cavalry and rifle squadrons lagging badly, he was ordered to assemble his squadrons in Skotina and make their way towards the eastern entrance of Pineios Gorge. Once there the unit was to come under the command of Oberstleutnant von Decker of I/3. Panzer-Regiment.[13]

In the meantime, that afternoon, covered by their carrier platoon, the bulk of 21 NZ Battalion withdrew to the eastern end of Pineios Gorge and dispersed under the trees by the river. Here Macky met Brigadier Clowes, who had come over on Anzac Corps' instructions. This was after Brigadier Rowell had concluded that Macky was in a 'blue funk' and needed some moral support. Someone was also needed to assess the situation.[14] At this point

Macky had proposed setting off the demolitions in the gorge and pulling back to Lamia, but this was countermanded by Clowes. Instead Macky and his men were to hold the western end of the gorge until 19 April 'even if it meant extinction'; their fallback position being the junction of the road and railway seven miles to the south of the western exit.[15] The only reassurance Clowes could give Macky was that he could expect reinforcements within 24 hours.

By the time Clowes had departed the rest of the battalion had arrived and the work of ferrying them across the Pineios River on a flat-bottomed barge began. This took the rest of the afternoon, the 25-pounders being taken over on the barge as well. Their Quads and the battalion's carriers were driven back along the railway line to Tempe, where they crossed by way of the bridge there. In the meantime the guns were towed back by some of the battalion's trucks that had come forward. With explosives in short supply the last carrier towed a boxcar into the first tunnel in the gorge, where the engineers blew off its bogie wheels. Craters were also blown in the line on either side of the tunnel. Some explosives found in a tunnel on the line were then used to demolish one of the culverts, the force of the explosion propelling the rails across to the other side of the river. Meanwhile, back at the ferry:

> Just when the ferry was due for destruction and the hauling ropes cut, there was an incident that could happen only in Greece or in a comic opera. Two shepherdesses arrived with small flocks of mixed sheep and goats and requested a passage. The pioneer platoon took time off from the war to haul them over before they ensured that nobody else would use the ferry for some considerable time.[16]

Craters were then blown in the road at two points selected by the engineers, 10 Platoon being left to cover the western one and the remainder of B Company taking up stations a mile inside the gorge up towards the village of Ambelakia, which itself was occupied by D Company. C Company took over the ridge running down to Tempe, the defence of Tempe becoming the responsibility of a platoon from Headquarters Company, while A Company was based south of Tempe. The mortar platoon was also assigned an infantry role after they discovered that, although they had loaded their heavy equipment onto the artillery tractors, some essential parts were missing, rendering their mortars unusable. In the final act the bridge over the river at Tempe was also collapsed into the river.[17]

Towards dusk Lieutenant Colonel Chilton arrived with his carrier platoon, followed shortly afterwards by his infantry, 2/2 Australian Battalion. Next to materialize was L Troop of 7 NZ Anti-Tank Regiment, followed later by 26 Battery, 4 NZ Field Regiment, at around midnight.

On the morning of 17 April, Chilton, Macky, Lieutenant Colonel 'Ike' Parkinson and some officers from the New Zealand artillery and anti-tank detachments conducted a recce up the gorge as far as the main road and tunnel demolitions. Discussions then centred on their defensive arrangements. Macky put forward the suggestion that he be given command of the entire force, though Chilton said that went against his instructions from Anzac Corps HQ. One thing they did agree on was the dispositions of their respective battalions. Macky's men were to hold their positions in the gorge, while 2/2 Australian Battalion was detailed to take up positions in depth around the entrance to the gorge. The Australians' tools arrived that morning and they began to dig their weapons pits. In addition three of the 2-pounders were placed in defilade positions along the defile in 21 NZ Battalion's area, while the fourth was set up commanding the southern exit from Tempe. The New Zealand 25-pounders were set up further back with two in anti-tank positions near Evangelismos.[18]

That morning the force was further strengthened by some Australian anti-tank guns, and these were dispersed around 2/2 Australian Battalion's positions. Brigadier Allen joined the force around midday to take command of what became known as Allen Force. Last to arrive was 2/3 Australian Battalion, which had ended up somewhere between Larissa and Trikkala before they were stopped. C Company was sent north towards Parapotamos, while the others were stationed around Makrikhorion. In the afternoon some sappers arrived from 2/1 Australian Field Company and placed naval depth charges in some culverts near L Troop's three 2-pounders, which were detonated that night.[19]

The local Greek population having left the area, the infantry of 21 NZ Battalion were instructed to make good their losses of tools from whatever they could find in the villages. The radio equipment they abandoned could not be replaced, but the Australians were able to supply them with enough captured Italian telephone cable to establish communications between Macky's and Chilton's headquarters. This meant that the companies and headquarters of 21 NZ Battalion would have to maintain contact by runners.[20] To further bolster the defenders at Pineios, Major John Russell of B Squadron, NZ Divisional Cavalry, was asked to send over an armoured car troop. Lieutenant Ernest Kerr's troop was dispatched, but one of his cars slipped off the road, resulting in Lieutenant Harry Capamagian's troop going instead.[21] Later, however, the rest of the squadron was also ordered to report to Allen's headquarters at Makrikhori.

That same morning, elements of 6. Gebirgs-Division reached the town of Gonnos, thus ending a long outflanking movement across the southern slopes of Mount Olympus. That move coincided with the drive of Panzer-Regiment 3 from the Panteleimonas ridge:

> 1 Coy was in the lead, as the other one was to the left on the coast and was held up by a blown tunnel. The descent from the ridge was even harder than the ascent. Time and time again tracks came off on the narrow mule path. Projecting rocks tore sprockets and tracks, and engineers had to knock or blow these rocks. Then the descent became easier, but was still slow. Unfortunately we had hardly any Mk II tanks left. Not until midday did the force reach the foot of the ridge and then it carried on along the railway line parallel to the coast, because the narrow track lost itself in swamp and sand. Now tank after tank bumped and rattled along the straight railway track. Early in the afternoon the leading company arrived at the Pineios River at the entrance to Tempe gorge. Here the enemy had blown or ruined every bridge or ford, and so we had to carry on along the railway tracks through the gorge. About the middle of the valley there was a gigantic demolition in the railway line right in front of the two blown tunnels, and it was impossible for the tanks to go on. There was no advance along this side of the river, even the engineers could do no good, so thoroughly had the English carried out their demolitions. The cycle squadron of a recce unit, which was attached to the regiment, pushed on as best they could.[22]

This advance of Balck's tanks did not go unnoticed by 21 NZ Battalion, 10 Platoon spotting one of their tanks moving along the railway line at approximately 5pm. Unfortunately, there was little the New Zealanders could do about it, as the forward observation officer was unable to make wireless contact with his guns thanks to the winding nature of the gorge and steepness of the hills. The infantry of 10 Platoon did open up on a party of cyclists from Aufklärungs-Abteilung 112, of 6. Gebirgs-Division, forcing the Germans to take shelter in the tunnel until the tank turned its gun on the New Zealanders who, themselves seeking shelter from the tank, climbed a further 200 yards up the ridge. Shortly after this Macky ordered the withdrawal of the platoon, the most exhausted being sent back to battalion headquarters and the rest joining 12 Platoon.[23]

In the meantime the Germans began a search for a place where they could get their tanks across the river:

> Finally Leutnant Brunenbusch and Leutnant Schmitthenner went to recce, and by swimming and wading through the river they discovered a point where it could to some extent be forded. Both were carried far downstream as they swam. The attempt was made. A Mark II tank drove determinedly down the high, steep embankment into the water. It struggled through the river like a walrus, with nothing to show except the turret; it appeared to be swimming. But the driver carried on calmly, although he was sitting up to his middle in water and the waves completely prevented him from seeing anything. Finally the tank clambered out on the other side amid loud cheers from the spectators and pushed on forwards.[24]

Though this necessitated a journey of several hundred yards upstream, it looked to be a viable way across the river, though not foolproof. The next five tanks followed, two slipping into holes in the river, whereupon their crews climbed out and abandoned them. The surviving tanks came upon one of the demolitions on the road, but on trying to bypass it came upon a swamp and, with the light fading, were forced to stop for the night.[25]

Audacious as this move was, there were signs of problems ahead for the Germans. In a message back to XVIII Korps that evening 2. Panzer-Division reported that their ammunition and petrol were only secured until the evening of 17 April. Thus it was imperative that railway line be repaired and that the army get some columns through to Katerini. Having advanced this far they were also in the invidious position of being unable to get their wheeled vehicles through the pass to Egani. As a result the tanks and infantry in the area of the gorge were now entirely without supplies.[26]

With the coming of dawn on 18 April Macky held his final meeting with company commanders, instructing them to make their own way back through the hills in small parties and rejoin the division if they were cut off. Across the river German troop movements were detected, mainly transport units in Gonos and small groups of infantry making their way into Itia. The New Zealand artillery opened up on them and the German artillery responded in kind.[27] The troops seen assembling in Gonos were from I/143. Gebirgsjäger-Regiment, who had been tasked with launching a feint attack

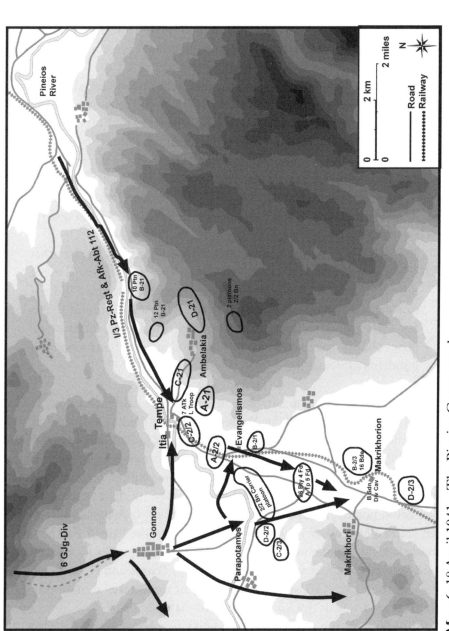

Map 6: 18 April 1941 – The Pineios Gorge attack.

to draw attention away from the real attack from the gorge. Thus they began what was to become a prolonged machine-gun and artillery duel, which also drew in A and B companies of 21 NZ Battalion until fire on B Company forced them to move further uphill. Around 10am the mountain troops began their move down to the river, aiming to cross it at a point to the left of D Company 2/2 Australian Battalion.

Chilton sent in his carrier platoon to deal with this and asked for support from Macky, who sent his carrier platoon. Though the Australian carriers came under heavy fire, two crewmen being killed and four others wounded, they and the New Zealand carriers hit the Germans hard, eliminating those that had managed to cross and killing some others in the river.[28] Under the cover of machine-gun fire the Germans then sent a battalion of infantry across in front of A and B companies of 2/2 Australian Battalion, this being met by a hail of Bren gun fire and mortar fire, as Charlie Green described:

> The only thing wrong with it for a mortar target was the fact that it was about 2,000 yards away, which was considerably in excess of the range for 3-inch mortars in those days. This however did not stop Sgt Coyle and his mortar platoon. The normal round plus a few extra primary charges were dropped into the barrel, the base plates almost disappeared into the ground and the mortars caused hundreds of casualties.[29]

By 11.30am the German attack was spent. The commander of I/143. Gebirgsjäger-Regiment, Major Weiser, then attempted to find another way across the Pineios River. Patrols sent to the west of Gonos had no luck. They found the river there too deep and wide for a crossing to be possible without the probability of suffering heavy casualties. Worse still, they had no material to make a bridge, their engineer platoon was not with them and most of his men could not swim. Upon learning that III/143. Gebirgsjäger-Regiment had crossed by way of a ferry they had found to the east of Parapotamos, Weiser sought permission to use this. This was refused and instead they were ordered to move by all available means to Tempe and cross there. This was something that Weiser was unwilling to undertake, as it would have involved a journey of five kilometres under flanking fire.[30]

Meantime, in the gorge itself, the tanks that had crossed the river the previous evening were in a difficult position until the demolition could be cleared. They were eventually joined by a platoon from 8/800. Brandenberg-Regiment who had managed to cross on kapok floats and, unable to advance beyond the tanks, they started work on opening up a route through the demolition. On the other side of the river Aufklärungs-Abteilung 112 attempted to move forward, but were forced to go to ground after coming under heavy machine-gun and mortar fire from the New Zealander infantry on the south bank and their artillery.[31]

Around 12.15pm the German tanks and their supporting infantry, having finally cleared the demolitions, appeared in front of 12 Platoon, 21 NZ Battalion, who, as the firing intensified from across the river, were forced to pull back up the slope towards D Company. This lessening of fire also opened up the way for Aufklärungs-Abteilung 112, allowing them to push on through the gorge towards Tempe. Then, at 12.30pm, five tanks emerged from the gorge, two of which closed up to the foot of the ridge, with the Brandenberger platoon in support, where they opened up on C Company. This forced 14 and 15 platoons to retreat further up the ridge, in the process abandoning 13 Platoon in their sangars on the flat between the road and the river.[32] Artillery fire was called down on the tanks, but only served to slow rather than halt their advance. Some of the tanks then turned their attention to 13 Platoon. According to their platoon commander, Lieutenant Michael O'Neill:

> Then O.P. called down to us 'Infanteers the tanks are coming.' A single file of about five tanks came out of the gorge. O.P. directed very good fire onto them. I saw two shells lob between tanks but no hits were scored. I lost sight of probably two tanks hidden behind the line of trees. Three tanks came forward to my position. ... Had they stood out a few hundred yards they would have blown us all to bits but their audacity saved us because they stopped at the very foot of the rise and thereby gave depth to our shallow weapons pits. At any rate we successfully withstood most of their cannon and machine gun fire and at less than 100 yards range. The two tanks dealt with us, the third closed to the point to recce the possibility of proceeding. Its crew got out while the other two tanks kept our heads down. The personnel crept round beyond my view. From midday for nearly an hour the most intense fire in which the tanks was kept up by both sides and then towards 1pm the fire behind me slackened.[33]

In the absence of infantry support the three tanks remained there for some time, the Brandenberg infantry still being heavily committed further back.

One of the tanks in front of 13 Platoon eventually moved off around 2pm, heading in the direction of the spur that C Company had formerly occupied. It was joined shortly after by two others.[34] An hour and a half an hour later the German infantry that had been working their way across C Company's ridge closed in on 13 Platoon's left flank, and with some others coming in from behind, forced the platoon to surrender.[35]

In the meantime Weiser's troops were still trying to find a way across the river. After leading a patrol from I/143. Gebirgsjäger-Regiment he discovered another crossing point, as he related:

> The recce patrol found had found that the river could be waded at the sandbank west of Evangelismos. About 1300 hrs an ever increasing noise of fighting from the gorge gave me the impression that the panzer division was making another attempt to break through. I decided at once to cross at the spot recced, and to attack the enemy at Evangelismos on the hills under fire.

Shortly after leaving 13 Platoon's position, the German tanks struck south towards C Company's spur and the demolished culverts, sighting and knocking out the 2-pounder commanded by Sergeant Quinn. For the next half hour Sergeant Daniel Cavanagh, in command of L4, sited behind C Company's spur, watched the tanks as they negotiated the demolitions:

> The German tanks reached the road block. One managed to cross and stopped while a second struggled to pass the demolition. The forward tank was well within view of L4 but Sergeant Cavanagh held his fire, wanting as many targets as possible within his field of fire before opening up. The range was little more than one hundred yards but the Sergeant relied on first class natural concealment, plus the canny use of his camouflage net, to keep the gun from German eyes. His confidence was well founded, for the second tank negotiated the road block and the men from both armoured vehicles climbed out and onto the road, while a third struggled across. With the third tank emerging from the bloc, the tank crews sprung into their vehicles again and started off along the road, and it was then that Sergeant Cavanagh gave the word to fire. At point blank range, L4 put 28 shells into the three tanks. The two leaders were definitely killed and the third put out of action, at least.[36]

According to the I/3 Panzer-Regiment report:

> The leading tanks came around the end of a hill and were greeted with anti-tank fire from the flank at very close range. In a moment both point tanks were burning. Some of the crews, including Leutnant Brunebusch, escaped into the thick scrub seriously wounded. The third tank spotted the enemy and opened fire at once. It kept on firing until the enemy was fought to a standstill and an ammunition wagon burst into flames and exploded. The unit MO came up quickly and had plenty to do. The driver of the HQ tank, Unteroffizier Greszek, saved both tanks before they blew up. By this time the infantry had arrived and set off in pursuit of the retreating enemy.[37]

In fact the German infantry called upon the gun crew to surrender. Realizing that the Germans did not know where they were, Cavanagh decided to make a break for it. Covered by Gunner Judd with his Bren gun, he and his crew ran back to their gun tractor 100 yards behind them and managed to get away in it. They eventually reached 2/2 Australian Battalion, only to be captured later.[38]

This left Balck's advance force with a PzKpfw III and his command tank, a PzKpfw III Befehlswagen. So more tanks were sent for and dispatched in the direction of Tempe to link up with the mountain troops, but all but one of these were disabled by direct hits, leaving it to carry on alone.[39]

At 3pm Allen received orders from 2 NZ Division Headquarters that they were to hold their positions until 3am the following morning, to allow time for 6 NZ Brigade and Savige Force to clear Larissa. Shortly afterwards Freyberg appeared at Allen's headquarters to investigate: having received disturbing reports of the situation at Pineios Gorge he had come forward to see things for himself. At 3.30pm Allen sent orders through to 2/1 Australian Battalion halting their impending withdrawal to Thermopylae. Instead they were ordered to take up defensive positions south of Larissa. For support they had some 25-pounders from 2/2 Australian Field Regiment and a troop from 2/1 Australian Anti-Tank Regiment.[40] Half an hour later Freyberg spoke to Chilton over the telephone and then went forward for a closer look (contact with Macky had been lost at midday). Realizing that the original timetable could no longer be adhered to, Freyberg issued new orders for Allen Force to break contact at dusk and withdraw. He managed to contact Parkinson, but was unable to reach Chiltern as radio communication with him had broken down. At this point he departed for Larissa. Another attempt was made to contact Chiltern at 5.30pm when an officer was sent forward in a Bren carrier, but he had only made it as far as the forward New Zealand artillery when he was wrongly informed that Chilton's headquarters had been overrun. By this stage Freyberg had reached Larissa, where he took it upon himself to direct traffic at the choke point where the columns of transport from Elasson and Trikkala met.[41]

At 3pm the Germans ramped up their assault on Tempe, overrunning HQ Company, 21 NZ Battalion, the survivors joining up with A Company on their small ridge behind the village. The Germans in Tempe were then joined by Aufklärungs-Abteilung 112, followed by three tanks from I/3 Panzer-Regiment half an hour later.

With Tempe taken, attention turned to the main objective of the German attack: Larissa. Throughout the afternoon Balck had been feeding tanks across the river and, as soon as a complete platoon had assembled on the south bank, it was sent off to the western end of the gorge. By late afternoon, he had assembled a large enough force of tanks and infantry to launch his main attack.[42] At 4pm 2. Kompanie, I/3 Panzer-Regiment, under Leutnant von Nostitz-Wallwitz, burst out of the gorge.[43] At this point the Germans turned their attention to A Company, 21 NZ Battalion, and two sections of carriers that had returned from the Australians. Machine-gun fire from the carriers initially kept the German infantry pinned down, but around 4.30pm A Company was eventually overrun, but not before, in one last desperate attempt, Sergeant Major Allan Lockett rammed the leading tank with his carrier, forcing it off the road. With this B and D companies of 21 NZ Battalion started to climb up into the foothills, where they were joined shortly afterwards by the remnants of A Company. The rest of A Company headed westwards. 7 Platoon under Lieutenant William Southworth linked up with 2/2 Australian Battalion, while other unarmed stragglers streamed through the Australian's position.[44]

At 4pm D Troop, 4 NZ Field Regiment, was withdrawn from the line and sent back to join Russell's squadron astride the railway at Makrikhorion.[45] At the same time D Company, 2/2 Australian Battalion, withdrew their patrolling platoon from the riverbank. What happened next, however, was somewhat unfortunate, as at 4.45pm, through a misunderstanding, D Company suddenly retired. They had been planning a counter-attack with the carrier platoon, but B Company 2/3 Australian Battalion had come forward with instructions that they were to withdraw with them. In fact the intention had been for it to happen the other way around, but somehow the message got mixed up. The two companies pulled back to Allen Force HQ at the Makrikhori railway station, leaving Chilton with the unfortunate impression, when firing ceased in their area, that they had run away.[46]

While the Germans had been fighting to secure Tempe, I/143. Gebirgsjäger-Regiment had been active over to the west of Evangelismos:

> The companies came forward and the attack began at 1400hrs. As soon as the enemy at and southeast of Evangelismos recognized our attack he opened heavy shell, mortar and machine gun fire on our bank and the river itself. But before the fire could have any effect 1. Kompanie (which had been directed to establish a bridgehead) had reached the other bank, thanks to the speed of the advance, which took the enemy by surprise. 3. Kompanie, Battalion headquarters and the signals platoon followed under extremely heavy fire. Our heavy mortars supported the attack from positions on our side of the river, and the MMG platoon (which was the last to cross) from positions further back. In about one and a half hours the whole of the battalion crossed the swift river. The companies were reorganized on the south bank, and then the attack was continued on Evangelismos.[47]

Next to cross the river was I/141. Gebirgsjäger-Regiment. Their orders were to push on towards Makrichori via the railway line. With them were some engineers who had been tasked with building a trestle bridge over the river:

> The bridge-building task was unnecessary, as a ferry was found. In any case the piles and trestles provided by the engineers were too short [the water was four metres deep in places]. The battalion crossed by the ferry, its leading troops at 1700hrs. During the crossing an enemy infantry gun was knocked out by one of our mortars. At 1750hrs the battalion carried on its attack on Makrichori.[48]

At 5.55pm at Evangelismos two German tanks swung into view from behind a spur over to the right of 2/2 Australian Battalion. Both were immediately engaged by a 2-pounder embedded with A Company headquarters, the round striking one and setting it on fire. The second tank with it was also hit but withdrew. The German armour then abandoned this line of approach and switched to one that took them across the fields that lay between the road and the river, fifteen to eighteen tanks surging forward with infantry from 7/304. Infanterie-Regiment and I/143. Gebirgsjäger-Regiment, who had just linked up with them.[49]

These German tanks were engaged by Sergeant John Franklin's gun from 5 NZ Field Regiment in his emplacement to the south of Evangelismos.[50] Franklin's gun hit the leading tank, setting it on fire, and then another shortly afterwards. Unluckily for the gun crew, another tank destroyed one of their lorries carrying petrol and ammunition, forcing them to withdraw. Sergeant Jeffrey Gunn's 25-pounder from 4 Field Regiment knocked out two more tanks, no crews emerging from them. The tanks burned for 10 minutes, giving out a dense cloud of smoke that provided cover for some other tanks following up.[51] These tanks then took up hull-down positions near the village of Evangelismos, where one of the tanks became engaged in a duel with Gunn's 25-pounder, until the gun crew ran out of armour-piercing ammunition.[52] One of Gunn's crew went back to get more, but while he was away the rest of the crew were wounded by shellfire and were forced to abandon the gun and escape in their tractor.[53]

At about 6pm, with the forward 25-pounders now neutralized, the leading tanks broke into the positions of A Company, 2/2 Australian Battalion, forcing them to ascend the ridges to the east of the road. C Company followed suit shortly afterwards. Around 6.30pm Chilton discovered that a 2-pounder and crew sited in defilade position near battalion HQ had also gone.[54] The tanks then nosed cautiously through the village, leaving Southworth's platoon and another from 2/3 Australian Battalion no choice but take to the hills as well. At 6.45pm, with more tanks appearing across the plain, Chilton ordered his headquarters and B Company to follow suit.[55] Chilton had a remarkable escape himself after passing some instructions to some troops near his headquarters:

> I then went back into the little mud hut we had been using as HQ to get my haversack, etc. and on coming out saw a couple of medium tanks about 50 yards away. They fired on us with their cannons and machine guns as we went up a slight open rise. At this stage I fell and hurt my knee. I realized I could not go on, so managed to get into a little dry creek bed where there was cover from the tanks' fire. Here I met up with three others: We decided there was no chance of getting away just then and tried to get into some low prickly bushes, but they were pretty thick and our arms and legs stuck out obviously. Some time later two German infantry

parties came right past us looking for anyone who might have been left behind. They were calling out 'Hello English prisoners' and firing odd shots about.

Chilton's party was exceptionally lucky not to have been seen. After dusk they set off in a south-easterly direction.[56]

Now, with signs of 2/2 Australian Battalion thinning out in front of 26 Battery, 4 NZ Field Regiment, Parkinson ordered the guns back towards Allen Force headquarters. First to go was F Troop, pulling back 2,000 yards. They then turned their guns around to cover E Troop, the latter withdrawing another 1,000 yards to cover F Troop, two more German tanks being destroyed and several others put out of action. An Australian infantryman later described the scene:

> The officer stood out in the open directing the fire, the crews crouching behind the shields and fed and fired the guns, while everything the enemy had was being pelted at them. ... They looked like a drawing by someone who had never been to a war but the whole thing was unreal. They got two tanks, lost one gun and pulled the other gun and their wounded out, having done what they could. There was nothing to stop the tanks then and they formed up and came on.

Having kept the German tanks at bay, and E Troop now in the clear, it became F Troop's turn to provide covering fire, disabling another tank in the process. They then pulled out leaving a section behind with the rearguard. The lack of ammunition ultimately forced E Troop to pull out completely and make for Larissa. [57,58]

Parkinson then went forward to contact Chilton and see how his two forward guns were doing, but all he found was an empty battlefield and both guns silenced. Instead he came across 150 men from 21 NZ Battalion, whom he sent back to 26 Battery positions, where some lorries were waiting to pick up any survivors of the fighting. By 7pm another fifty men had drifted in and they too were loaded into the trucks. The convoy then set off southwards.[59]

While the New Zealand artillery had been providing cover, Allen had pulled his headquarters back to the road and railway crossing at Makrikhorion at around 6pm. There he found himself with a mixed force of infantry and light armour. Among them were B and D companies, 2/3 Australian Battalion, D Company 2/2 Australian Battalion, elements of the carrier platoons of 2/2, 2/5, 2/11 Australian and 21 NZ battalions, and Russell's squadron from NZ Divisional Cavalry, plus D Troop 4 NZ Field Regiment. After being bombed and strafed by the Luftwaffe, twelve to fifteen German tanks came along the road sometime round 7.30pm, their turrets traversing and firing in all directions. Several men were hit and two were run over by one tank, one of them being saved from serious head injuries by the soft ground and his tin hat.[60]

The Australians withdrew in their trucks to a new defence line 1,000 yards to the south, and took up a line astride the road. Then, around 9pm in the fading light, they prepared to meet the tanks again. This time they decided to allow the tanks to penetrate their line, while lying in wait for the German infantry following close behind. However, after driving into the Australian position, the tanks soon became aware of them and opened fire:[61]

> In a few minutes the leading tank appeared. A man who was standing waist high in the turret of one of them peering out was riddled with bullets and slumped forward. Lamb shouted to the men to make every shot tell and that the tanks could not fight in the dark. The tank stopped and fired shells and tracer bullets at random and fire appeared to be coming from other tanks behind it; an ineffective hail of rifle and machine-gun fire answered this. The tank withdrew.[62]

Allen then ordered Russell's squadron from the NZ Divisional Cavalry to cover the withdrawal of the Australians to where the road crossed a swamp north of Larissa.[63] This they did, leapfrogging back as the German tanks advanced through the trees. Frank White recalled his escape:

> The Jerry tanks – light tanks – came through in front of us and took hostile action. They hit us twice, but luckily one 20mm bullet went into a blanket roll. It went up the full length of the blanket roll and hopped in beside the driver. The driver was a short little fellow and he tried to pick it up. It was hot. So he got it out quickly. At the same time the other one hit us on the steel of the towing rope and burst there and set the carrier alight. We managed to put that out. Bill McCready had an armoured car further back and he came to help us.[64]

Further back D Troop, 26 Battery, covered Russell's squadron with a hail of fire on the tanks, hitting several of them, F Troop joining in shortly afterwards. Under this combined weight of fire the Germans were forced to fall back.[65] However, the Germans themselves were spent and in no position to follow up, as their report stated:

> It was by now very dark, and one company reported by wireless to Unit HQ that it thought it was being fired on by the other one. Leutnant Statten (the adjutant) came on a convoy of trucks at 10 yards range and was fired upon but got away. It was better to halt. The regimental commander fired flares, and we formed a laager round his, covered by infantry and the recce troop. The petrol situation was bad. We had enough to reach Larissa, but we did not know how much further. We were almost out of ammunition. All the ammunition was taken from the knocked-out tanks, and ammunition was ferried across the Pineios River in open barges, for all other vehicles were waiting for a bridge to be built.[66]

Some of the Anzac troops escaping towards Larissa then ran into a roadblock that had been set up north of Larissa by 2. Kompanie, 143. Gebirgsjäger-Regiment.[67] This company had crossed the river unseen earlier that morning and had made a wide flanking movement that had gone unseen by the Australians as they withdrew. This eventually brought them onto the plain north of Larissa. From there they set out for their objective, the point where the road to Larissa crossed the railway line:

> Using dead ground and skirting of all enemy positions Leutnant Jacob succeeded in reaching the area north of Kuluri about 1700hrs. At 17.30hrs the leading elements of the company tried to save a German airman forced down 2 kilometres away from being captured by English troops who hurried up in trucks. The leading three sections went forward at a run, but when 600 metres away from the spot they were seen and engaged with machine gun fire. Immediately after that the English MT drove away to the south with the captured airman. The company immediately swung towards the railway embankment and carried on toward Larissa. Two English MT moving along the Tempe-Larissa road from the north in an attempt to make a quick getaway southwards were engaged with two LMGs and an HMG. After a short exchange of fire their crews were forced

to surrender. The road–railway crossing 3.5km northeast of Larissa was reached about 1900hrs. All telephone lines (which were all in use) were cut, and a roadblock was made on the railway with the two captured trucks. The company took up all-round defence positions, for which the terrain was very favourable, paying particular attention to the north-south withdrawal route. A fully loaded ammunition truck convoy with nine or 10 trucks was captured. At 2130hrs a long MT convoy, whose lights could be seen as far as the foot of the mountains, approached the block. The leading vehicle (a light tank) came up to the block at 40 to 50mph and immediately opened fire. It was engaged with several LMGs, 2 HMGs and an anti-tank rifle and destroyed. The rest of the convoy had stopped, and the troops took cover on either side of the road and opened a heavy fire with rifles and machine pistols. At 2330hrs two armoured cars came up, firing with all weapons and tried to crash through the block to the southeast. In the darkness they came forward with no lights along the railway embankment and stopped. Leutnant Jacob fired flares, collected all the heavy infantry weapons, which were on the embankment, and opened fire again in volleys on the vehicles further away. The effect was terrific. In the first pause in the firing the rest of the Australians left the vehicles and made a determined attempt to overrun the positions on the embankment by coming in to very close range. Our accurate defensive fire inflicted heavy casualties on the enemy.

In the confusion of night the mountain troops appear have mistaken one of Balck's tanks, a PzKpfw II, for the enemy:

> About 0100hrs a heavy tank with a quick-firing gun was knocked out by several direct hits with the anti-tank rifle. The attack collapsed. About 30 Australians came in to surrender and the rest ran in all directions across the fields trying to escape to the south-east.

With all the Australians in the leading lorry appearing to have been either killed or wounded by a burst of machine-gun fire, the party of Germans, estimated at about fifty, then called upon the rest of the column from 2/3 Australian Battalion to surrender. As Lieutenant C.M. Johnson later recalled:

> Upon proceeding 100 yards the leading carrier ran onto what I presume was a land mine, slewed across the road and blocked any

further movement forward. The efforts of approximately six men failed to roll the carrier off the road, it still being under continual machine-gun fire and sniping, and the troops were told to take cover off the road. [I and Gunner J. Aldridge] contacted a second lieutenant of the NZEF who had with him several of his own men. He expressed his determination to attack the machine-gun nest on the left of the road and wanted personnel to accompany him. Bombs were obtained from one of the carriers and we attempted to encircle the nest. During this time fire from the enemy was still kept up. As far as I can ascertain it took us nearly an hour to overrun this position. It was situated between the rails and sangared in with stones. ...All four men were killed. After destroying the gun we withdrew back on to the flat ground. During the operation several New Zealanders received wounds. Owing to the casualties it was decided not to attack the other machine-gun post but to make our way round to Larissa.[68]

Having failed to break through, Johnson and Aldridge worked their way down the column of trucks and managed to gather a few others also willing to escape. They then split up into smaller groups, skirted the main German position and made their own way back to Larissa. The rest of the column further back, having seen the tracer fire, turned off the road and made their way south across country or along boggy tracks.

D Company 2/2 Australian Battalion, along with their B Echelon, part of their carrier platoon and regimental aid post, had a lucky break, as their regimental medical officer Captain Armati later related:

At 0100 on the 19th, having brought my RAP [Regimental Aid Post] 15 miles in 6 hours across country to the Larissa Road, we were within a couple of miles of Larissa and in a dilemma. Behind us the Germans must be pushing forward, ahead of us in Larissa itself could be heard the crackle of enemy machine guns. Our escape seemed to be cut off and it was decided that the one hope was to bypass Larissa and during daylight to lie low in the foothills. It was at this critical junction that we heard the noise of AFVs – friend or enemy? We scattered into the enveloping darkness and strained our ears. After and interminable time a solid British curse rent the air: as one man we rose to our feet and ran towards the welcome voice. We had contacted a NZ armoured unit [Russell's squadron], which had been cut off north of Larissa and were attempting to escape. We joined their carriers, traversed an ill-marked road, more mud and water than solid earth, were lost more times than can be imagined and then as dawn was breaking we found the southern road and sped on as fast as our carriers could go. On the Larissa–Volos road we met a 2/2 Battalion truck and continued in it towards Lamia.[69]

The last of 6 NZ Brigade cleared the town by 1.30am the next morning, followed by Savige Force around 4am and not a moment too soon.[70] Just two hours later the leading elements of the panzer and mountain troops entered the town and to their astonishment found 'a rich haul of best quality goods.' But their luck was only temporary, as the report of Panzer-Regiment 3 later recorded:

The Mk II tanks still had a little petrol, so on they went. But after 40km their petrol gave out and they had to stop. If we had found during our search in the morning the English petrol that was discovered about midday, the Thermopylae battle might never have taken place, because we would have not allowed the Australians to take their positions there.[71]

Thus the Anzacs narrowly escaped entrapment north of Larissa, but as the British would have said, it was a 'near run thing'. Nevertheless, there is no doubt that the drive by Balck's battlegroup towards Platamon and through the Pineios Gorge was a remarkable feat of arms, but not without risks. Certainly the nature of the terrain and roads over which they travelled was not the easiest. At Platamon the determined defence by 21 NZ Battalion must have come as a shock: it certainly was a shock for the New Zealanders, who had been told not to expect tanks and had not been provided with anti-tank guns. In the end, after doing all they could under the circumstances, the battalion withdrew, leaving Balck with many of his tanks disabled in the rough ground of the ridge or mine-damaged, and he lost valuable time recovering them. In forcing his way across the Pineios River he again showed his mettle in his drive towards securing Larissa, but in doing so over-extended his force by pushing dangerously beyond their logistical support. While the platoon tanks and company of infantry that first broke out of the gorge had an effect on 21 NZ Battalion that far exceeded their actual combat effectiveness, they they had too few infantry with them to really achieve much. The infantry platoon and the two tanks with them were able to force the bulk of 21 NZ Battalion further up the hill, but the other three tanks could not deal with a single platoon. This is possibly because of their fear that the area in front of 13 Platoon was mined, and may also have been because of an unwillingness to lose Balck's command tank, but the lack of infantry was telling. The lack of infantry also worked against the tanks when they attempted to push on further and lost three tanks to one anti-tank gun. This ultimately cost the Germans, as by the time Balck launched his main attack the day was almost over and the New Zealand artillery exacted a terrible toll on his tanks as the light faded. The reality was that the infantry of both 21 NZ and 2/2 Australian battalions were virtually impotent against the German tanks, their anti-tank rifles being next to useless. Forced to retreat over the hills to the east, both battalions ceased to exist as coherent fighting forces thanks to the terrain they had to traverse.

Nevertheless Balck's force had suffered heavily in the attack. Among his tank crews he had lost four killed and thirty-seven wounded. Just how many operational tanks he had left is less clear. While his men in Larissa were rummaging around for more fuel, his tank recovery teams would have been assessing the damage done to the tanks left behind in the Vale of Tempe and further forward. What they found out was grim. Their first casualties had been in the Pineios River, where two PzKpfw IIs and two PzKpfw IIIs had drowned in a position where there would have been little chance of their early recovery. Of those lost in combat, the panzer regiment records stated that two PzKpfw IVs had been totally destroyed, and a further eleven PzKpfw IIs and two PzKpfw IIIs knocked out. Though initially assessed as long-term repairable (ie. after their return to Germany), these tanks were eventually re-categorised as so badly damaged they were not worth repairing. In addition, the damage to a further three PzKpfw II, twelve PzKpfw IIIs and two PzKpfw IVs necessitated them being pulled out of the line for three to eight days of repair work.

Records of 2. Panzer-Division stated that 3. Panzer-Regiment had started the campaign with 116 tanks (forty-five PzKpfw IIs, fifty-one PzKpfw IIIs and twenty PzKpfw IVs). Based on their regimental organization, I/3. Panzer-Regiment could have started the attack through Platamon and Pineios Gorge with fifty-four tanks (there were eight in their regimental headquarters).[72] Based on the reliable and conservative estimate made by Captain Caldwell from 2/2 Battalion, from observations during the latter stages of the battle, there had been up to fifty tanks in the valley.[73] Assuming no losses for breakdowns earlier in the campaign, by the end of the day's fighting Balck's battle group would have been left with four PzKpfw IIs, eight PzKpfw IIIs and six PzKpfw IVs, representing an effective combat loss of two-thirds during the battle. For Balck, whose panzergrenadiers were first to cross the Meuse in the campaign in France in 1940, this must have been a huge disappointment. Worse still, he had the ignominy of seeing both 6 NZ Brigade and Savige Force slip through his trap. As to the Greeks in Albania, their fate would ultimately be decided by someone else.

Chapter 9

The Thermopylae Line

T hough the Anzac Corps had come perilously close to failure in the Vale of Tempe, they had managed to hold off the Germans long enough to extricate all their forces north of Larissa. They also ended up with several days' grace. Not only was Balck's battlegroup from 2. Panzer-Division short of petrol, but their other battlegroup had also been held up south of Olympus Pass by the demolished bridge over the Pineios River. They, in turn, were blocking traffic from Servia Pass. To make matters worse, the troops coming through Servia Pass were ordered to give priority to Luftwaffe ground staff. Over to the west, 5. Panzer-Division was still somewhere between Grevená and Kalabaka, and hardly in a position to take over the advance. Nevertheless, XII. Armee commander, Generalfeldmarschall List, made the decision that Generalleutnant Stumme's XL. Panzer-Korps was to be given priority over Generalleutnant Böhme's XVIII. Gebirgs-Korps. Whether Böhme's troops would abide by that decision was another matter.

On 19 April, concern over the deteriorating situation in Greece saw General Wavell fly into Athens. He met first with General Wilson, at W Force Headquarters, who at this stage was still of the view that they could hold the Thermopylae Line for some time. However, after some discussion, both agreed that abandoning Greece was their best option, even if that meant they might be lucky to save only 30 per cent of the force. Later, at the Royal Palace, they put these views to the king, General Papagos and representatives from the Greek government. At this meeting Wavell and Wilson made it plain that they would not leave Greece unless the Greeks gave their consent. As it transpired the Greeks were of a similar mind and were only too happy to agree, having concluded that the country would be devastated if the war continued for another month or two.[1]

Unfortunately for Greece, the rot had started to set in, with the military facing a revolt among some senior officers. That very day, in fact, General Georgios Tsolakogou, having abandoned his Macedonian army and his two corps commanders three days previously and driven to Epirus, had sacked the commander of their army, General Ioannis Pitsikas, and commenced surrender negotiations with General Sepp Dietrich of the LSSAH. Papagos tried to intervene by having Pitsikas dismiss Tsolakogou, but it was already too late. The following day Tsolakogou signed the surrender agreement at Larissa.[2]

With the withdrawal to Thermopylae in full swing on 19 April, over 10 miles of the main road south of Larissa was jam-packed with Anzac Corps lorries, all heading south, and not just them. It would appear that further north, several German divisions were all vying for access to the same stretch of road, the difference being that they were not subject to heavy attacks from the air. What they did have to deal with, though, was 40–50 miles of cratered roads and blown bridges and culverts left behind by the departing Anzacs.[3]

Over on the east coast a second rearguard was established at Volos, utilising 24 and 25 NZ Battalions that had arrived there that morning. Not that they stayed for long.[4] Some stragglers from 21 NZ and 2/2 Australian battalions reached them later that morning and, when it became apparent that no more were coming, the rearguard was able to pull out that evening.[5] For those troops retreating along the main road, the morning started clear, but around 7.30am the first heavy air attacks began, forcing the columns to halt temporarily. Typical was the experience of Lieutenant Jack Bedalls of 2/11 Australian Battalion:

> We hadn't gone very far when the Germans started an intense strafe of the road, dive-bombing and machine-gunning the 20 mile or so from the Brallos Pass to Domokos. The planes came over in relays and aimed their bombs at the vehicles on the road and then machine-gunned the area at the side of the road where the troops had taken cover. This lasted well over two hours.[6]

Lou Williams also of 2/11 Australian Battalion described his experience:

> Our first dose was about 7am – our next at 9am – again about 11 (till 1 o'clock this one lasted – the best yet). But worse was to come – he copped us on a flat about half way up Lamia Pass and we stopped our truck alongside a petrol dump. I thought I would have to hitchhike the rest of the way, but Lady Luck was with us and no one was hurt, not even the truck.[7]

Despite what the troops were experiencing, the actual damage done by the air attacks was not as great as it seemed. Australian records indicate that although many vehicles were hit, few were disabled. The casualties suffered by 2/5 Australian Battalion were thirteen killed and twenty-four wounded, while losses by 2/11 Australian Battalion were four killed and eleven wounded, and those were the heaviest that day. In fact the troops were usually well dispersed during these attacks by the Luftwaffe, and often the soft ground dulled the blast of the bombs or the strafing of their supporting fighter aircraft.[8]

That evening news was received that the last New Zealand troops had passed through Lamia, though there was still no word of the last formation, 16 Australian Brigade. Nevertheless, the rearguard at Domokos started to withdraw around 7pm, and as they left they blew several craters in the road, somewhat hastily, it would appear, as some of them were behind 2/6 Australian Battalion's positions, forcing them to abandon two anti-tank guns. An hour later several trucks appeared carrying British engineers and Cypriot pioneers, who started to fill in the craters. The rearguard opened fire on them, but on realising their mistake sent a patrol to collect these stragglers, then destroy their trucks. The rearguard then made their way back to a new position 10 miles further south at the southern exit from the hills between Lamia and the plain of Thessaly.[9]

The day started off badly for the RAF as well, for at breakfast time the airfield at Menidi was attacked by Messerschmitt Bf 109s. Their first victim was a Vickers Valentia cargo plane that had only recently returned to 11 Squadron. Leaving it ablaze, the Bf 109s turned their attention to a line of Blenheims, which were then attacked by Messerschmitt Bf 110s. By the time they had finished all twelve were ablaze. Over at Eleusis 33, 80 and 208 Squadrons came in for some attention by a flight of Messerschmitt Bf 109s, with five Hurricanes sustaining damage. After the firing had died down the ground crews dragged them back to a hangar. Over the rest of that day and night they cannibalized enough parts to get three functional. To their dismay, just after first light the next day some Ju 87 dive-bombers showed up and attacked the hangar, destroying it and the Hurricanes inside. For a time the leak of information was blamed on fifth columnists. It was only later that they learned that the Germans had been monitoring the national telephone system from Larissa.[10]

Things were not much better for the Germans. For 5. Panzer-Division the journey on to Kalabaka turned out to be worse than the day before. The road they were taking was in poor condition, there were continued delays as the pioneers with them continued to build more bridges, and to make matters worse the division was hit by a heavy thunderstorm. When they did eventually reach Kalabaka they were told they were now to push directly onto Phársala. After the division set off on 20 April they were hit both by the RAF and by an even worse thunderstorm than the day before. There were more blown bridges and demolitions in every possible bottleneck to deal with, plus there was still no sign of the retreating Australians. When they eventually reached the junction with the main road south of Phársala they became involved in a quarrel with 2. Panzer-Division about who had the right of way on the road to Lamia. Worse still, they were now cut off from their supply column thanks to an order that resulted in the dispatch of LSSAH southwards along the same route they had taken. Instead they were forced to live off the land, their divisional quartermaster, Hauptmann Voss, having the unenviable task of searching all petrol stations, barracks and airfields for whatever petrol he could secure.[11]

Later that afternoon one of the Anzac rearguards came in for some unwanted German attention. Having taken up a new position north of Lamia the previous night, two companies, one from each of 2/6 and 2/7 Australian battalions, along with 2/1 Australian MG Battalion, had been reinforced by eight 2-pounders from 31 NZ Anti-Tank Battery, some armoured cars from the NZ Divisional Cavalry and the five remaining A13s of 1 Armoured Brigade's Headquarters Squadron.[12] By daylight on 20 April the troops and guns were well dug in and concealed: the company from the 2/7 Australian Battalion astride the road, and that from the 2/6 Australian Battalion to the left, while the A13 tanks were concealed in a small copse a mile further forward.

At approximately 2.15pm four German motorcycle and sidecar combinations from Aufkläurungs-Abteilung 8 of 5. Panzer-Division appeared in front of the rearguard and drove into the middle of the Australians, where they were hit by a heavy volley of fire. Though all were killed or wounded, a fifth, some 500 yards back, on seeing the wrecked motorcycles, turned smartly around and got away. The A13s then returned to the main force, but later two were sent forward to two knolls and when an armoured car hove into view it was disabled out by one of the tanks. This was followed shortly afterwards by a German light tank and, though it was hit several times by armour piercing and high-explosive shells, it managed to back off and escape. During a rainstorm the Germans recovered their damaged armoured car and brought up some mortars, but these were soon dealt with by the Vickers machine guns. Around 5pm two of the A13s withdrew to the main position, while a third was hit and caught fire in a crop field to the east of the road. That evening, on receiving news that the last convoys had passed through

Lamia, the rearguard began to withdraw.[13] Two of the A13s then held the road under German fire until the infantry withdrew, and as a parting gift the engineers blew some craters in the road. Later two of the A13s broke down and were used to block the road, after which they were set on fire.[14] A third A13 had to be abandoned on the northern bank of the Spercheios River after 7 NZ Field Regiment blew the Alamana Bridge.[15]

Around breakfast time that morning the Luftwaffe turned their attention to 5 NZ Brigade, bombing and strafing 22 NZ Battalion's position. Four Hurricanes did put in a brief appearance, but only after the Germans had flown off. Another lone Hurricane returned later and shot down a Junkers and 'as one man the troops along the front, regardless of exposing themselves, rose from their trenches to cheer'.[16] That afternoon the Luftwaffe launched an air attack on Piraeus with 100 aircraft, against which the RAF had only fifteen serviceable Hurricanes. Nevertheless, in the ensuing dogfight they managed to shoot down twenty-two German aircraft for the loss of only five themselves.[17]

By the morning of 21 April the bulk of the Anzac Corps was back at the Thermopylae position, preparing for what they thought would be a protracted defence, but unaware that the Germans were still struggling to make their way forward. Anzac demolitions had added to the Germans' problems, heavily restricting their movement up the pass. Though their lead elements had reached Lamia, the road through the pass between Phársala and Lamia was completely jammed by troops from both 2. Panzer-Division and 6. Gebirgs-Division. One thing was certain: both units seemed to be unwilling to relinquish the road to 5. Panzer-Division from Stumme's corps, despite the latter having the right of way. As a result his infantry units, Infanterie-Regiment 120 among them, were still stuck on the road to the west of Phársala.[18]

At this stage the Australians were inland at Brallos and with 2/1, 2/5, 2/11, 2/4 and 2/8 Australian battalions, though the latter was very much understrength. To their right 2 NZ Division had deployed 5 NZ Brigade along the coast road, in the foothills south of Lamia and along the Spercheios River, while 4 NZ Brigade was to their right and 6 NZ Brigade was in reserve. Freyberg also had 5 NZ Field Regiment and elements of 7 NZ Anti-Tank Regiment, to which were added 102 Anti-Tank Regiment and 2 Royal Horse Artillery when they reached the Thermopylae position on the night of 20/21 April. The rest of 1 Armoured Brigade was further back: 3 Royal Tanks in Athens and 4 Hussars at Glyphada, the latter having lost seventeen tanks on the Lamia Pass. 1 Rangers had been sent to Khalkis to hold the bridge to the island, while a detachment from NZ Divisional Cavalry investigated a report of possible landings by German troops on Euboea.[19]

As it turned out, W Force would not be in Greece for long. Earlier that morning Blamey received a visit from Wavell and was told that they were to be evacuated. In the first phase a covering force was to be established on the night of 22/23 April on the road to Athens south of Kriekouki, with the view to holding it until the 26th. The following night one brigade from each division was to move to a concealed position near its place of embarkation. The Australians were to go to Megara and the New Zealanders to Marathon, the embarkation to take place on the night of 24/25 April. The next group would leave the following night and the covering force the night after that.[20] In Alexandria, meanwhile, with the Mediterranean Fleet due back in two days time from bombarding Tripoli, the Royal Navy was beginning to assemble its evacuation force. Commanded by Rear-Admiral Pridham-Wippell it was to include the cruisers HMS *Orion*, *Ajax*, *Phoebe* and HMAS *Perth*; the anti-aircraft cruisers HMS *Calcutta*, *Coventry* and *Carlisle*, twenty destroyers and three sloops; the infantry assault ships HMS *Glenearn* and *Glengyle*, two liners converted to assault landing ships with twelve Landing Craft Assaults, (LCAs) and one Landing Craft Mechanised (LCM); nineteen medium-sized troopships; four A-lighters (an early tank landing craft) and some miscellaneous craft.[21]

To conform with the new plan, 25 NZ Battalion was moved up from Molos on 21 April to take over the position occupied by 22 NZ Battalion, 24 NZ Battalion already being in place opposite Ay Triada. The two battalions were also reunited with 26 NZ Battalion, which had come through from the Australian sector, and they were sent into reserve just to the west of Molos. Behind 6 NZ Brigade, 4 NZ Brigade, now in reserve, was preparing to take over its anti-parachute and coast-watching role, although 19 NZ Battalion was then dispatched that evening to find suitable defensive positions in Delphi Pass.[22]

The only activity around Brallos that day involved two 25-pounders that 2/2 Australian Field Regiment had set up on the forward slope of the escarpment. Throughout the previous day German vehicles had been seen moving into Lamia and, though largely confined to the town, from time to time the odd tank or group of infantrymen would emerge to the south of it. The situation started to change around 6pm, when some vehicles began to move out more purposely on the road south of the town. Having previously ranged on that stretch of road, the gunners were able to loose off only three rounds before hitting one of the trucks. This forced the rest to pull back into

Lamia. That night the Australians had ringside seats to what seemed like lights of hundreds of vehicles entering the town.

On the morning of 22 April the two 25-pounders came under fire from four German medium guns in a wood to the south-east of Lamia. As these guns were out of range of the 25-pounders, all the Australians could do was fire on any vehicles that came into range along the road south of Lamia. This enabled the German artillery to slowly close the range with the Australian guns, until they eventually hit a truck carrying smoke shells and later one of their ammunition limbers. By 1pm, when one of the guns was out of action through a leaking recuperator, some Germans reached the base of the escarpment and began to unload infantry.[23]

This was 55. Kradschützen-Bataillon, which had managed to cross the Spercheios River that day. They had set out from Lamia around 4.30am, debussed at Beki, a small railway station, formed up under a short artillery barrage and then advanced on the river:

> On reaching the blown bridge 1km north of Kostalexis it was discovered that it was still passable to infantry, and could be made passable for motorcycles and heavy infantry weapons ... in a very short time. The crossing of the Spercheios went off quickly and with no enemy interference. The heavy weapons could not get over the river then, but had to wait for the engineer platoon. The advance from the Spercheios into the mountains, which rose steeply from Kostalexi, made a change in formation necessary. 3. Kompanie was put in front, with 2. Kompanie, Batallion HQ and 4. Kompanie behind. The further into the mountains the advance penetrated the harder did the going become. A few kilometres south of Kostalexi all the roads ceased and the general direction had to be kept by bridle paths. The advance at first was over hills covered with vineyards, but soon these gave place to rocky peaks covered with thorn bushes. The higher the sun rose, the more oppressive did the advance become. Some men carrying ammunition boxes or heavy mortar equipment had to sit down and rest in what shade the thorn bushes offered. Mountain horses and donkeys grazing near by were commandeered and loaded up with weapons and ammunition. On reaching the Gorgo Stream the company stopped for a short rest. The animals had to be left behind, for the stream could only be crossed over a deep gulley, which was impassible to the horses and donkeys. The men again hoisted their burdens on

their backs and took up the ammunition boxes and went up the rocks in the glowing heat of midday. About 1400 hours small British outposts were discovered on the hills east and southeast of Delfino. On the appearance of German troops they immediately evacuated their positions without offering battle, withdrawing south and east.

The 'British' outposts included the crew of the surviving gun from 2/2 Australian Field Regiment. To deal with the Germans they had lifted its trail onto the edge of the pit to gain more depression and fired fifty rounds into them. The Germans responded with even heavier fire, forcing the gun crews to retire, but when the Australians returned they found the gun had been put out of action. On trying to get the other gun operational six men were killed and two wounded, bringing an untimely end to their duel.[24]

By now the leading companies of 55. Kradschützen-Bataillon were completely exhausted and had become badly mixed up, so they took up defensive positions around the town. The following day, with the bridge repaired, the battalion managed to bring over their light infantry artillery and anti-tank guns. Not that they were of much assistance: the terrain the battalion was in was so rough that the gun could not be brought up to the forward companies. So the Germans rested and reorganized for the rest of the day.[25] As it so happened, their advance had had a minimal impact on 2/1 Australian Battalion, the arrival of the motorcyclists having forced back the battalion's forward outposts. Nevertheless, Vasey decided to withdraw to a more compact position north of Brallos and set about arranging transport to achieve this. When it did not arrive the troops had to make an arduous climb on foot back up to their original positions.[26]

Though things were quieter in other sectors of the Thermopylae Line that day, the RAF had another serious setback. Both airfields around Athens were hit again and this time those Blenheims that remained at Menidi were flown out of Greece, while the rest of the squadron personnel left in trucks.[27]

The NZ Divisional Cavalry returned from Euboea, having found no signs of activity on the island. That evening the rest of 4 NZ Brigade moved out to link up with 19 NZ Battalion, now near Delphi, and were joined there by 2/3 Australian Field Regiment, an Australian anti-tank battery, 2/8 Australian Field Company and a company from 2/1 Australian MG Battalion. This completed, 5 NZ Brigade began pulling out from the Sperchios River at 9pm, their destination Ay Konstandinos fifteen miles back. The next to go was 6 NZ Field Regiment, though to a position just to the west of Molos.[28]

On 23 April the NZ Divisional Cavalry, on another search for Germans on Euboea, found some eighty Australian and New Zealand refugees from the Pineios Gorge action. After they returned to the mainland, engineers from 1 Armoured Brigade set off demolition charges on the mechanism of the swing bridge.[29] Concern that the Germans might reach Delphi led to a party of engineers conducting a spree of destruction along the road from Amfissa to Levadia, blowing bridges and culverts, and cratering roads along a 30-mile stretch. A blocking force was then set up at the last demolished bridge, consisting of 2/5 Australian Battalion, a troop of field guns and a company of machine-gunners.[30] To the south the Greek Reserve Officer's College Battalion and some field artillery were sent to Navpaktos, to block any attempt by the Germans to cut off the retreat through Delphi Pass. Finally, 4 Hussars, now with only six carriers and twelve Light Mk VIs, crossed the Corinth Canal and dispersed along the south side of the canal as far as Patras, leaving four tanks around Corinth itself.[31]

On 23 April, at approximately 5am, the last seven Hurricanes flew out of Eleusis for Megara, as Pilot Officer Roald Dahl later recalled:

> Soon we were circling the little village of Megara, and we saw a green field alongside the village and there was a man on an ancient steam-roller rolling out a kind of makeshift landing strip across the field. He looked up as we flew over and then drove his steam-roller to one side and we landed our planes on the bumpy field and taxied in among some olive trees for cover. The cover was not very good so we broke some branches off the olive trees and draped them over the wings of our planes.[32]

Their stay was quite short. Dahl had been ordered to fly to Eleusis to deliver an important package to Air Commodore Sir John D'Albiac Dowding, commander of the RAF in Greece, and on his return to Megara flew with the other planes to Argos, where a furtther six Hurricanes were based. At approximately 4.30pm a lone Messerschmitt Bf 110 flew over the camp and made three passes before departing. Shortly after this the adjutant of the squadron came over with orders that they were to send a patrol over the fleet at 6pm. Dahl and his fellow pilots, figuring that the German squadron would return about then, asked for permission to leave earlier. When this was refused they came up with their own solution:

At five minutes to six I was in position at the end of the strip with my engine running, ready for take off. David [Coke] was to one side, all set to follow me. The Ops Officer stood on the ground nearby looking at his watch. The five other pilots were beginning to taxi their planes out of the olive trees. At six o'clock the Ops Officer raised his arms and I opened the throttle. In ten seconds I was airborne and heading for the sea. I glanced around and saw David not far behind me. He caught up with me and settled in just behind my starboard wing. After a minute or so, I looked around expecting to see the other five Hurricanes coming up to join us. They weren't there.[33]

In fact three others had got airborne, but when the sixth was lifting off forty Messerschmitts appeared on the scene and attacked and shot it down, killing the pilot. The pilot of the seventh plane was luckier: he leapt out in time and took cover in a slit trench while the Germans proceeded to shoot up the entire airstrip. By the time Dahl and Coke returned an hour later, having failed to locate the navy ships, they found the airstrip covered in a thick blanket of smoke. That brought to an end the RAF's presence in Greece. The five remaining Hurricanes were sent to Crete and the rest of the pilots flown back to Alexandria.[34]

Further north, on the Thermopylae Line, 55. Kradschützen-Bataillon made another attempt to dislodge the Australians above them. Around mid-afternoon they sent out a number of patrols towards Delfino and the lower zigzag road to the east of it:

A large enemy concentration and heavy traffic were seen on the high ground 1km south-west of Skamnos. A large number of strongly-built MG nests were also seen on either side of the road on the eastern slopes of Tridendri, as well as tank traps and prepared demolitions. We sent out fighting patrols commanded by officers in an attempt to surprise the enemy and disconnect the charges, but none of them was successful. The enemy held most favourable positions from which he could see our patrols approaching and immediately put down heavy and accurate MG and shellfire on to them, making it impossible for them to get forward. The enemy was also aware of penetration to his left flank and reorganized his defences accordingly, as could be seen from the regrouping of his artillery.

Attempts to deal with the Australians by calling down German artillery fire from around Lamia were also unsuccessful, as they were too far away to be effective.[35]

That evening some German motorcyclists reached the Alamata Bridge over the Spercheios River and tried to cross. Second-Lieutenant Alan McPhail from B Company, 23 NZ Battalion, was ordered to take a patrol to out to the right flank and cut them off. Unable to reach his forward positions despite some covering fire from a Bren gun, he attacked them himself, killing three and forcing them to retire.[36]

Later that night the first stage of the evacuation of W Force began. In the New Zealand sector 4 NZ Brigade moved back to the Kriekouki Pass to prepare the next defensive line. Early the following morning some British anti-tank guns were brought forward early to cover E Troop, 5 NZ Field Regiment at Thermopylae, who were set up in an anti-tank role. At the same time 22, 23 NZ and 28 (Maori) Battalion set out for Marathon, passing through Athens itself before first light.[37] At Brallos 17 Australian Brigade withdrew around dusk, and by dawn the next morning were settling in at Eleusis, where they found good cover for the day.[38]

That evening Blamey reported to Wilson only to be told that he had been ordered back to Egypt. His last act, before departing for Alexandria by flying boat the following morning, was to inform Anzac Corps headquarters that it had now been dissolved and the evacuation plans had changed. Blamey was allowed to take six members of his staff and easily came up with five names to form the basis of his new Western Desert headquarters. When it came to the sixth name he kept rejecting all suggestions, until in the end he finally said 'We might as well take young Tom', meaning his 28-year-old son, Major Thomas Blamey. And that is what he did, much to the enduring annoyance of many of his fellow Australians.[39]

In fact the plans for the evacuation had also undergone a considerable revision. The sinking of twenty-three ships between 21 and 22 April by the Luftwaffe, and the departure of the RAF from Argos, had convinced Wavell and Cunningham that the only solution was to use fast-moving destroyers for the evacuation wherever possible. The ships would also have to depart earlier in the morning to enable them to be covered by aircraft based on Crete.[40] Nor was it going to be possible to evacuate all the troops from the beaches around Athens. Instead 16 and 17 Australian Brigades and around 4,000 base personnel were to be taken off from the Peloponnese, either Argos or further south at Kalamata.

To protect against a possible German paratroop attack against the bridge over the Corinth Canal, reinforcements needed to be sent to the troops already based there, some anti-aircraft artillery at Corinth and the four Light Mk VIs of 4 Hussars.[41] First to go was 6 NZ Field Company, with instructions from Freyberg to maintain the highway and prepare the bridge for demolition. Once there the engineers strapped the girders with gun cotton and placed extra explosives under the abutments and TNT or gelignite in the centre of the bridge itself.[42]

On the morning of 24 April the Germans finally launched their attack on the Thermopylae position. Their initial focus was on the main road up to Brallos but, in anticipation of meeting little resistance, they were also hoping to detach a platoon of tanks from the attacking force to advance on Molos. They began by bombing the camouflaged but empty artillery pits of 2/2 Australian Field Regiment that they had hammered the previous day, 125 Stuka attacks being made before the artillery took over, concentrating on the same targets. The main assault was launched by I/31. Panzer-Regiment, reinforced by four PzKpfw IVs from 3. Kompanie, plus some 88mms from 1/61. Fleigerabwehrkanone-Regiment, backed up by engineers, motorcyclists and assault guns. This force crossed the Spercheios River via a temporary bridge and made for Brallos pass. The first demolition they bypassed with ease, but the wrecked bridge and larger crater beyond it brought any further progress to an end. To the west of this, 55. Kradschützen-Bataillon launched their attack on 2/11 Australian Battalion at Brallos, after a dawn attack by Stukas, but soon ran into trouble:

> Targets could be engaged by our artillery only with great difficulty, because wireless contact between the forward observers and the guns could not be established. The light artillery did not fire at all but the heavy artillery engaged the enemy battalion at Kato Brallos and scattered its fire uselessly round the eastern slope of the ridge southwest of Skamnos. At 1030 hours, as the leading troops of the battalion reached the broken ravine area south of Elefterochori after moving round the Elefterochori spur, the first enemy HMG fire opened from isolated nests on the high ground southwest of Skamnos. At the same time the enemy began to shell the troops still in the valley. It seemed almost impossible to get out of the zone of fire and advance. Any movement, even by individual men, was seen by the enemy and engaged at once with HMG fire. We lost one killed and several wounded. It took several hours for the troops to approach the enemy and reach the northern slope of the height just west of Skamnos. Here too the enemy was trying to land shells

in the ravines and partially succeeding. Elements of the battalion in the course of the attack came out from behind their sheltering hill and were literally pinned to the ground by fire. Mule columns coming up after the battalion with food and ammunition from Delfino were hit and scattered. The battalion had to again recourse to emergency rations, which with stream water formed the men's sole meal.

With this line of attack temporarily blocked, the second part of the German plan was put into effect.[43] A platoon of tanks from 1. Kompanie was diverted along the road towards Molos, but as soon as they hove into view around a bluff at 11am they came under fire from some New Zealand 25-pounders, one tank being destroyed, after which the rest were forced to retire.[44] Their report of 'Unexpected and extremely heavy opposition. Artillery firing like mad. Road block removed. Danger of mines', did not deter Stumme. He now ordered 1. Kompanie, under Hauptman Prince von Schönburg, to: 'pass through to Molos and destroy the artillery'. It was at this point that advance elements of 72. Infanterie-Division, with Aufklärungs-Abteilung 112 under its command, met up with the tanks and discovered that they both had orders to advance on Molos. An agreement was made on the spot that the tanks would support the infantry in the forthcoming attack.[45]

Later, at approximately 2pm, five German tanks were observed attempting to cross the salt marsh on the eastern side of the road, but after one tank was hit by artillery fire the others withdrew behind an aqueduct. The Germans then proceeded to bomb and strafe the area before Molos for half an hour, after which some cyclists rode down the road, but fire from the hills drove them back. However, a more serious situation developed when Aufklärungs-Abteilung 112, exploiting a gap in the line left by the withdrawal of 5 NZ Brigade, managed to gain the high ground behind and above 25 NZ Battalion. By 4.30pm two sections from 14 Platoon, C Company were forced to give ground, despite covering fire from 13 and 15 platoons and 3-inch mortars. Prompted by this the Germans continued to infiltrate behind C Company, forcing it to withdraw behind A Company. In response B Company withdrew two of its platoons to allow it swing around and face westwards.[46]

Later in the afternoon Freyberg received a cable 'ordering me forthwith to take my staff to the Gulf of Athens and emplane in a "Sunderland" flying-boat and fly to Cairo'. His response to GHQ Athens said: 'I was being attacked by tanks, fighting a battle on a two-brigade front, and [I] asked them who was to command the New Zealand troops if I left'. When told it was Movement Control, he said: 'I naturally went on with the battle'.[47] Major-General Mackay, of 6 Australian Division, received a similar order and set off with his headquarters staff for Argos. His staff departed in a cruiser that night, he and his aide-de-camp leaving the following morning in a flying boat.[48]

At 4.15pm, having apparently exhausted all possibilities, von Schönburg's 1. Kompanie finally launched their attack towards Molos, preceded by some motorcyclists:

> With Leutnant Weistein's platoon leading, nineteen tanks in file charged along the yellowish country road. Ahead of us the first shells burst on the road. While clouds of dust shot up, mixed with powder smoke and were carried away swiftly by the wind. We could not deploy. On our right the hills rose 800 metres, and on our left stretched the dreaded Thermopylae swamp. Again and again the tanks were shaken as by giant fists. Then the dust rose in front of the tracks. The shells screamed more and more madly into the attacking company. In the shallow ditches our forward infantry, who a few hours before had been halted here, lay pressed into the ground. They could do no more. Suddenly we came under fire from six or eight guns. Without halting we swung our turrets round to the right and answered the fire with great effect. Our guns fired as rapidly as they could and our 50mm tank shells spread death and destruction. But at the next curve all hell broke loose.[49]

There Lieutenant Allen Dickinson from 27 NZ MG Battalion witnessed what happened next:

> The lead tank halted at the approach to the bridge, within 25 yards of my No.1 Gun and the rest closed up behind him. Being closed down he was fairly blind and he didn't see the 2-pounders nor the 25-pounder sitting within fifty yards of him. ...The 25-pounder whipped off his net and slammed a shot in at point-blank range. So did the 2-pounder only about 200 yards away. ...Seeing their leader go west the other three turned tail and fled. Unfortunately vision was limited to less than half a mile of the road but our guns got two more tanks and only one managed to get round the bend again and I think he was badly hit.[50]

Having set those three tanks on fire, Second Lieutenant Howard Parkes's 25-pounder knocked out five medium tanks and one light tank, while another E Troop gun got two more. Shortly afterwards Parkes and his crew found themselves in trouble when the crew of one tank started to stalk them, their own infantry having long departed:

> the gun team left their shallow pit and salvaged a Bren gun left behind by the infantry. They then fought a fresh duel with the tank men, killed or wounded them all, and then carried on with their anti-tank action. ...Still they came on, through the smoke from the blazing tanks ahead of them, somehow working their way round the derelicts and on towards Molos.

Three more German tanks were claimed by F Troop, while one 2-pounder from E Troop, 31 Anti-Tank Battery, sited near a bridge, knocked out one tank at 6–800 yards range and damaged a second, which was then destroyed by another 25-pounder.[51]

Around 5.45pm the surviving tanks withdrew, with the news that four or five tanks were burning on the road, though another report indicated 'that eight tanks of 1. Kompanie had been knocked out and for the most part brewed up'.[52] In fact the losses were much more severe, the New Zealand artillery reporting fifteen knocked out, most of them in flames, while the Germans reported eighteen or nineteen damaged, of which twelve were total losses.[53] The rest had been disabled through track or engine damage, among them that of the company commander, von Schönburg.[54]

Spectacular as the tank thrust had been, the real danger lay with the advance of 72. Infanterie-Division on the high ground above 25 NZ Battalion. The next to face encirclement was A Company, a section from which had moved up to occupy some ruins that the Germans had been seen approaching, only to briefly come under fire from their own supporting 25-pounders. The company then found themselves on the receiving end of fire from the German troops who had moved into C Company's old positions. Later, when A Company detected German voices below their company HQ, they drove them off with grenades, rifle fire and a bayonet attack. Using this opportunity they were able to disengage from the Germans and start withdrawing, the platoons leap frogging back until they reached B Company's area. From there the two companies pulled back towards D Company. Now, with daylight fading and German activity ceasing, the withdrawal began in earnest, D Company holding on for another fifteen minutes before pulling back to a bridge north of their battalion headquarters, where they were picked up by their transport. Not so lucky were the men of the carrier platoon. When their turn came to pull out, their carriers were mistaken for German tanks and fired on by some anti-tank gunners, with two carriers and their platoon truck knocked out for the loss of three killed, seven wounded and one missing. The rest of their platoon abandoned their vehicles and made their way back on foot.[55]

Unfortunately, the gradual withdrawal of 25 NZ Battalion had put the artillery down by the road in a difficult situation, some crews from 5 NZ Field and 7 NZ Anti-Tank Regiment being all but surrounded. Nevertheless, they continued to fire until dusk, by which time, with no supporting infantry nearby, it was impossible to get the guns out. Before departing, some of them spiked their guns; others drained the buffer-recuperators of oil and all removed the breechblocks and firing mechanisms before retiring.[56]

Fortunately for 6 NZ Brigade, the Germans were slow to follow up and did not occupy Molos until 2.30am the following morning,[57] some three hours after 25 NZ Battalion had cleared the town.[58] After their drubbing earlier, the tanks of 31. Panzer-Regiment were not too keen to push on that night and did not join the infantry from 72. Infanterie Division until later, no attempt being made by the Germans to advance further that night.[59]

In contrast to the intense battle at Molos, at Brallos it had been quiet for most of the day. So it was not until late in the afternoon that 2/11 Australian Battalion, under the command of Major Ray Sandover, detected an increase in enemy activity on its front, the troops being from 55. Kradschützen-Bataillon. Shortly afterwards D Company, on the left flank, found themselves under a heavy mortar barrage and suffered many casualties. Under increasing pressure, one platoon of D Company was forced to withdraw to the reverse slope, followed by a party of twenty Germans hard on their heels until a short burst of Thompson submachine-gun fire saw them off. Soon after another party of Germans mounted an attack up a small re-entrant between D and B companies. To counter this, two platoons of A Company, along with a section of Vickers machine guns, were moved up behind them and level with C Company. By 6.15pm the increasing pressure being put on the battalion led to the forward companies being pulled back, covered by machine-gun fire.

Now, however, a wider encircling movement by II/141. Gebirgsjäger-Regiment forced Brigadier Vasey to speed up the withdrawal of his units, 2/1 and 2/4 Australian battalions now needing to embus at 8pm and 2/2 Australian Field Regiment half an hour later. As a result Sandover's troops had to hold his positions for a further hour. Concern that the Germans might bring up armour led Sandover to send five Bren carriers from his carrier platoon across to the left flank and form a protective screen. Sandover was therefore relieved to learn, when they returned, that the country was impassable to their carriers. Fortunately, no attack developed, the Vickers guns having served to discourage the Germans, and Sandover was able to organize his next line of defence. Nevertheless, the situation continued to deteriorate and when II/141. Gebirgsjäger-Regiment reached Gravia, to the south-east of Brallos, threatening to cut off their line of retreat, he sent three carriers over to bolster the company of 2/1 Australian Battalion there. The other two carriers were sent over to C Company when an attack developed on its front, as 2/8 Australian Battalion had withdrawn to Brallos. Fortunately this attack developed so slowly that both A and C companies were able to withdraw unmolested at around 8.50pm, followed by B and then D companies soon after, the last truck departing at 10.15pm.[60]

Thus ended the battle for the Thermopylae Line. Though there were a few critical moments, the Anzacs had redeemed themselves well, something that could not have been said for the Germans. Even in the advance to Thermopylae the Germans had been caught out by the poor nature of the Greek road system. As the Anzacs found out during the retreat, the best line of escape was via the main road from Larissa, through Domokos to Lamia, especially as the road to Volos became virtually impassable in heavy rain. For this reason the Larissa–Lamia route could also easily be blocked by demolitions, especially where it passed through the mountainous region between Domokos and Lamia. It was partly because of these demolitions that the Germans were not in a position to attack the Thermopylae Line until five days after taking Larissa. It also did not help the Germans that they had to divert 5. Panzer-Division through the Grevená–Kalabaka route: the poor nature of the road, coupled with the demolitions left behind by the retreating British and Anzac troops, considerably delayed their progress. Then, when they reached the main road south of Phársala, they became involved in a dispute with 2. Panzer-Division about who had the right of way. The dispatch of the LSSAH behind them on the same road also cut them off from their own supply line, forcing them to forage for petrol. Whether the Thermopylae Line could have been held by W Force and the Greeks indefinitely, as Wilson had claimed, is another matter. Certainly they could have blocked the German advance for a while, but it would have been at a cost both to their own troops and the Greek army, thanks to the overwhelming air superiority of the Germans at this time. The Germans could also have exacted a considerable toll on civilians and infrastructure in southern Greece. This command of the air would also have severely constrained the ability of the Royal Navy to maintain supplies to W Force in Greece. The reality was that Wavell needed all the troops he could muster to help defend their holdings in the Middle East. There was the issue of the defence of Crete, something that Churchill was not prepared to give up willingly. As it turned out W Force would prove to be an ideal source of reinforcements for the forces stationed there.

Chapter 10

Evacuation

The first evacuations took place on the night of 22/23 and 23/24 April, when some 1,300 base troops, British civilians and the 150 Germans captured at Servia Pass set sail from Piraeus in a number of small Greek ships. On 24 April the luxury yacht *Hellas* arrived in Piraeus offering to take on 1,000 or so passengers. Loading began in the afternoon, with reports indicating that some 500 civilians had boarded, comprising a mixture of mostly Maltese, Cypriots, about 400 from 26 British and 2/5 Australian general hospitals and a New Zealand workshops unit. Unfortunately, just as it was about to leave, the harbour was subjected to an air raid and the *Hellas* was set on fire. With the only gangway destroyed, no one could escape and eventually the yacht rolled over and sank.

On the night of 24/25 April orders were received at 5 NZ Brigade headquarters to the effect that soldiers were to take precedence over equipment. That evening they set off from their various hiding places with what they could reasonably carry: small packs, respirators, steel helmets, weapons plus 100 rounds of ammunition, groundsheets and one blanket. The rest was destroyed, while their trucks were made inoperable by draining oil from the sumps and water from the radiators, then running the engines till they seized. Sometimes more extreme measures were taken and trucks were pushed over bluffs. The troops then made their way, under strict control, the final two miles to their embarkation point at Porto Rafti, when, shortly after dark, HMS *Calcutta*, HMAS *Perth* and HMS *Glengyle* hove into view. By the time they departed at 3.40am the ships had lifted almost the entire component of 5 NZ Brigade. With them were a mixture of headquarters and other supporting units from 2 NZ Division, plus a few British troops including some from 64 Medium Regiment. In all a total of 5,750 were rescued that night. This still left 500 troops on the beach and, rather than leave them there, they were loaded onto *Glengyle*'s LCM and deposited some fifteen miles away on Kea island. There the crew, before departing, warned them to be prepared to find their own way to Crete.[1]

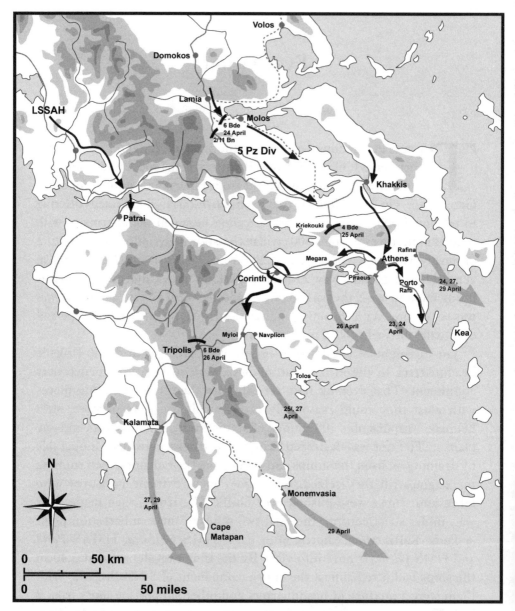

Map 7: 24–29 April 1941 – The evacuations from Greece.

Luckily for those on the evacuating ships, low cloud and fog limited the attention they received from the Luftwaffe and no damage was suffered, nor was there any loss of life before they reached Crete the following day. Instead the ships managed to shoot down two German bombers.[2]

The embarkation from Navplion did not proceed as smoothly. Some 7–8,000 men, largely from base units, had gathered there throughout the day, mostly in the town. At around 6.30pm they were organized into their respective units and sent out to separate dispersal areas, each of which housed around 1,000 men and 150 vehicles. Embarkation began at 10.30pm with the arrival of *Glenearn*, the cruiser HMS *Phoebe*, the corvette HMS *Hyacinth* and the destroyers HMAS *Stuart* and *Voyager* and the MV *Ulster Prince*. This continued without a hitch until the latter ran aground at the harbour entrance. It was refloated, but ran aground again at the wharf and had to be abandoned. Nevertheless, 6,685 men and women, including some New Zealand nurses, were loaded on to the remaining ships and at 3am departed for Crete. The *Ulster Prince* was destroyed the following day by dive-bombers.[3]

Independent of the navy-organised effort, a number of parties from 2/2 Australian Battalion also got away that night. They had been forced to make their way over the hills from Evangelismos after the German breakthrough at Pineios Gorge. As Colin Smith later recalled:

> They got within sight of the coast and met up with Major Cullen and Lieutenant Dunlop, who gave them £3 in drachmae and a handshake before moving on. On the 26th April they got hold of a rowing boat at a coastal village and after rowing all night, almost made it to the Gulf of Volos. Here they bought a sheep for 400 drachmae and cooked it in their tin hats. The next night they set out for Skiathos and met heavy seas and a strong wind and the boat sprang a leak but they kept bailing all night with their tin hats and made it to Skiathos before daylight. A German patrol boat arrived shortly afterwards but they were hidden by the village policeman and next night rowed to the island of Skopelos. Here the Greeks provided them with a benzina (motor boat) and a skipper who took them on to the island of Skyros, where 200 Germans were in the town, but a guide hid them in an old mine tunnel until the Germans left the following day. They were now joined by sixteen new arrivals led by Sgt. Tanner, who made a deal with a Greek skipper to sail for Turkey in a boat 20 feet long and 6 feet wide for the price of £350, to be paid by the British consul on arrival. They set off on 5 May with a fair wind but by dark the wind had dropped to a dead calm, so they all took turns to row, including a Kiwi officer who had three tommy-gun bullets through his shoulder. They pulled into the Gulf of Smyrna at midnight on 6 May but Turkish guards on

the shore opened up on them with rifle fire and they came ashore with hands in the air and were marched off to the barracks. The CO spoke French and was very friendly, and after a good meal invited them to play soccer against a local team. They lost! Here they joined Colonel Chilton, who had already arrived with another party and they all travelled by train to Alexandretta, where they embarked on the *Aclides* and landed back in Palestine on 24 May.[4]

Major Cullen actually played a key role in the escape of many men from 2/2 Australian Battalion and some New Zealanders, some 270 men coming together at Spelia at one point. Using regimental funds he purchased food for them and when they were unable to find a naval vessel to take them off Greece he distributed the remaining regimental funds among them before they split up into small parties:

Major Cullen and Captain King now joined forces and arranged for a caique to take 120 men to the island of Skopelos. They concluded a bargain with the Greek skipper to keep to the smaller islands and make for Crete for 120,000 drachmae (£240) and they sailed for the island Skyros where they bought 16 sheep and bread and cheese. Then on to the island of Psara and from there to Chios, which they reached on the morning of 29 April, this being ten miles off the Turkish coast. It was tempting to push on to Cesme in Turkey, but Major Cullen was of the opinion that Turkey meant internment and it was Crete or nothing. He arranged to borrow £300 from Mr Lemos, the Deputy-Mayor of Chios and Captain Lemos a shipowner, to obtain accommodation on an iron steamer which was sailing for Crete that night with some 400 Greek officers and men. Major Cullen's party comprised fourteen officers and 108 men, but that same night Lieutenant Fairbrother and his party of ninety-seven arrived at Chios and again had to be left behind because there was no room for them on Major Cullen's ship. Captain King remained behind with them. Major Cullen sailed from Chios at 2000 on 29 April and reached the island of Tinos on the 30th, but that night the engine broke down, and after making the island of Naxos, Lieutenant Baird, Sergeant Sandow and Sergeant Carle remained on board all day and helped the crew repair the engine. The following morning they reached the island of Santorin[i] and finally landed on Heraklion on Crete at 0700 on 5th May.[5]

A Universal Carrier Mk I and Marmon–Herrington armoured car from
2 NZ Divisional Cavalry on the road from Volos to Lamia. (Frank Horton)

German troops in captured British vehicles pass a horse-drawn column
outside Lamia. (Aris Kosionides)

During the German attempt to break through the Thermopylae Line this PzKpfw III from I/Panzer-Regiment 31 was knocked on the road to Molos after its crew turned it around in an attempt to escape the carnage. (Archer/Auerbach Collection)

By 26 April, with German command of the air overwhelming, 2 NZ Divisional Cavalry were forced to take shelter among trees at Tatoi until dusk when they could make their way through Athens, Frank Horton (with pipe) among them. (Frank Horton)

On Anzac Day New Zealand troops were given a warm farewell on their way through Athens to their evacuation beaches. (Ian Collins)

Greek troops pass through the 4 NZ Brigade rearguard at Kriekouki. (Sir John White Collection)

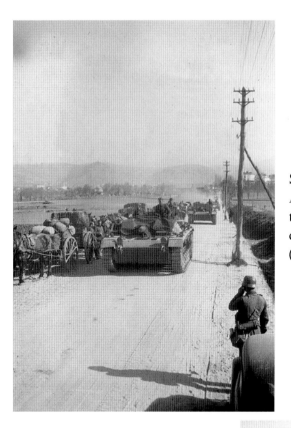

Sturmgeschütz IIIs from StuG-Abt 191 make their way forward through a horse-drawn supply column on their way to Athens. (Gunter Geucke)

Athens became a trophy city, with rival columns seeking to get there first, eventually falling to the Germans on 27 April. (Gunter Geucke)

German troops guard both sides of the destroyed bridge over the Corinth Canal after the abortive attempt by their paratroopers to take it by a *coup de main*. The signpost indicates there was a 16km drive to the nearest bridge to the Peloponnese peninsula. (Mike Smythe Collection)

Troops from the Australian 16 and 17 Brigades entering Kalamata on 26 April. (Australian War Memorial)

After departing from Kalamata a stray bomb from a Stuka damaged the SS *Costa Rica* causing it to start to sink. Here some of the troops on board are being taken off by HMS *Hereward* (H93). (Australian War Memorial)

RAF personnel were evacuated from Kalamata by Short Sunderland flying boat, this one from 228 Squadron. (Alexander Turnbull Library)

Infantry from 26 NZ Battalion making their way down to Monemvasia on the evening of 28 April. (Frank Keyes)

New Zealand troops rescued from Monemvasia on their way to Crete on HMS *Ajax*. (Sir John White Collection)

A group of Australian prisoners of war on their way back to Megara after their capture at Corinth. (Mike Smythe Collection)

A PzKpfw IV from 3. Panzer-Regiment, 2. Panzer-Division in the process of being loaded onto a freighter at Patras on 19 May. (Plowman Collection)

On the morning of 25 April Major General Freyberg met with General Wilson at W Force headquarters, where he was informed of the change in plans for the evacuation. These required 4 NZ Brigade to hold its position for another day, 1 Armoured Brigade to cover the beaches at Rafina and Porto Rafti, and 6 NZ Brigade to proceed south to the Peloponnese.[6] While this meeting was in progress 16 and 17 Australian brigades, with their attached troops under Brigadier Allen, had departed for Argos from their hiding places among the olive groves around Eleusis. They had just started to cross the Corinth Canal bridge at 1.30am when Brigadier Savige was asked to detach a battalion to join Isthmus Force and help guard the area. Accordingly three companies and two platoons from 2/6 Australian Battalion were pulled from the column. Captain H.A. Dean's Company was stopped north of the bridge and attached to 4 Hussars. Another company was halted near Argos and Captain James Jones's Company was sent to Corinth. Freyberg met Jones that evening on his way south to his headquarters at Myloi, informing them that the road through Corinth was impassable thanks to recent attacks from the Luftwaffe and needed to be cleared to allow the passage of 6,000 troops through the town. On Freyberg's suggestion Jones's men began clearing a new route and, after completing it later that night, they took up a position south of the town on a ridge parallel to the road.[7]

On 25 April (ANZAC Day), 25 NZ Battalion rejoined 6 NZ Brigade and together they passed through 4 NZ Brigade's positions at Kriekouki before taking cover from air attack in a forest of young pine trees.[8] Their supporting artillery carried on south through Eleusis and Athens and, as one veteran recalled:

> As we approached the centre of Athens there was a roar of cheering, and the vehicles were mobbed by crowds of young and old of both sexes, applauding and thrusting flowers and gifts upon us. I thought I was pretty tough but tears came to my eyes as this tribute, usually reserved for the victors, was spontaneously rendered to a beaten army – and moreover by a people who well knew in a day or two they would soon be under the Nazi heel.[9]

From there the artillerymen turned eastwards to an area just inland of Rafina and Porto Rafti, where they lay up for the day. As soon as it was dark 6 NZ Brigade set off again, receiving their orders at the canal that they were now to proceed to Tripolis.[10]

The original plan had been to embark 19 Australian Brigade at Megara on the night of 25/26 April, but around midday Wilson decided that the brigade and the 1,100 wounded there would have to be moved to another beach. The trouble was that by the time word got through to the troops at Megara most of their vehicles had been destroyed, leaving only enough to carry 300 men.[11] At 9pm the men began to move out in groups of fifty to the beaches where they were gradually shipped out to the SS *Thurland Castle*, the cruiser HMS *Coventry* and the destroyers HMS *Havock, Hasty, Decoy, Waterhen* and HMAS *Vendetta*.[12] Not all went smoothly for 2/4 Australian Battalion though:

> A start was made in the direction of the harbour to board our old friend the *Pennland*. Word was received that the *Pennland* had been sunk in a brave attempt to run the gauntlet of the German bombers. The next message received was that transport was available for a move to Argos via the Corinth Canal. Some other units were attached to the 2/4th Battalion for this move, and because of a shortage of serviceable transport it was necessary to break the battalion and attached groups into two groups. After a long march back the tired troops of the first group to be moved, crawled and scrambled into the vehicles, and settled in for another forced night drive. The convoy was about to move when a further message was received that four destroyers had pulled into the bay and we were to get there with all speed to embark, time being a most important factor. Back down the track and a further halt! All vehicles had been destroyed – then to be told there were no ships at all. This we found out shortly from a patrol was a false report as the ships were in fact there and were due to pull out at 0300 hours. The time was then 0230 hours. With all possible speed, the whole group moved in the direction of the harbour – then into boats and water craft of all descriptions and out to the destroyers, and so we left Megara and Greece. The battalion embarked on HMS *Hasty* close on 3am on April 26.[13]

In the end, with 5,900 loaded, 500 had to be left behind, some of whom were captured later at the Corinth Canal.[14]

On 26 April a further attempt was made to bolster Isthmus Force with the dispatch of C Squadron, NZ Divisional Cavalry under Captain Roy Harford, along with carriers from both 22 NZ and 28 (Maori) Battalion.

They passed over the canal bridge around 3am.[15] Some infantry from 19 NZ Battalion were also sent down. The last through was 9 Troop from C Squadron, 3 Royal Tanks, which had been assigned to escort Wilson's own headquarters to Myloi. Leaving Athens in their three trucks some time after 4am, Robert Crisp recalled their arrival at the canal at around 6am:

> We came round a headland and there was the deep cleft of the Canal and the gleaming metalwork of the bridge. Troops were digging themselves in or seeking rock-protected positions. As we passed over the bridge we saw the demolition charges in position. We stared down at the ribbon of sea over 200 feet below. What a tank trap! Once across the Canal I stopped our little procession; I wanted to find out what was happening and whether the H.Q. party had got over safely. After all I was still supposed to be their escort. An officer told me that General Wilson and the Admiral had crossed the bridge shortly after 4am. We were exchanging information about the overall situation, none of it very encouraging, when there came a warning shout and simultaneously we heard the planes. They came over the dark, indistinct mass of Mount Parnassus in the north. Scores of dots defining themselves as they drew noisily nearer as Heinkels and Stukas, and the Messerschmitts cavorting above them in the sky they had made their playground.[16]

Crisp and his troop were able to get away, but the defenders of Corinth had to endure the aerial assault, losing one heavy anti-aircraft gun in the first attack. Half an hour later a further wave of 120 medium and dive bombers appeared and turned their attention to any vehicle or gun they could see, while fighters strafed anything else that moved. Within a short time the remaining anti-aircraft guns had been put out of action. Then at 7.25am Ju 52s arrived, bringing Colonel Alfred Sturm's Fallschirmjäger-Regiment 2.[17] As seen by Harford's men:

> Literally in seconds the air was filled with the fascinating but chilling sight of hundreds of parachutes in several colours, mainly white. When Harford gave the order to open fire, everything possible was turned on them, belt after belt, magazine after magazine. ...It takes only a matter of seconds for a paratrooper to descend 300 feet. It was an impossible task for any squadron to wipe out a thousand men in this time. These well-drilled soldiers seemed to fall out of

their harness as they touched the ground, take a quick look around for a red coloured parachute – the leader's – rally there, and each group was off to its appointed task in short, quick rushes.[18]

As the parachutists descended, gliders landed near the bridge, disgorging their occupants, who took charge of it and started to clear the demolition charges. But it all came to naught. Those who were there recall the loud clap of thunder as the charges on the bridge exploded, but there were various stories about how the charges were detonated. After the war some German senior officers voiced the opinion that the parachute officer in charge of removing the explosives had piled them up on the bridge. When a stray round stuck this pile and detonated it, the resulting explosion dropped the bridge into the canal.[19]

Dean's company from 2/6 Australian Battalion soon found themselves under pressure from the paratroopers. A couple of bombs falling on one platoon kicked up sufficient dust to jam their automatic weapons and, finding themselves heavily outnumbered, they were soon forced to surrender. Two gliders landed among Lieutenant George Richards's platoon and, though their occupants were all killed or wounded, Richards's position was eventually overrun and the survivors captured. Lieutenant William Mann's platoon and company headquarters also came under heavy attack, the latter holding out until around midday, when, nearly out of ammunition, they too were forced to surrender.[20] The Germans did pay a heavy price, however, suffering some 237 casualties in the attack.[21] Further back, when Jones's company started to pull back they became aware that the paratroopers were advancing on them. Their luck held, as they continued their withdrawal towards Argos, when some German aircraft mistook them for their own troops and dropped weapons and supplies. They eventually met up with A and D companies from 26 NZ Battalion, who had been sent north from Argos to help extricate the troops around Corinth.[22]

Realizing that there was nothing further they could do, Harford decided to withdraw his squadron and any of the other carrier platoons he could contact. With radio communications failing, he made for their rendezvous point and waited for those who were able to disengage from the fighting. Eventually, his two Marmon-Herringtons and six carriers were joined by two carriers from the 28 (Maori) Battalion, the whole group setting off along a road that led into the hills south of Corinth. After a couple of miles it terminated in a village, from which a goat track led into the hills. Rather than go back they collected all the food and weapons they could carry, destroyed their vehicles by running them into a deep ravine, and set off south with a guide from the village. They eventually reached the village of Myloi,[23] where Crisp and his troop from 3 Royal Tanks also found themselves at the end of the day.[24]

One unfortunate consequence of the destruction of the canal bridge was that it had split W Force in two. Among those north of Corinth Canal were 4 NZ Brigade, a mixture of New Zealand and Australian artillery units, part of the NZ Divisional Cavalry and part of 1 Armoured Brigade. South of it were 6 NZ Brigade, 16 and 17 Australian brigades, the rest of NZ Divisional Cavalry and 1 Armoured Brigade, plus a mixture of reinforcement units and base and lines of communication troops.

South of the canal, Jones's company from 2/6 Australian Battalion and the two from 26 NZ Battalion drove off some paratroopers, then withdrew to the high ground north of Argos. While they held that position further readjustments were made that afternoon. 24 NZ Battalion was sent south to set up defensive positions around the road junction at Tripolis. When word was also received that the Germans had crossed over to the Peloponnese at Patras, Freyberg attempted to contact the three squadrons of 4 Hussars based nearby, there being no chance of rescuing their headquarters at Corinth. An officer was sent, followed by two others towards evening, with Greek money, petrol and orders for the Hussars to withdraw towards Tripolis. Greek guides were posted along their route to direct the Hussars and though their advance guard made it to Tripolis, the main body of 300, possibly mistrusting the Greeks, continued south to Kalamata.

That night Freyberg and his staff headed south towards Tripolis, eventually setting up headquarters ten miles south of the town. At the same time the small force of troops in Argos, consisting of the remnants of 2/6 Australian Battalion, 3 Royal Tanks and 2 Heavy Anti-Aircraft Battery, plus two Bofors guns, set off for Monemvasia, with orders to establish a defensive position there. The other two battalions of 6 NZ Brigade also made their way down to Tripolis, taking up positions along either route to the north of the town.

*****

North of the Corinth Canal, 4 NZ Brigade at Kriekouki and their supporting Australian artillery were now in a somewhat more perilous position as they were in danger of being isolated and captured. Nevertheless, the brigade remained undetected in their positions on the reverse slopes for the rest of the day, no anti-aircraft fire being permitted, and only moving to the forward slopes again that night. After trying to contact the commander of 4 NZ Brigade, Brigadier Edward Puttick, by radio, Freyberg eventually got a message through to Brigadier Charrington at 1 Armoured Brigade headquarters with instructions to contact Puttick about the change of plans, sending the message in the clear as all codes had been destroyed.[25]

Around 11am a German column of some 100 vehicles, led by motorcyclists along with a light tank, the latter from I/31. Panzer-Regiment, was seen driving down from Thebes towards 4 NZ Brigade's positions. When the German column came within range their supporting artillery opened up. Though it was a little wide of the road at first, as they had not registered their guns, it did force the Germans to abandon their vehicles and scatter. The next salvo was on target, setting eight vehicles on the road on fire, forcing the Germans to retire. Around midday the Australian artillery came under attack from the air and an hour later became engaged in a duel with some German artillery, which lasted for the rest of the afternoon. A few German tanks did come forward as well but were chased off, one suffering a direct hit, while some German infantry who appeared on the left flank were driven off by machine-gun fire. Towards the end of the afternoon the Australians carried out a registration shoot to give the impression that more artillery had arrived.

The bulk of the German force, including I/31. Panzer-Regiment, had meanwhile turned eastwards towards Khalkis, with 9. Auflklarungs-Abteilung reaching as far as Malakasa to the north of Athens. Almost at the same time 2. Kradschützen-Bataillon and 8/800. Brandenburg-Regiment crossed over to Euboea and reached as far south as the bridge near Khalkis, which they managed to repair later that afternoon. Now poised to strike on Athens, it would appear that XVIII. Gebirgs-Korps had instead disregarded Stumme's orders and were intent on being the first into Athens.[26]

As it so happened, this movement of the Germans towards Khalkis did not go unnoticed by 4 NZ Brigade at Kriekouki, particularly as it suggested that the Germans were attempting to by-pass their position. Puttick had also been concerned about reports of other German activity in the area, and the appearance of German paratroopers near Megara, but it was not until 6pm that confirmation of this was received. Nevertheless Puttick, unaware of the destruction of the Corinth Canal bridge, was still committed to withdrawing via this route and forcing his way over the canal. So it was fortunate that half an hour later he received a visit from an officer carrying Freyberg's message to Charrington with new orders for the brigade. To prevent any interference from the Germans, two platoons and five Bren carriers were sent to take up a position west of the Eleusis road junction. The route through Athens was picketed and an advance party sent through to Porto Rafti. The main withdrawal began at 9pm and continued through the night without interference until the brigade was all under the cover of olive trees on a small plain to the north-west of Markopoulon.[27]

*****

A number of evacuations were carried out on the night of 26/27 April. At Rafina the *Glengyle* and the destroyers HMS *Nubian*, *Decoy* and *Hasty* were faced with rescuing one anti-aircraft, two anti-tank and two artillery regiments, together with the NZ Divisional Cavalry (less C Squadron), 1 Armoured Brigade and detachments from other units. Among those taken on board the ships that night was Murray Loughnan of the Divisional Cavalry:

> On my way out I heard a whistle and I said to the fellow next to me: 'There are only two people in the Northern Hemisphere who know that whistle, one is my brother Bob who is in Cairo, therefore the other is my brother Ian who is in 4 NZ Field Regiment.' He was a little distance ahead. I waited before I think we had travelled a hundred yards and gave the reply. I was then aware of two figures silhouetted against the absolute blackness and one of them said 'Where are you?' and I recognized my brother's voice. I said: 'I'm here'. So I said: 'this is C Squadron, wait till Div Cav have gone through, down to the beach and onto the ship.' So he joined us. We went aboard the *Glengyle*.[28]

Unfortunately, a heavy swell meant that the *Glengyle* had to remain a mile and a half offshore and, in order to meet their sailing deadline of 3am, 1,167 men from 1 Armoured Brigade and many New Zealanders, including some from 34 NZ Anti-Tank Battery, 4 NZ Machine Gun Company and A Squadron Divisional Cavalry, had to be left behind. They took cover under the shelter of some trees at the southern end of the beach.

The evacuation at Porto Rafti could not commence until the *Glengyle*'s LCM, their sole means of loading, had picked up the men who had been shipped over to the island of Kea. Fortunately a naval officer had spent the afternoon rounding them up, most of whom were loaded onto the troopship

SS *Salween* and the cruiser HMS *Carlisle*, which had arrived earlier with the destroyers HMS *Kandahar* and *Kingston*. Though this delayed the start of the main evacuation, all the troops on the beach were uplifted, including three artillery regiments, some New Zealand engineers and machine-gunners. Better still, the convoy was still able to meet its sailing deadline.

*****

At Navplion on the night of 26/27 April the evacuation of the base troops and W Force headquarters was beset by problems. With the wreck of the *Ulster Prince* preventing destroyers from getting alongside the quays, the troops had to be ferried out to the waiting ships, but the sea was too rough to use small boats. To make matters more complicated the *Glenearn* had been disabled by dive-bombers and its LCAs sent to Monemvasia, so the naval ships were forced to use the *Glenearn*'s motor caique and LCM. These carried the men out to the troopship SS *Slamat*, the cruiser *Calcutta* and four destroyers. At Tolos the *Stuart* was soon full, so it was sent around to Navplion where it transferred its load to the cruiser HMS *Orion* and then went back with the *Perth* to Tolos to take on more troops. Eventually 1,559 were taken off the beach at Tolos, leaving some 1,300 behind. At Navplion 2,968 men were taken off, leaving another 1,700 on shore. The LCM then took on board 600 Australian troops and set off the following morning for Monemvasia. Among those left behind at Navplion were elements of 3 Royal Tanks and C Squadron of the NZ Divisional Cavalry, the latter having reached the beach after the embarkation was complete.

Force headquarters, across the bay at Myloi, ended up waiting until midnight for the HMS *Havock* to arrive, whereupon they were taken down the coast towards Monemvasia. Here they came across the ten LCAs from the *Glenearn* in a bay four miles north of the port and went ashore in them. In the meantime Wilson, Prince Peter of Greece, some Greek ministers and members of the British Military Mission had to wait until it was light for their Sunderland flying boat to depart, as the pilot could not safely land in Suda Bay, Crete until daylight. With Wilson's departure Freyberg became responsible for what was left of W Force,[29] or at least those elements he was aware of, the troops at Kalamata still being unknown to him.[30]

At Kalamata the troopships SS *Dilwarra*, *City of London* and *Costa Rica* arrived with five destroyers to find that instead of 8,000 men there were some 16–17,000. The Australians were determined that fighting troops be given priority, so the evacuees were divided into four groups, with those of 16 and 17 Australian brigades afforded highest priority. Around 10pm the ships appeared in the bay, the first two destroyers tying up at the wharf shortly afterwards. By 2.45am some 8,650 had been loaded and those on shore were told that the ships were full but would return the following night.

*****

With the coming of dawn on 27 April the evacuation ships had to run the inevitable gautlet of attacks from the air. Most had managed to get a reasonable distance from Greece but, in leaving its departure till 4.15am, the *Slamat* was more at risk. At 7am some aircraft swooped into the attack, hitting and disabling it. HMS *Diamond* set about rescuing the survivors and was soon joined by HMS *Wryneck*, which had left Suda Bay earlier. By the time both ships had taken on board the last of the survivors, *Slamat* was afire from one end to the other, so *Diamond* torpedoed and sank it before departing. It was all to no avail. Early in the afternoon *Wryneck* and *Diamond* were attacked and sunk by a swarm of Messerschmitt Bf 109s and Junkers Ju 88s, with only fifty men surviving.

That same morning the convoy from Kalamata was sighted by a mass of Stukas shortly after dawn. This brought forth a mass of anti-aircraft fire from not only the ships' guns, but also the small arms of the troops they were carrying. The *City of London*, for instance, bristled with eighty-four Vickers, Bren and Hotchkiss machine-guns and anti-tank rifles. No ships were lost in that attack, nor in the nine raids that followed, though seven planes were shot down. However, at 2.40pm a lone Stuka, coming in out of the sun, dropped a bomb on the *Costa Rica*, and although it hit the water some seven feet from the stern of the ship, it sprung out some plates and caused the ship to stop and start to sink. The *Defender* came alongside first and started to take troops off. When she was full the *Hereward* took over, followed by the *Hero*. By now the *Costa Rica* was listing badly and troops were able to step directly from the upper decks onto the destroyer. Eventually all 2,500 evacuees were transferred, with only one life being lost, when one man jumped from the ship and was crushed between the ship and a pom-pom battery. Luckily, as it turned out later, the convoy was diverted to Alexandria, as Suda Bay could not accommodate any more ships.[31]

*****

On the morning of 27 April 4 NZ Brigade was in a difficult position. Having only had time to disperse in their new location, no thought had been given to its defence in the event that they could not be evacuated the previous night. Realising this, Puttick ordered his battalions to take up positions to the east of Markopoulon and astride the road to Porto Rafti, knowing that this was not the best time of the day to do so. Still, the operation went well until around 11am, when twenty aircraft pounced on them. The brigade would have survived this attack more or less unscathed, had it not been for the chance explosion of a 25-pounder shell initiating a chain reaction that set the surrounding fields and pine plantations on fire. In the process it destroyed several trucks and nine guns of one of the units nearby, killing six gunners. Both 18 and 20 NZ battalions suffered casualties too.

Not that the Germans were overly concerned with dealing with the New Zealanders, assuming they were even aware of them. Instead their attention was focused on reaching Athens first. Early that morning, 47. Panzerjäger-Abteilung's motorcycle platoon abandoned their supporting armoured cars at a demolition south of Malakasa and joined up with 8/800. Brandenburg-Regiment in the race to the city. On entering it at around 8am they made their way straight to the Acropolis and raised the swastika flag. Shortly after 2. Kradschützen-Bataillon from 5. Panzer-Division reached the city, but was ordered to make for Lavrio. This small force, backed up by some light tanks, arrived at Markopoulon around 3pm. Here they were told: 'between Markopoulon and Porto Rafti there were English troops who were abandoning their vehicles and fleeing towards the coast'. However, every time the Germans probed forward with light tanks they came under a hail of artillery fire. Lacking artillery, their commander tried to call up some Stukas without success. Eventually they resumed their advance southwards. In the meantime, the bulk of 5. Panzer-Division turned west towards Corinth where they relieved the paratroopers. With the main bridge down they then began assembling their own bridge over the canal at its eastern end, while, almost simultaneously, III. Bataillon, LSSAH crossed the Gulf of Corinth at its western end.[32]

Having been completely overlooked by the Germans, 4 NZ Brigade and its attached elements were now free to complete their final stage of withdrawal. At 8.45pm the 25-pounders were wrecked, leaving the anti-aircraft guns to cover their withdrawal. The troops then made their way to the beach in stages and were ferried out to *Ajax* and the destroyers HMS *Kingston* and *Kimberly* until all 3,840 were on board. At Rafina Charrington had arranged for some men to be taken off by a caique. That done, he then set out with 600 from 1 Armoured Brigade to march up to Porto Rafti, unaware that arrangements had been made for them to be uplifted at

Rafina. They eventually had to retrace their steps. This was partly because some Germans were blocking their way, but Puttick had also managed to get word through to them of the change of plans. They were successfully uplifted and the next morning a German patrol reported that all British troops had gone.[33]

The only major loss occurred at Tolos–Navplion, where 1,500 men had been left behind. The 'Australian Composite Battalion', who had been sent back from Tripolis to cover the evacuation, provided a detachment to act as rearguard to cover the beach at Tolos. When it became apparent at around 3am on 28 April that no transports were likely to arrive, the troops waiting on the beach dispersed. The rearguard itself was overrun by a detachment from 5. Panzer-Division later that afternoon, the main body having pushed on via Tripolis to Kalamata.[34] Also picked up was a party of engineers from 6 NZ Field Company under Captain Douglas Kelsall, who had made their escape from Corinth:

> Kelsall and some fifteen other ranks crawled through the low vines, came unexpectedly upon a farmhouse occupied by Germans and scattered. Kelsall and another sapper escaped, joined two Australians and two English soldiers from the anti-aircraft batteries and with them went over the hills hoping to reach Navplion. Informed by the Greeks that embarkation from that port had ceased, they turned south-east through wild romantic country and eventually reached the coast, from which on 29 April they were ferried across the bay to Spetsai Island. Here two officers and forty other ranks of 4 Hussars appeared with some Australians. The combined parties hired a caique and sailed to Velpoula, where they picked up a sub-lieutenant from Piraeus, whose boat had been shot up off the island. That night, 1–2 May, the party weathered a severe storm and reached Milos with a disabled ship. When they were attempting to obtain another, more escapees arrived and other ships called on their way to Crete. Finally on 8 May, after a Cretan colonel had forced the Greeks to produce a ship, the party prepared to sail – in all 320, including 180 Cretans from the Albanian front. But next evening, as the ship was about to leave Milos, three German motor boats appeared and the odyssey came to an end.[35]

Nevertheless, some of those left behind at Navplion managed to get away, among them the men from C Squadron, NZ Divisional Cavalry:

One group, European and Maori, led by Harford and Lieutenant Michael Studholme, seized an 18-foot boat, crossed the bay and went down the coast, rowing in shifts from island to island and eventually reaching Crete in a Greek fishing boat. Another group had hired a caique and was about to leave the bay when a German patrol boat appeared. The caique was sunk but Lieutenant Ian Bonifant and others took to the hills, joined up with British and Greek troops, and about ten days later slipped away in another caique to Kithira and thence to Crete.[36]

Snow Nicholas also got off at Tolos that night:

We were then told to go to another bay they called Tolos about another 10–12 miles that the navy would pick us up the following night. We were there a few hours and the German army came in. There was a major on a motorbike running around us all saying 'Surrender, surrender don't fight'. I still wonder whether he was a British major or a German dressed as a [British major]. But I had no intention of becoming a prisoner of war so I took off with my driver and we got to the beach and we saw some Greeks in a small boat who were going to row out to a small island for protection. We hopped in the boat with them and went to the island. We were on the island for several hours when we talked the Greeks into letting us have their boat and we started rowing with the idea of eventually getting to Crete if possible. We rowed for three days. After the third night there was a small motor boat passing and in this motor boat was a member of our troop. He recognized me and he stopped and they picked us up and they finally took us to Crete. We went to another small island, stayed there that night and on the fifth day out and landed at Glyphisia on Crete. The Cretans came out and showered us with food and wine.[37]

*****

On the 27th it was discovered that the Germans were moving south faster than first thought, to the extent that there was an expectation that they were likely to reach the positions of 24 and 25 NZ Battalions north of Tripolis before dusk. This led to an acceleration of the withdrawal, with 26 NZ Battalion departing in convoy from Tripolis around midday. Though they were soon spotted by a German reconnaissance plane and subjected to the now-usual strafing and bombing, they suffered little in the way of casualties or damage. Around dusk their trucks pulled into a wooded area around Malaoi, ten miles from Monemvasia, and the men spread out among the trees of an olive grove. The rest of the brigade and those still in Tripolis pulled out that night and joined them later without incident.[38]

Throughout the rest of 28 April 6 NZ Brigade remained under the cover at Malaoi. A German reconnaissance aircraft discovered the LCM that had brought the Australians from Navplion and sent over dive-bombers to destroy it, though they did not discover the LCAs. In the meantime 6 NZ Field Company and the Divisional Cavalry, in an effort to block any German advance on their position during their evacuation, obtained a few depth charges from a Greek destroyer that had run aground at Monemvasia. These they used to demolish a bridge 16 miles out of town. This done the brigade, having done all they could, and now reduced to small arms and a limited supply of ammunition, settled down to wait. Fortunately for them the Germans were unaware of their presence and in the end bypassed them and carried on to Kalamata.

With the fall of night 6 NZ Brigade started making their way down to the beaches, 4 NZ Field Ambulance in the lead, reaching them around 9pm. After contact was established with *Ajax*, *Havock*, *Hotspur*, *Griffin* and *Isis* the embarkation began around 11.50pm, the troops leaving from two piers and the causeway connecting Monemvasia with the mainland. Eventually all 4,320 troops were loaded. Last to leave were Freyberg and several other senior officers, including Brigadier Harold Barrowclough, who were taken on board the *Ajax*. The convoy departed at 3am, reaching Suda Bay eight hours later. There the troops from 6 Brigade and 3 Royal Tanks transferred to SS *Thurland Castle* and *Comliebank* and three hours later were on their way to Alexandria. They were some of the lucky ones. In offloading troops on Crete to reduce the turnaround time of the rescue ships, the navy had unwittingly provided Churchill with his defence force for the island. This was something Freyberg was unaware of when he and his senior staff officers elected to stay the night on the island. Instead of flying out the next day he spent a little longer there than intended.[39]

*****

The most serious loss of personnel occurred at Kalamata, where it had not been possible to embark the remaining 8,000 men on the night of 26/27

April. Of these there were some 1,500 Yugoslavs, 4,500 unarmed and largely leaderless base troops, Palestinian and Cypriot labourers, Greeks and Lascar seamen. Also with them were the New Zealand Reinforcement Battalion, 380 Australians, fifty men from 3 Royal Tanks and 300 from 4 Hussars, the latter providing the outer screen to their defensive perimeter.

When 5. Panzer-Division arrived around 6.30pm the Hussars were quickly brushed aside, as Clive Dunn recalled:

> A reconnaissance plane flew over and had a look at us, and half an hour later the expected armoured brigade came down the road in a cloud of dust. ... The sun-drenched patch of hillside was now shattered by rifle and machine-gun fire, but I seemed to be alone – everybody was well hidden from view. Then a voice from my far left rang out, calling us back to the lorry. I gratefully ran down the hillside in a sort of nervous stoop to avoid the bullets. We now stood in the open waiting for further instructions. His plan was to put a machine gun in the back of the lorry and, with everyone lying flat except the Bren operator, we should drive like hell to the main road down which the enemy were coming, do a sharp turn left with our guns blazing, and drive as fast as possible away from the German tanks towards Kalamata. ...Unfortunately the Bren gun was still halfway up the hill where it had been abandoned. The captain ordered two men to go bring it down. They didn't exactly refuse – they just didn't go. He then ordered someone else to go, and they remained rooted to the spot. To end this embarrassing situation I went, not out of bravery but out of pure embarrassment for the captain. Then we sat the machine gun on the tail of the lorry and tumbled in. Away we went down the road, screeched to a halt, turned round with great difficulty and hurried back the way we had come. The Germans were now so close that our madcap scheme was foiled. There was now nothing to do but keep driving down the dusty track towards the hills. We did this for a hundred yards, but then as we rounded a bend the track petered out into a hillside. The next plan was to destroy the lorry.[40]

That done they set off on foot into the hills.

Some infantry, backed up by armoured cars from the panzer division, then pushed on into the town, crossing the bridge over the dry creek. After they reached the Customs House opposite the West Quay, where the embarkation was to take place, they turned eastwards through the town, thereby blocking the escape route of the Anzac troops sheltering in the olive groves on the eastern edge of Kalamata. More serious was the capture of Captain Clark-Hall of the Royal Navy and his signalman just before they departed for the waterfront, thus denying the evacuees their chance to communicate with the incoming ships.

It was at this point that Major Basil Carey from 3 Royal Tanks and Major Pemberton, Royal Signals, came upon some men retreating along the waterfront. Carey obtained a Bren gun and took up the fight against the Germans, while Pemberton went back to get help. Carey was soon joined by more men who had been rounded up by a Lieutenant-Colonel Hubert Geddes. Independent of this action B Company from the NZ Reinforcement Battalion set up roadblocks on the eastern end of Kalamata, while other elements of the battalion, accompanied by the Australians, set off into the town. Initially they made their way along the inner roads of the town, but in the general confusion, with mortar rounds dropping on them and sporadic German small-arms fire from doorways, the attack switched to the waterfront. Here they discovered that the Germans had set up two heavy artillery pieces, which prompted Sergeant Jack Hinton, under covering fire from some Australians, to tackle them. What happened next is described in his citation for the Victoria Cross:

> When the order to retreat to cover was given, Sergeant Hinton, shouting: 'To Hell with this, who'll come with me' ran to within several yards of the nearest gun; the gun fired, missing him, and he hurled two grenades which completely wiped out the crew. He then came on with the bayonet followed by a crowd of New Zealanders. German troops abandoned the first 6" gun and retreated into two houses. Sergeant Hinton smashed the window and then the door of the first house and dealt with the garrison with the bayonet. He repeated the performance in the second house and as a result, until overwhelming German forces arrived, the New Zealanders held the guns. Sergeant Hinton then fell with a bullet wound through the lower abdomen and was taken prisoner.[41]

From there the fighting continued along the waterfront, the troops advancing one block at a time. Eventually the Anzac troops called upon the Germans to surrender, whereupon the firing stopped. The Germans sent over an officer to negotiate, pointing out the rest of their force outside and mentioning in the process the hopelessness of the situation. Still, in the end it was the Germans who surrendered.

By this stage the rescue force of *Perth* and *Phoebe*, along with *Nubian*, *Defender*, *Hereward*, *Decoy*, *Hasty* and *Hero* were approaching the harbour. Contact was made with *Hero* at 8.45pm using signal lamps, informing them that Germans were in the town and still controlled the quay. The *Hero* approached the beach and, after sending someone ashore, concluded that the beach was suitable for evacuating troops. Unfortunately, wireless problems prevented this news reaching the *Perth* until 10.11pm. In the meantime the convoy commander of the *Hero* had learned that the convoy commander had abandoned the operation some 40 minutes previously, having observed explosions and firing on shore. Nevertheless, naval authorities on Crete had sent *Kandahar*, *Kingston* and *Kimberly*. These arrived around 1am and managed to evacuate 332 all ranks, leaving the bay two and a half hours later. At 4.30am the British in the town, realising the hopelessness of the situation, finally approached the Germans and negotiated a surrender.[42] Thus ended a remarkable turn of events, whereby small bands of Anzac troops forced a temporary surrender on a numerically superior German force. It was a pity that the naval ships were too quick in abandoning their attempt to uplift the troops in the town.

Nevertheless, some troops managed to get away from Kalamata after the surrender, among them a few from 6 NZ Field Regiment:

> Not confident of getting away Lieutenant Reid and his party had been encouraged by McKenzie to arrange for their own evacuation. During the morning they had found a caique anchored well out from the mole and had left Sergeant Fenton, Sergeant Lydster and Gunner Hodgetts to prepare her for the open sea and to keep guard over until nightfall. Unfortunately for them the Germans arrived just before dark, came along the mole and took the caretakers back to join the prisoners near the Customs House. The other members of the party, after the counter-attack and the announcement of no evacuation, returned to the caique, took aboard the supplies McKenzie had collected and remained hidden all through 29 April – not smoking, not talking, very hot and sometimes worried by the sounds of German voices. No investigation was made, however, and when darkness came two men used the rowing boat and towed the caique beyond the mole and out to sea. Thence they made their way down the coast and across to Crete where they landed eight days later.[43]

They were not the last to escape, however. Many others attempted to get away in small parties in commandeered Greek boats, some successfully. One party of twenty-two made their escape through some olive groves to the west of the town, where they acquired three boats. Those in the largest boat were eventually picked up by the *Isis*, which was part of a flotilla that had been sent over from Crete to collect any survivors. Another party set off from the Greek shore in a rowing boat and was also picked by the *Isis*. At least one party chartered a 30ft motor boat, while others stole Greek caiques and sailed all the way to Crete. By this means, even though 13,958 troops from W Force had to be left behind, the navy managed to rescue some 50,172 others from Greece. Though this was a substantial loss of men, it could have been worse. Somehow, in their haste to seize Athens and the Kalamata, the Germans failed to locate and round up two entire brigade groups.

Chapter 11

Operation Lustre in Retrospect

There are several reasons to believe that, while the German invasion of Yugoslavia was another example of their blitzkrieg doctrine, it broke down in Greece. While both countries were notable for their mountainous terrain and poor roads, all ideal for delaying actions by the defenders, Yugoslavia was beset by internal dissention and conflicting loyalties, with the Croatians and Slovenians having leanings towards the Axis and the Serbians favouring the British. The Yugoslav army also barely had time to mobilize before the Germans launched their attack, besides which much of their weaponry dated back to the First World War. To cap it all off the punitive air attack by the Luftwaffe on Belgrade effectively cut all communications between the Yugoslav high command and their troops in the field. When the Germans and their allies did invade the country the Croatians welcomed their forces and ultimately changed sides. As a result things were heavily weighted against the Yugoslav army and it was very quickly overwhelmed by the invaders.

This was not the case in Greece, and there are a number of reasons why. The Greeks had already mobilized to face the Italians and, even though they lacked the mobility of modern armies, had nonetheless proved their mettle in battle. On the other hand the British and Commonwealth commanders, on realising the inadequacies of the Greek forces, saw that their only solution was to withdraw to more defensible positions further south and hence only committed themselves to holding the existing line until the redeployments could be completed. This inadvertently set the tone for the rest of the campaign to one of progressively falling back through a series of defensive positions until they ultimately left Greece. In this they were aided more than once by the breaking of the German codes through Ultra. On most occasions they were able to hold off the Germans long enough to enable them to disengage and withdraw to the next position. In fact there were times when the German superiority in numbers worked against them, particularly after the fall of Larissa when several divisions were competing for the same stretch of road. Skilful use of demolitions by the Anzacs also gave them several days' grace on this occasion.

There were, however, times when the Anzacs nearly came unstuck, the defence of Kliedi Pass at Veve being a case in point. Here the sudden withdrawal of the Rangers unhinged the defence line and upset the Australians, even though it may have been partly due to the withdrawal of some Australian infantry in the first place. Worse still, what had been a solid defence soon turned into something resembling a rout for 2/8 Australian Battalion. On this occasion many men from the battalion discarded their weapons as they retreated (some under their officer's orders), something that would not have been expected of a combat-blooded unit. Not that it was entirely their fault: the men were physically exhausted after being in transit for five days, with little sleep, and then thrown into battle shortly after arriving at the front. The fault lies further back in the chain of command, with Blamey's decision to have 6 Australian Division sent first. While there was some merit in sending a formation with battle experience ahead, it is possible that Blamey had not appreciated the time it would take to extricate it from Libya, or the need for another unit to take its place before it left. In fact Lavarack's 7 Australian Division acquitted themselves well in the defence of Tobruk, despite not having been deployed in action, and it is possible that it could have been brought up to combat readiness and sent to Greece much earlier than 6 Australian Division. So other factors may have been at play here, notable among them the enmity that existed between Blamey and Lavarack, which dated back to the First World War and had come to the fore in Australia at the start of the Second World War.[1] Instead, thanks to the battle of Matapan and the bombing of Piraeus, the dispatch of the bulk of 6 Australian Division to Greece was delayed and this severely hobbled W Force in the early stages of the campaign. The poor mechanical state of the A10 Cruiser tanks of 3 Royal Tanks also played a part. Had they been more reliable, the unit might have been able to take a more active part at Kliedi. Nevertheless, they did provide an effective block at Sotir and later Ptolemais with those tanks they had left, both fall-back positions having been carefully chosen. The Germans were also let down by poor logistics and were unable to follow up because they ran out of petrol.

The outcome could not have been more different at Servia Pass, where the destruction of the bridge over the Aliákmon River and the control by the Anzac artillery of the battlefield placed a severe constraint on the Germans' ability to deploy across the river. The pass itself severely restricted the German deployment. They were also let down by their reconnaissance, thinking that the Allied troops had left the battlefield, with the capture of two Greeks further reinforcing that view. The survivors of the attacking companies later maintained that they had been ambushed, but that was no excuse for poor reconnaissance.[2] The Germans were so thoroughly beaten there that the Anzacs were able to abandon their positions without interference. Olympus Pass imposed even stronger constraints on the Germans, with the narrow mountain road meaning that it was easy to block their armoured support.

South of Larissa the nature of the Greek roads provided another constraint on the German advance and one that worked to the advantage of the Anzacs as they demolished bridges and cratered roads as they retreated. Not only did this delay the German advance, but they also seemed to throw caution to the wind in their haste to break through the Thermopylae Line. During the attack on Molos von Schönburg's company of tanks continued to attack after their supporting infantry had been forced to ground. In fact the New Zealand artillery appear to have stolen a march from them by separating the German infantry from the tanks. The result was a shambles. In fact some measure of his discomfort over their performance can be seen in von Schönburg's combat report. In a departure from his normally precise and accurate accounts, his exaggerated claims bordered on the outrageous and even upset Stumme, his corps commander. Rather it appears to have been an attempt to cover up his failure.

It is possible that the German success in bypassing the Maginot Line by driving through the so-called 'tank-proof' Ardennes was partly responsible for their undoing in Greece. Caught by surprise, this unsettled the French army sufficiently to lead to its rapid collapse. The Germans may have considered Greece in the same light but, instead, appear to have underestimated the difficulties that these routes imposed on their mobility. While there were a number of parallel routes through the Ardennes in Belgium, the four possible avenues of approach to Athens all ultimately passed through Larissa, something that must have elevated the strategic importance of this town. In fact there were only two good routes available to the Germans: Salonika–Katerini–Olympus and Kozani–Servia, both of which could be easily blocked at the passes in the mountains. The German response was to outflank them, but with mixed success. It may have seemed a good idea sending 5. Panzer-Division via Kozani–Grevená–Kalabaka, the same route that was so costly in tanks to 3 Royal Tanks, but it considerably slowed their advance and they never made contact with Savige Force. Not only was the road poor, but it was also easily blocked by demolitions, of which there were many, and this involved diverting a lot of the combat troops of the division into road-building activities. The decision to send LSSAH along the same route as 5. Panzer-Division effectively cut them off from their supply train. Likewise the Katerini–Platamon–Tempe axis of advance also had potential as a way of outflanking the main blocking positions, but there were logistical issues with it that 2. Panzer-Division could not have foreseen when they embarked on that course of action. Balck's combat group were effectively out of supply once they crossed over the pass into the Pineios Valley. Then, despite the somewhat haphazard response of the Anzacs, they were ultimately defeated their attempt to reach Larissa. After the fall of Larissa, with rain turning parts of the Larissa–Volos road into a morass, the only real option was to use the Larissa–Lamia route, but there the liberal use of demolitions could be used to maximum effect. This threw the two panzer divisions into conflict over who had the right of way and slowed their advance further.

To some extent the Anzac conduct of the campaign in Greece was reminiscent of the way the Germans handled the Italian campaign, but in reverse. This could be put down to the exit strategy of the Anzacs. Outgunned and outnumbered, they had no choice but to leave Greece; the only question was how they could extricate their troops with minimal losses. In that they had the support of the majority of Greeks, who understood their need to go, while at the same time wanting to minimise the damage to their own country. The Anzac Corps also exhibited a degree of flexibility not normally seen in the British army. Ad hoc formations were formed, broken and new ones re-formed from various combinations of Australian, British and New Zealand units as the circumstances permitted. This was something that the Germans did with such finesse later in the war. This plasticity also demonstrated that, by and large, the Australian and New Zealand troops could work well together. Though Freyberg thought that the breaking up of the brigades was wrong, given the physical constraints of the terrain in Greece and the rapidly changing situation, there was often no alternative.[3]

Perhaps the final word here might lie with 2. Panzer-Division:

> Particularly it may be noted that the English soldier is a good fighter, and the Australian and New Zealand soldiers fought an outstanding defensive battle in the craggy wooded country in which they had to fight. Their choice of ground, use of ground, adaptation of the ground and construction of positions were good and made things very hard for the attackers. The siting and use of the British artillery was also very skillful. The shellfire was heavy and accurate. The British made great use of anti-tank weapons, which were always sited in good, well-camouflaged positions. Anti-tank rifles were

used a great deal. The English made a lot of use of mines, choosing his minefields and blocks well. He had large stocks of mines and explosives. His road and bridge demolitions hindered our advance greatly.

The British sensitivity to his flanks was again confirmed. The British soldier cannot stand up to determined tank attacks supported by accurate fire from our artillery and other weapons.[4]

*****

What happened at Pineios Gorge has long been a source of controversy among historians. In particular the focus has been on how 21 NZ Battalion could perform so well against an armoured battlegroup at Platamon, then fall apart so quickly when faced with a small detachment of infantry and tanks. Ultimately their commander, Macky, was sacked by Brigadier Hargest for his performance at Pineios. Certainly Macky went from his masterful effort at Platamon to a man showing signs of defeatism and despair when he met up with Brigadier Clowes at the Pineios River. It also would not have gone down well with Hargest that his final orders to his company commanders were to escape over the hills if the Germans broke through in force. The failure to provide them with a rallying point was a factor in the dissolution of the battalion. The nature of the terrain over which they withdrew was another, as the same thing happened to Chilton's 2/2 Australian Battalion when the tanks fell upon their position. What does seem strange is that, when first sent to Platamon, 21 NZ Battalion was not given some anti-tank guns; Freyberg's assurance that they were not to expect tanks does not cut it. Some provision should have been made for that eventuality. Even stranger was that when the Anzac Corps learned that tanks had reached Platamon, all they sent was Clowes. Surely, at that stage, some 2-pounders would have been of more use?

When it came to the matter of the defence of Pineios Gorge, the editor-in-chief of the New Zealand official histories, Howard Kippenberger, came to the view that the problem with 21 NZ Battalion's defence at Pineios Gorge was largely that it had been sited to meet a frontal attack across the river.[5] What was not considered was that its dispositions were based around dealing with an infantry attack, certainly not one involving armour. Like most historians he had the benefit of hindsight; in this case he knew that the German tanks had been able to ford the river. Most accounts have made the assumption that this was by way of a simple ford that took them directly across the river. The map in the New Zealand official history of the Greek campaign reflects this view, showing the location of the ford as being just to the east of the tunnel demolition.[6] If such a ford existed then it would have been evident to Macky, Chilton and Parkinson when they conducted their recce as far as the road demolition. The fact is that no such ford existed.

The Nazi regime was big on propaganda, to the extent that it embedded photographers with combat units to record their successes for publication in such magazines as *Signal*. The Pineios Gorge action was no exception. In a remarkable series of photographs they recorded the advance up the gorge on the northern side and the crossing of the river by Balck's tanks. These photographs show that at their point of entry the rise from the water would have been too steep for the tanks to climb, let alone clamber over the abutment of the road. Other photos in the series show that the tanks had to advance several hundred metres upstream before exiting, three of the tanks drowning close to the south bank. This was certainly not anticipated by the Anzac unit commanders on the spot and probably led them to the view that the main threat lay across the river with the arrival of the mountain troops.

One of the mistakes attributed to Macky was the withdrawal of 10 Platoon on the evening of 17 April. In reality, having discovered the inadequacy of their Boyes anti-tank rifles, there was little that they could do. Though this weapon was capable of penetrating 22mm of armour at 100 yards, it would only have been really effective against the side armour of the PzKpfw II (originally 15mm of armour all round) as this tank had been fitted with additional plates of 20mm on the hull and turret fronts, or the PzKpfw IV if its round struck its side or rear armour. However, the armour on their main combat tank in Greece, the PzKpfw III Ausfrungs E and F, had 30mm on the front and side, while the Ausf G had 30mm all round, making it impervious to fire from the Boyes anti-tank rifle. There were also some Ausf H's in Greece with additional 30mm armour on the hull front, making this part of them impervious to fire from the Anzac's 2-pounder anti-tank guns. The only thing 10 Platoon could have done was report that German tanks had crossed the river, which might have given them time to prepare Molotov cocktails, as Chilton had suggested, though this was only a close-in defence weapon.[7] Thus the infantry of 21 NZ Battalion (and 2/2 and 2/3 Australian battalions, for that matter) were entirely dependent on their supporting 2-pounders and 25-pounders to deal with the tanks. Just what benefit the knowledge that tanks had crossed the river would have been to the Anzac commanders at Pineios is not clear. Repositioning their 2-pounder anti-tank guns could have helped, assuming that they were not discovered before having a chance to deal with the tanks, as some were. Any success against the tanks would only have been short lived. Ultimately it would have just delayed the inevitable. Everything points to Balck as being able to shift the entire complement of I/3. Panzer-Regiment across the Pineios that afternoon, something in the order of fifty tanks. Thus the Germans could have easily made good their tank losses in the first wave from the gorge, which is what they actually did. Ultimately Balck was forced to stop feeding them piecemeal into the battle and allow time for a sufficient number to build up before unleashing them on the hapless Anzacs.

Post-war, Macky expressed the view that the major mistake at Pineios was the siting of the demolition in the gorge, and he has a point.[8] The terrain in the gorge where it was located, coupled with the trajectory of the 25-pounder, meant that they would not have been able to land shells in the vicinity of the demolition. Coupled with this was the fact that radio contact between observers in the gorge and their attendant artillery was nigh on impossible. Macky was of the view that the proper place for the roadblock was where the gorge road broke into the valley running up to Ambelakia, where it could be kept under shellfire by artillery and, hence, make its repair difficult, if not impossible. The Australians did attempt to demolish the road there, but by that stage they lacked the explosives to be really effective, as events showed. The trouble was that little consideration appears to have been given to the need to prevent the Germans clearing the gorge demolition by New Zealand engineers. In a way this was symptomatic of the way the entire campaign had been conducted. The Anzacs literally seemed to be making things up as they went along. Sometimes they worked out and sometimes they did not. No one had really expected the Germans to send an armoured force along this route in the first place.

While preparing the official history of the Greek campaign, one of McClymont's concerns was how the Germans could have so easily overcome the Anzac defenders at Pineios Gorge, particularly when the two forces were more or less equivalent in size. However, there was one vital difference: the Germans were able to call upon the support of tanks, whereas Allen Force could only muster thirty or forty Bren gun carriers and half a dozen armoured cars. On that score McClymont somehow gained the impression that the first six tanks to emerge from the gorge were all PzKpfw IIs, but where he got that idea from is not clear. Balck's report talks of four tanks crossing the river on 17 April, only one of which was a PzKpfw II. Later on in the same report Balck mentions two tanks, a PzKpfw III and a tank with a dummy main armament and only one machine gun, essentially a command tank with a single box-shaped aerial over the engine deck, the Panzer III Befehlswagen.

Ultimately, as the British were to slowly learn, the best defence infantry had against tanks were tanks of their own, preferably ones of equivalent performance to the enemy. Unfortunately, by this stage of the campaign they had too few left and they were too far away to be of any use. Clearly the British decision to send only one armoured brigade was a factor here, but there is more to it than that. From the time of their first sortie towards Panteleimon on 11 April, to their arrival at the Venetikos River on 17 April, 3 Royal Tanks lost forty-six of their fifty-two A10 Cruiser tanks, all but one to mechanical breakdowns of one sort or another, of which over half succumbed to track failure. The latter was a result of the mud congealed to the sprockets stretching and breaking the tracks.[9] To some extent this could have been alleviated by the crews cannibalizing some of the broken-down tanks for their tracks and track pins, as their compatriots had done in North Africa a few months earlier, but this did not seem to occur to them.[10] Contrast this with their Brigade Headquarters Squadron, who travelled the more circuitous route from Edhessa to Kalabaka, via Katerini, Larissa and Trikkala before losing their first A13 Cruiser on the final stage between Trikkala and Kalabaka. Charrington considered that the performance of the Light Mark VIs and the A13s was excellent; the only real problem with the former was that over a period of eight days they could never find four consecutive hours to change their brake linings.[11] In the case of 3 Royal Tanks their problems can be put down to the decision of the Middle East high command to strip 3 Royal Tanks of their two squadrons of A13s and replace them with the worn-out, substandard A10s. Thus the question needs to be asked: what could have been achieved if this had not happened?

Just how well did the Germans fare that day? From their point of view the attack started to go wrong the moment Balck's force exited the gorge. When the Brandenburg platoon, with two tanks in support, swung away to deal with the New Zealand infantry on the hill, that left the other three tanks with no infantry support at all. Though this would normally have been enough to secure the surrender of 13 Platoon, they refused to do so despite the fact that there was no way they could escape. Unable to deal with the New Zealanders, possibly through fear of the position being mined and of losing their command tank, the two armed tanks proceeded to shell 13 Platoon ineffectually for the next one and a half hours, and in doing so threw the whole attack out of whack. The dearth of infantry also worked against the Germans when three of their tanks attempted to tackle the culvert demolition, allowing Cavanagh's gun to successfully take out all three before their infantry support caught up. Balck was forced to feed more tanks in to cover that loss and then more after most of those tanks were knocked out as well. This slowed the build-up of the rest of his tanks in the gorge and hence delayed the launch of his main attack until 4pm, and by then time was fast running out. Thus it would appear that 21 NZ Battalion, and in particular 13 Platoon, imposed a delay of some two hours on Balck's attack, which ultimately proved crucial to their failure to reach Larissa by nightfall.

In pursuing his attack beyond the gorge entrance, Balck was also not prepared for the reception he received from the Anzac artillery and anti-tank guns, in what was a textbook withdrawal by the New Zealand field artillery. By the end of the day his operational tank strength had been reduced by two-thirds, and the survivors were desperately short of fuel and had been forced to make up some of their ammunition losses by stripping it from the disabled tanks. Just why he had allowed this to happen is not clear. Balck had clearly ignored warnings that they would be out of supply once they crossed into the Pineios Valley. This was possibly because he had hoped that they could break through to Larissa and meet up with the rest of 2. Panzer-Division there, or open up a supply route along the railway, or bridge the Pineios River.

*****

If Britain had not sent troops to Greece, would they have been better employed in North Africa? There has certainly been the view in some quarters that Wavell should have been allowed to continue his offensive in Libya against the Italians to secure Tripoli. This argument ignores the fact that the first German troops arrived in Tripoli a matter of two to three days after the battle of Beda Fomm. Furthermore, there were issues of logistics. Their Mediterranean Fleet was concerned about its ability to support an assault on Tripoli. Both the ports of Tobruk and Benghazi had been badly damaged in the campaign, two weeks being needed to get Tobruk operational, and even then it could not accept tanks for quite some time; Matildas were not shipped round till October on lighters. Unfortunately, as a result the army had to divert a large proportion of its front-line transport to servicing these ports and their associated supply dumps at the expense of its front line troops, resulting in the withdrawal of Australian troops from the forward area. Mechanically exhausted by the fighting, 7 Armoured Division had to return to Egypt to rest and refit, while its replacement, 2 Armoured Division, was now little more than a weak armoured brigade after having had to make its way over to Cyrenaica under its own steam, losing many of its tanks through breakdowns on the way. Only enough tanks survived the journey to equip one regiment. The other had to make do with captured Italian M13/40s. When the division did get there it had to rely on a series of dumps that had been set up, thus denying it what mobility it had.

There was also the issue of the current British armoured doctrine. Unfortunately, this was something that Operation Compass, and in particular the battle of Beda Fomm, if anything, only served to reinforce. To be more specific the British had developed three different classes of tanks – light, cruiser and infantry – of which the aptly named cruiser tank was seen to have the same operational role as its naval cousin, to the extent that, in some quarters, cooperation with infantry by cruiser tank-equipped units was seen as anathema. This was an attitude that seemed to persist in some armoured units right up until the First Battle of Alamein in July 1942. There is no doubt that the British failure to develop a reliable high-explosive round for their 2-pounder was a contributing factor, but this was no excuse once they started to receive quantities of American armour (such as the Stuart and Grant tanks), for which such ammunition was available. Given that during Operation Crusader they somehow managed to turn a superiority of tank numbers into an inferiority in a short space of time, it seems unlikely that any other outcome would have been possible from Rommel's Operation Sonnenblume. Not that this in anyway justifies Operation Lustre, though had it been cancelled the British and Commonwealth troops would have been spared the grievous losses in men and materiel of that campaign and later on Crete.

By all accounts the campaign was doomed before it began. Fighting on as many fronts as they were after the fall of France, Britain could not spare the ten divisions requested by Greece. In fact, they could not deliver two complete divisions and an armoured brigade to Greece on time. Of course, whether it would have been possible to deploy ten motorized divisions in Greece was another matter. More importantly they could not supply sufficient modern fighter aircraft or bombers either. Just why they persisted with their desire to support the Greeks is not clear. Certainly what started out as a genuine effort to contain Italy, in combination with France, soon degenerated into a futile attempt to set up a Balkan Front against the Axis, before morphing into some sort of moral obligation to support Greece. Ultimately, Britain, Australia and New Zealand lost a great deal, both in men and materiel. This does not mean that W Force did not give a good account of itself, which it did despite a multitude of shortcomings. The German performance in Greece was also less than spectacular. Nor did that stop them from continuing their blitzkrieg approach. However, Russia was too vast for it to work properly, while in North Africa the British command of the air and sea placed severe constraints on German logistical support of their troops there.

Appendix I

Composition of Opposing Forces

Allied Forces

W Force (General Henry Maitland Wilson)

1 Armoured Brigade (Brigadier Harold Charrington)
   - 4 Queens' Own Hussars
   - 3 Royal Tank Regiment
   - 1 Rangers King's Royal Rifle Corps
   - 102 Anti-Tank Regiment
   - 2 Royal Horse Artillery (2 batteries)

2 New Zealand Division (Major General Bernard Freyberg)
   - New Zealand Divisional Cavalry Regiment
   - 4 Brigade (Brigadier Edward Puttick)
      - 18 Battalion
      - 19 Battalion
      - 20 Battalion
   - 5 Brigade (Brigadier James Hargest)
      - 21 Battalion
      - 22 Battalion
      - 23 Battalion
   - 6 Brigade (Brigadier Harold Barrowclough)
      - 24 Battalion
      - 25 Battalion
      - 26 Battalion
   - 27 MG Battalion
   - 28 Maori Battalion
   - 4 Field Regiment
   - 5 Field Regiment
   - 6 Field Regiment
   - 7 Anti-Tank Regiment

Australian Imperial Force (Lieutenant General Sir Thomas Blamey)

6 Australian Division (Major General Sir Iven Mackay)
    16 Brigade (Brigadier Arthur Allen)
        2/1 Battalion
        2/2 Battalion
        2/3 Battalion
    17 Brigade (Brigadier Stanley Savige)
        2/5 Battalion
        2/6 Battalion
        2/7 Battalion
    19 Brigade (Brigadier George Vasey)
        2/4 Battalion
        2/8 Battalion
        2/11 Battalion
    2/1 MG Battalion
    2/1 Field Regiment
    2/2 Field Regiment
    2/3 Field Regiment
    2/1 Anti-Tank Regiment

Greek Army (Field Marshall Alexandros Papagos)

Eastern Macedonia Army Section (Lieutenant General Konstantinos Bakopoulos)
    7 Infantry Division (Major General Christos Zoiopoulos)
    14 Infantry Division (Major General Konstantinos Papakonstantinou)
    18 Infantry Division (Major General Leonidas Stergiopoulos)
    19 Motorised Division (Major General Nikolaos Lioumbas)
    Nestos Brigade (Colonel Anastasios Kalis)
    Krousia Detachment
    Evros Brigade (Major-General Ioannis Zisis) detached as a covering force for western Thrace

Central Macedonian Army Section (Lieutenant General Ioannis Kotoulas)
    12 Infantry Division (Colonel G. Karamatos)
    20 Infantry Division (Major General Christos Karassos)

German Forces

XII. Armee (Generalfeldmarschall Wilhelm List)

XL. Panzer-Korps (Generalleutnant Georg Stumme)
  9. Panzer-Division (Generalleutnant Alfred von Hubkicki)
  73. Infanterie-Division (General der Infanterie Rudolf von Bünau)
  Liebstandarte SS Adolf Hitler Motorised Regiment (SS-Obergruppenführer Josef 'Sepp' Dietrich)
  Later: 5. Panzer-Division (General de Panzertruppe Gustav Fehn)

XVIII. Gebirgs-Korps (Generalleutnant Franz Böhme)
  2. Panzer-Division (Generalleutnant Rudolf Veiel)
  5. Gebirgs-Division (General der Gebirgstruppe Julius Ringel)
  6. Gebirgs-Division (Generalmajor Ferdinand Schörner)
  72. Infanterie-Division (Generalleutnant Phillipp Müller-Gebhard)
  125. Infanterie-Regiment (reinforced) (Major Friedrich Niemeyer)

XXX. Infanterie-Korps (Generalleutnant Otto Hartman)
  50. Infanterie-Division (Generaloberst Karl-Adolf Hollidt)
  164. Infanterie-Division (Generalleutnant Josef Folttmann)

Deployed later in the campaign:
  7. Flieger-Division (Generalleutnant Wilhelm Süssmann)
In reserve in Romania:
  L. Infantry Korps (Lieutenant General George Lindemann)
In reserve on the Turkish–Bulgarian border:
  16. Panzer-Division

Appendix II

Commonwealth and Axis Commanders

Commonwealth commanders

General Archibald Wavell

General Archibald Wavell was born on 5 May 1883. He was educated at Summer Fields near Oxford, Winchester College and then the Royal Military College, Sandhurst. After being commissioned in 1901 into the Black Watch he fought in the Second Boer War before being transferred to India, fighting in the Bazar Valley Campaign in 1908. He served on the Western Front from 1914–15, first in General Headquarters of the British Expeditionary Force, before being posted to 9 Infantry Brigade, being wounded and losing his left eye at the Second Battle of Ypres in 1915, where he won a Military Cross. In 1916 he was assigned to the Russian Army of Caucasus until 1917 when he was posted to the Egyptian Expeditionary Force headquarters. After the war he held various War Office appointments until he was given command of 6 Infantry Brigade in 3 Infantry Division in 1930. In 1932 he was appointed ADC to the king, a position he held for a year. Promoted to major general in 1933, he was appointed commander of 2 Division the following year. In 1937 he was promoted to lieutenant general and posted to Palestine as general officer commanding British forces in Palestine and Trans-Jordan. In 1938 he became general officer commander in chief of Southern Command in the United Kingdom, a post he held until July 1939, when he was named as general officer commander in chief of Middle East Command as full general. During the early years of the war Wavell was called upon not only to defend Egypt and Cyrenaica, after it was captured during Operation Compass, but also to provide forces for the defence of British Somalia, Eritrea, the campaign in Greece and later the defence of Crete, and to send troops to invade Syria and Lebanon. He was eventually sacked by Churchill after the failure of Operation Battleaxe and posted to India as commander in chief, India.

General Henry Maitland ('Jumbo') Wilson

Born in London on 5 September 1881, Maitland Wilson was educated at Eton College and Sandhurst. Commissioned into the Rifle Brigade as a second lieutenant in 1900, he served in the Second Boer War in South Africa. He was then posted to Egypt, India and Ireland. In the First World War he was sent to France in December 1915 and served as a general staff officer two with 41 Division on the Somme and Passchendaele. In October 1917 he was appointed general staff officer one to the New Zealand Division as a temporary lieutenant colonel. For his war service he was awarded the Distinguished Service Order in 1917 and mentioned in dispatches three times. Between the wars he served for a time at Sandhurst, then as a lieutenant colonel as second in command of 2 Battalion, the Rifle Brigade. In 1927 he took over command of 1 Battalion, Rifle Brigade on the Northwest Frontier in India. Back in England in 1930 he became an instructor at Camberley before taking command of 6 Infantry Brigade in 1934 with a rank of temporary brigadier. In 1937, with the rank of major general, he took over command of 2 Division. In June 1939 Wilson was appointed general officer commanding the British troops in Egypt, with the rank of lieutenant colonel, a role that saw him responsible for providing military advice to a range of countries from Abyssinia to the Persian Gulf. Wilson's initial response to the Italian entry into the war was to invade Libya, but he was forced to pull these forces back when the Italians invaded Egypt. In December 1940 Wilson launched Operation Compass, which under the command of General Richard O'Connor saw the Italians evicted from Cyrenaica. On 1 February 1941 he was offered and accepted the position of military governor of Cyrenaica, a position that he soon had to withdraw from when he was appointed to lead the Commonwealth expeditionary force to Greece. After being evacuated from Greece he was appointed general officer commanding British forces in Palestine and Trans-Jordan, overseeing the successful offensive in Lebanon and Syria.

General Thomas Blamey

Born on 24 January 1884 in Lake Albert, New South Wales, Australia, Blamey attended Wagga Wagga Superior Public School and later Wagga Wagga Grammar. Initially training and working as a teacher, Blamey joined the Cadet Instructional Staff of the Australian Military Forces and was appointed to a position with responsibility for school cadets in Victoria in 1906 as a lieutenant. Promoted to captain, he became brigade major of the 12 Brigade Area in 1910. After attending staff college he served with the British army on the North-West Frontier in India. At the outbreak of First World War he was initially based in the War Office, but was posted to Australian Imperial Force (AIF) as a general staff officer grade three on the staff of 1 Division, sailing for Egypt in November 1914. Blamey landed on Gallipoli on 25 April 1915, where he was mentioned in despatches in May for a patrol he led in an effort to locate some guns. In July he was promoted to general staff officer two to 2 Division, serving with them at Gallipoli for the rest of the campaign. He then returned to 1 Division as general staff officer one and went with them to the Western Front until he was hospitalized in September 1917. In June 1918 he became the corps brigadier general, general staff to the Australian Corps until the end of the war. Between the wars Blamey was appointed deputy chief of the general staff until he took up the position of chief commissioner of the Victoria Police in 1923, being forced to resign in 1936 while trying to cover up details of the shooting of the superintendent of the criminal branch. In 1938 he was appointed to the Commonwealth government's manpower committee as controller general of recruiting. In October 1939 Blamey was promoted to lieutenant general and put in command of 6 Division. In February 1940 the army raised 7 Division and grouped them with 6 Division into I Corps under the command of Blamey. I Corps was dispatched to Palestine in the Middle East as the AIF under Blamey, remaining there until 15 February 1941, when it was given responsibility for Cyrenaican Front. Dispatched to Greece, he eventually assumed command of all fighting troops, the Anzac Corps. After his evacuation he was appointed deputy commander in chief in Middle East Command, only to see Wilson promoted above him to ensure that command did not pass to him if anything happened to Wavell. He then resumed command of the AIF and took part in the campaign in Lebanon and Syria. He returned to Australia in 1942 to become commander in chief of the Australian military forces and later took the role of commander of Allied land forces, south-west Pacific area.

Major General Sir Iven MacKay

Iven MacKay was born on 7 April 1882 in Grafton, New South Wales, Australia. Educated first at Grafton Superior Public School and Newington College, he eventually graduated with a Bachelor of Arts degree in 1904 from the University of Sydney. He taught for five years at the Church of England Grammar School before returning to the University of Sydney to teach physics. Starting with the cadets while at Newington College, he reached the rank of lieutenant in the Cadet Corps in 1911, transferring to the military two years later and becoming adjutant of 26 Infantry Battalion in July of that year. At the start of the First World War, at the rank of captain, he was posted to 4 Battalion as their adjutant, but missed the embarkation of his battalion after he punctured a lung in a riding accident. Rejoining his unit early in 1915 as its transport officer he observed the landing on Gallipoli from one of the transports, only finally going onshore in May and being given command of a company in August. During the battle of Lone Pine he was wounded and eventually evacuated to Malta. For his actions at Lone Pine he was mentioned in despatches and eventually awarded the Distinguished Service Order. MacKay rejoined his unit in February 2016 in Egypt and sailed for the Western Front a month later. In France, promoted to lieutenant colonel, he took over command of 4 Infantry Battalion in 1 Division, leading it in the battle of Pozières, receiving a second mention in despatches. He commanded them during the advance to the Hindenburg Line, later taking over temporary command of 1 Infantry Brigade for a second time, this time during the Battle of Bullecourt, being awarded a bar to his Distinguished Service Order. MacKay led 4 Battalion during the battle for Broodseinde, gaining a fourth mention in despatches. In 1918 he was put in command of 1 Machine Gun Battalion, leading them in the Battle of Hazebrouck. In August 1918 he led his unit in the Battle of Amiens. For his services as a brigade commander he was appointed a Companion of the Order of St Michael and St George in the 1919 New Year honours and the Croix de Guerre by the French. After studying physics under Ernest Rutherford he returned to Australia in 1920, first to teach and later as a headmaster. He continued to serve with the military with the rank of honorary brigadier commanding a number of brigades. In 1937, promoted to major general, he took command of 2 Division. On the outbreak of the Second World War he assumed command of 6 Division on 4 April 1940, sailing with it to Egypt. In 1941 the division was sent forward in Libya, capturing Bardia in January, for which he was made a Knight Commander of the Order of the British Empire. Following this the division attacked and captured Tobruk, Derna and Benghazi. After the campaign in Greece MacKay returned to Australia to take command of the Home Forces there.

Major General Bernard Freyberg

Born in Richmond, Surrey, England, on 21 March 1889, Freyberg moved to New Zealand with his parents when he was two. He was educated at Wellington College and qualified as a dentist in 1911, practising in several towns in New Zealand before leaving in 1914. On the outbreak of war in Europe, he travelled to England and joined 7 Hood Battalion of the Royal Naval Division, eventually gaining a commission in it. He served in the defence of Antwerp in 1914, before travelling to the Middle East and taking part in the landings at

Gallipoli on 25 April 1915, where he was awarded the Distinguished Service Order. In 1916 he went to France with the Hood Battalion, In November 1916, in temporary command of the Hood Battalion on the Somme, he earned the Victoria Cross for exploits during the capture of Beaucourt and Beaumont-Hamel. In April 1917, in the rank of temporary brigadier general, he took over command of 173 Brigade, 58 Division, aged twenty-seven, reputedly making him the youngest general in the British army. He was awarded a Companion of the Order of St Michael and St George later that year. Returning to the front in 1918, after being wounded, he commanded 88 Brigade, 29 Division during the German Spring Offensive, gaining another bar to his DSO. At the end of the war he led a cavalry squadron from 7 Dragoon Guards in their capture of a bridge at Lessines, one minute before the Armistice, earning a second bar to his DSO. The French also awarded him a Croix de Guerre. Between the wars he was granted a regular commission in the Grenadier Guards in 1919, serving in various command and staff roles until the diagnosis of a heart problem obliged him to retire in 1937. Though classed as unfit for service he returned to the active list in December 1939, after which he was approached by the New Zealand government and given command of the New Zealand Expeditionary Force and 2 New Zealand Division in the Mediterranean. Freyberg commanded the division in Greece in May 1941, taking over command of all forces on Crete in May. After the evacuation from Crete he resumed command of 2 NZ Division, a position he continued to hold until the end of the war, apart from a brief period in command of the New Zealand Corps at Cassino in 1944.

Brigadier Harold Charrington

Born in 1886, Charrington joined 12 (Prince of Wales's Royal) Lancers in 1905 as a second lieutenant. Promoted to a lieutenant two years later, he served with the Egyptian army from 1913–14. Promoted to captain in 1914, he served in France and Belgium during the First World War. After the war he undertook several postings from the War Office to the Royal Military College, Sandhurst, rising from major to lieutenant colonel in 1927. From 1927–31 he commanded 12 (Prince of Wales's Royal) Lancers and then 6 Midland Cavalry Brigade (Territorial Army) until 1932, when he retired to become a director of Charringtons Brewery. Re-called to service in the Second World War he served as a general staff officer one in Aldershot Command until 1940, when he took over the command of 1 Armoured Brigade, moving with the unit to Egypt in 1941. He was invalided back to England in July 1941.

General Alexander Papagos

Born in Athens on 9 December 1883, Papagos entered the Brussels Military Academy in 1902 and then studied at the Cavalry Application School at Ypres. Promoted to lieutenant in 1911, he participated in the Balkan Wars of 1912–13 attached to the field headquarters of the crown prince, and from 1913 under King Constantine. After the Balkan Wars he served in 1 Cavalry Regiment and on the staff of III Army Corps. Promoted to major in 1916, he was appointed as chief of staff of the Cavalry Brigade, but as a confirmed royalist he was dismissed from the army in 1917 as a result of the National Schism. Re-called to active service in 1920 following the electoral victory of the royalist parties, with the rank of lieutenant colonel, he served as chief of staff of the Cavalry Brigade and of the Cavalry Division during the campaign against the Turks, being sacked again in 1922 after their disastrous defeat and the subsequent outbreak of a military revolt. He was re-called in 1926, with the rank of colonel, and the following year was appointed commander of 1 Cavalry Division. Promoted to major general in 1930, he was named deputy chief of the Hellenic army general staff a year later. In 1933–35 he served as inspector of cavalry, followed by commands of I and III Army Corps. He was promoted to lieutenant-general in 1935. That same year, along with the service chiefs of the navy and air force, he toppled the government of Panagis Tsaldaris, becoming Minister for Military Affairs in the new cabinet of Georgios Kondylis. He remained in this role through this and the next government of Konstantinos Demertzis. On 5 March 1936 he was named inspector general of the Army, holding the post until 31 July, when he was promoted to chief of the army general staff. Following the outbreak of the Greco-Italian War on 28 October 1940, he became commander in chief of the army, successfully halting the Italian advance in November 1940, forcing them to withdraw deep into Albania, and then repulsing a second Italian offensive in March 1941. He held his post of commander in chief of the army until the capitulation of the Greek armed forces following the German invasion of Greece in April 1941. Papagos remained in Greece after the fighting ended until his arrest in July 1943, when he was transported to Tyrol, along with 140 other prominent inmates of the Dachau concentration camp. He was liberated by the Americans in May 1945.

Axis Commanders

Generalfeldmarschall Wilhelm List

Born in Oberkirchberg in the kingdom of Bavaria, German empire, on 14 May 1880, List entered the Bavarian army in 1898. In 1913 he joined the general staff, serving as a staff officer during the First World War. He remained with the Reichswehr after the war, rising to a Generalleutnant in 1932. In 1938, after the Anschluss of Austria, he received the task of integrating the Austrian armed forces into the Wehrmacht. List took part in the invasion of Poland at the start of the Second World War in command of 14. Armee, taking part in an encircling manoeuvre on the extreme southern wing. After the conclusion of that campaign List's army remained in Poland as an occupying force. In May 1940 List, now in command of 12. Armee, took part in the thrust by Armee Gruppe A through the Ardennes, making the breakthrough on 15 May that cut off the British Expeditionary Force from their supply lines and spread panic through the French army. Promoted to Generalfieldmarshall after this, List was delegated to negotiate with the Bulgarian general staff, which led to the signing of a secret agreement that allowed German troops free passage through Bulgaria. On the night of 28/29 February his 12. Armee, along with other German troops, entered Bulgaria, the country joining the Tripartite Pact the following day. List took command of Armee Gruppe A during the summer offensive in 1942, but was eventually relieved of his command by Hitler due to his apparent loss of momentum. After the war he was arrested and convicted at Nuremburg of ordering reprisal killings of Serbian hostages in Yugoslavia, serving four years of his sentence.

Generalleutnant Georg Stumme

Born on 29 July 1886 in Halberstadt, Germany, Stumme fought in the First World War before joining the German general staff after the war. In 1933 he was promoted to Oberst, then Generalmajor in 1936, taking command of 2. Leichte-Division when it was formed on 10 November 1938. Achieving the rank of Generalleutnant at the outbreak of the Second World War, he commanded the division during the invasion of Poland. After it was converted into 7. Panzer-Division he relinquished command to Erwin Rommel and was appointed commander of XXXX Armeekorps in 15 February 1940, leading it in action in the Ardennes campaign and being awarded the Knight's Cross of the Iron Cross for bravery. He was also promoted to General der Kavallerie on 1 June 1940. Stumme served under Field Marshall Fedor von Bock in Operation Barbarossa and later led the advance of 6. Armee on Stalingrad in 1942. After some plans fell into Soviet hands Hitler had him court-martialled, and he was sentenced to five years. Bock secured his release and pardoning. He was then posted to the Afrika Korps, taking over at El Alamein from General Erwin Rommel when he was relieved through ill health. During the fighting in October 1942 Stumme's staff car was attacked and he was later found dead.

Generalleutnant Alfred von Hubkicki

Born on 5 February 1887 in Hungary, Hubkicki served in the Austrian army and by the time of the Anschluss of Austria in 1938 he had reached the rank of Generalmajor as the commander of the Austrian army motorized division. Thereupon he transferred to the Wehrmacht with the same rank and was appointed commander of 4. Leichte-Division after its formation in Vienna. Prior to the start of the Second World War the unit was renamed 9. Panzer-Division, and Hubicki commanded it through the invasion of Poland, taking part in the Battle of Jordanów and Battle of Jaroslaw. He then took part in the invasion of France and the Netherlands in 1940, being promoted to Generalleutnant in August 1940. He was awarded the Knight's Cross of the Iron Cross for his role in the Balkans campaign. In October 1942 he was promoted to General der Panzertruppe, later serving as the head of the German Military Mission to Slovakia, retiring in March 1945.

SS-Obergruppenführer Josef 'Sepp' Dietrich

Born on 28 May 1892 in Hawangen, near Memmingen in the kingdom of Bavaria, German empire, Dietrich joined the Bavarian army in 1911, serving with 4. Bayerische Feldartillerie-Regiment 'König' in Augsburg, and served in the First World War with the Bavarian field artillery. During the war he was first promoted to Gefreiter in 1917 and awarded the Iron Cross second class, then in 1918 he was promoted to Unteroffizier, also being awarded the Iron Cross first class and Bavarian Military Merit Order third class with swords. After working in several jobs after the war he joined the Nazi Party (NSDAP) in 1928, being given a job with *Eher Verlag* (the NSDAP publisher). Around that time he also became commander of Hitler's Schutzstaffel (SS) bodyguard. In 1930 he was elected to the Reichstag as a delegate for Lower Bavaria. By 1931 he had become SS-Gruppenführer, rising swiftly through the hierachy after the Nazi Party seized power in 1933 to become commander of Leibstandarte SS Adolf Hitler (LSSAH) and a member of the Prussian state council, taking part in the Night of the Long Knives the following year. He led LSSAH in the attack on Poland at the start of the Second World War and then into the Netherlands in 1940. After moving into France, in defiance of OKW orders, he sent III Bataillon, LSSAH, across the Aa Canal, south-west of Dunkirk, where the British Expeditionary Force was trapped, and drove British artillery observers off the heights beyond. For this act of defiance he was awarded the Knight's Cross of the Iron Cross. After Greece he was promoted to head of 1. SS Panzer-Korps, serving on the Russian front and then in Normandy in 1944, rising to command 5. Panzer-Armee later in the campaign. He took over command 6. Panzer-Armee in the Battle of the Bulge and later in Hungary, surrendering to the Americans in Vienna. After the war he was tried for his involvement in the Malmedy Massacre, serving ten years in prison.

Generalleutnant Franz Böhme

Born on 15 April 1885 in Zelteg, Duchy of Styria, Austria–Hungary, Böhme commanded 30. Infanterie-Division and 32. Infanterie-Division during the opening years of the Second World War. He took part in the invasion of Poland in September 1939 and in the Battle of France in May and June 1940. On 29 June 1940, he was awarded the Knight's Cross of the Iron Cross. After the Greek campaign he took over as commanding general and commander of Serbia, where he ordered the execution of 2,000 Jews and communists in Topola as a reprisal for a partisan assault on twenty-two soldiers. He served as 2. Panzer-Armee's commander in the Balkans and later as armed forces commander of Norway and commander in chief of 20. Gebirgs-Armee. He was arrested and tried for the war crimes he committed in Serbia. Before being extradited to Yugoslavia he committed suicide by jumping out of the fourth storey of his prison.

Generalleutnant Rudolf Veiel

Born on 10 December 1883 in Stuttgart, German empire, Veiel joined the army in 1904 and was commissioned as an officer in 1905, serving in the cavalry during the First World War. In 1919 he joined the Freikorps in Württemberg and then in October 1920 became part of the Reichswehr. In 1933 he was promoted to Oberst and then Generalmajor in 1937 and Generalleutnant in 1938, when he was put in command of 2. Panzer-Division. He commanded the division during both the invasion of Poland in 1939, and the Battle of France in 1940. After Greece he took part in Operation Barbarossa, commanding XLVIII Panzer-Korps after the battle for Moscow. In 1944 he was relieved of his command because of his complicity in the plot to kill Hitler, and placed on officer reserve.

General der Gebirgstruppe Julius Ringel

Born on 16 November 1889 in Völkermarkt, Carinthia, Austria, Ringel joined the military academy in Vienna in 1905, graduating on 18 August

1909. Assigned to the k.u.k. Landwehr Infanterie-Regiment 4 he was promoted to Leutnant. At the outbreak of the First World War, he served with Gebirgs-Schützen-Regiment 2, where he took part in the operations in Galicia and the Italian Alps, becomin a prisoner of war in 1918. After the war he returned to the newly formed Republic of German Austria and fought against the Serbians, Croatians and Slovenians occupying his native Carinthia. After the Carinthian Plebiscite and the creation of the First Austrian Republic, he was transferred to the Austrian federal army, where he was first promoted to Major in 1930 and then Oberstleutnant in 1932. Two years later he was joined to 5. Gebirgsjäger-Brigade. After the Anschluss he joined 3. Gebirgs-Division in the Wehrmacht, where he was promoted to Oberst on 1 February 1939 and took over command of Infanterie-Regiment 74. At the start of the Second World War he was transferred to 268. Infanterie-Division, taking over command of Infanterie-Regiment 266 in October 1939, commanding them during the battle for France. He returned to 3. Gebirgs-Division, taking over command on 14 July 1940. At the end of October he was promoted to Oberstleutnant and took over command of the newly established 5. Gebirgs-Division. After taking part in the battles for Greece and Crete Ringel took over 3. Gebirgs-Division and took part in the invasion of Russia. In December 1943 he moved with his division to Cassino until being promoted to command LXIX Armee-Korps in Croatia; he was later in charge of Wehrkreis XVIII, serving with it until the end of the war.

Generalmajor Ferdinand Schörner

Born on 12 June 1892 in Munich, German empire, Schörner served in the First World War. He was awarded the Pour le Mérite when, as a Leutnant, he took part in the Austro-Hungarian and German Battle of Caporetto, which shattered the Italian lines in the fall of 1917. He served as a staff officer and instructor during the interwar period. In 1923 he was adjutant to General von Lossow, the commander of Military District VII in Munich, and participated in the defeat of the Beer Hall Putsch. During the invasion of Poland at the start of the Second World War he commanded 98. Gebirgsjäger-Regiment before taking over command of 6. Gebirgs-Division prior to the invasion of the Balkans. He received the Knight's Cross for his role in breaching the Metaxas Line. After Greece he fought in Russia, rising to command XIX. Gebirgs-Korps in Finland, XXXX Panzer-Korps in 1943 and later Army-Gruppe A and then Army-Gruppe-Ukraine in 1944. In April 1945 he was promoted to Fieldmarschall and named as the new commander in chief of the army by Hitler, a position he nominally held until the end of the war.

Movement of W Force to Greece

Date	1 Armoured Brigade	2 New Zealand Division	6 Australian Division	Corps Troops
March				
7-9	102 Ant-Tank Regt (2 batteries)	18 Battalion		12 Heavy AA Regiment
10-12	4 Hussars 3 Royal Tank Regiment			
15-17	1 Rangers KRRC	19 Battalion 20 Battalion		
18		24 Battalion 25 Battalion		
19			2/3 Battalion	
20		4 Field Regiment		
21		NZ Divisional Cavalry Regiment 26 Battalion 27 MG Battalion		64 Medium Regiment
22			2/1 Battalion 2/2 Battalion	
25	Italian attack on Suda bay, *York* and *Pericles* hit damaged			
27		5 Field Regiment 6 Field Regiment 23 Battalion 28 Maori Battalion		
27-28	Battle of Matapan			
29		7 Anti-Tank Regiment 21 Battalion 22 Battalion		

Date	1 Armoured Brigade	2 New Zealand Division	6 Australian Division	Corps Troops
April				
3			2/2 Field Regiment 2/3 Field Regiment 2/1 Anti-Tank Regiment 2/4 Battalion 2/8 Battalion	
6 /7	Pireaus harbour bombed and *Clan Fraser* blown up putting harbour out of action			
9			2/1 MG Battalion	7 Medium Regiment
12			2/1 Field Regiment 2/5 Battalion 2/6 Battalion 2/7 Battalion 2/11 Battalion	

Appendix IV

British Tank Losses in Greece

3 Royal Tank Regiment (A10 Cruiser tanks)					
Date	Location	RHQ	A Squadron	B Squadron	C Squadron
11 April	Amyntaio – Panteleimon				1 (engine) 6 (tracks) (all repaired)
12 April	Panteleimon – Ptolemais			4 (tracks) 1 (blown up)	2 (engines) 5 (tracks)
13 April	Ptolemais – Kozani – Aliákmon		1 (clutch) 1 (clutch & engine) 2 (tracks)	2 (tracks)	1 (steering) 1 (engine) 5 (tracks)
14 April	Aliákmon – Grevená		1 (engine) 1 (steering) 1 (tracks)	2 (engine) 3 (steering)	
14 April (morning) across the Aliákmon – composite squadron formed from: 2 tanks from RHQ, 9 tanks from A Squadron and 2 tanks from C Squadron					
15 April	Grevená – Venetikos		4 (tracks)	2 (steering) 1 (engine)	C Sqdn left for Larissa
	Total Regimental tank strength of 6 A10s				
17 April	Venetikos – Larissa		2 (tracks)	1 (tracks)	
18 April			1 (tracks)		
18 April	Larissa – Lamia		1 (steering)		
19 April			1 (tracks)		

Reason for tank loss in brackets.[1]

1 Armoured Brigade Headquarters Squadron (A13 Cruiser tanks)	
Date	Details
14 April	1 abandoned on way from Trikkala to Kalabaka and later destroyed
16-19 April	1 lost between Kalabaka and Domokos – cause unknown
20 April	1 knocked out and set on fire at Domokos 2 broke down on Domokos/Lamia Pass 1 abandoned on Alamana bridge over Sperchios river
26-29 April	1 damaged by Stukas and destroyed by crew

Appendix V

Embarkations from Greece

Date	Location	Ships involved	Numbers lifted	Units involved
22/23 April & 23/24 April	Piraeus	Small Greek ships	1,300 150	Base troops & British civilians German POWs
24/25 April	Porto Rafti Navplion	*Calcutta, Perth, Glengyle, Glenearn, Phoebe, Hyacinth, Stuart, Voyager,* *Ulster Prince**	5,750 6,685	5 Brigade Group, 2 NZ Division HQ and support troops, 64 Medium Regiment HQ Anzac Corps, Base Units, RAF
25/26 April	Megara	*Thurland Castle, Coventry, Havock, Hasty, Decoy, Waterhen, Vendetta, Wryneck*	5,900	19 Brigade Group

Date	Location	Ships involved	Numbers lifted	Units involved
26/27 April	Rafina	*Glengyle, Nubian, Decoy,*	3503	1 Armoured Brigade (part), NZ Divisional troops
	Porto Rafti	*Hasty, Salween, Carlisle,*	4720	Corps and NZ Divisional troops
	Navplion/ Myloi/Tolos	*Kandahar, Kingston, Slamat*, Calcutta,*	4,527	Force HQ, Base Troops, 1 Armoured Brigade (part)
	Kalamata	*Stuart, Orion, Perth, Khedive Ismail, Wryneck*, Diamond* Dilwarra, City of London, Costa Rica*, Defender, Hereward*	8,650	16 & 17 Brigade Groups
27/28 April	Porto Rafti	*Ajax, Kingston,*	3,840	4 Brigade Group
	Rafina	*Kimberly, Havock*	850	1 Armoured Brigade (part)

Date	Location	Ships involved	Numbers lifted	Units involved
28/29 April	Monemvasia	*Ajax,* *Havock,* *Hotspur,*	4,320	6 Brigade Group
	Kalmata	*Griffin,* *Isis,* *Perth,* *Phoebe,* *Nubian,*	332	Miscellaneous
	Klithera	*Defender,* *Hereward,* *Decoy,* *Hasty,* *Hero,* *Kandahar,* *Kingston,* *Kimberly,* *Hyacinth*	820	Miscellaneous
29/30 April	Kalamata area	*Isis,* *Hero,* *Kimberly*	33	Miscellaneous
30 April/1 May	Kalamata area	*Isis,* *Hero,*	201	Miscellaneous
	Myloi	*Kimberly* *Hotspur,* *Havock*	700	Miscellaneous

* Beached or sunk[1]

Appendix VI

Casualties

The total strength of the forces committed to Greece by the Allies was 62,571, composed of: British army, 21,880; Australian, 17,125; New Zealand, 16,729; RAF, 2,217; Palestinans and Cypriots, 4,620. The losses suffered by these contingents were as follows:

	Killed	*Wounded*	*Prisoners*
British army	146	87	6,480
Palestinians and Cypriots	36	25	3,806
Royal Air Force	110	45	28
Australians	320	494	2,030
New Zealanders	291	599	1,614
Total	903	1,250	13,958

As announced by Hitler at the end of the campaign, losses for Germany were reported as: 1,160 killed, 3,755 wounded and 365 missing. However, to this must be added what happened to 2. Panzer-Division after the campaign was over. In May 1941 the division was shipped back to Germany by way of Italy, the first convoy reaching Taranto on 19 May. The rest of the division left Patras on 21 May, but two miles south of Cape Lefkada the *Kybfels* ran into a minefield laid the previous night by the minelayer HMS *Abdiel*. *Kybfels* was struck in quick succession by three mines and began to sink. The *Marburg* set off at full speed to assist it, but struck two mines itself and caught fire. The Italian cruisers escorting the convoy came forward to help and were later joined by some torpedo boats and destroyers from Patras, continuing the search well into the night illuminated by the light of the burning *Marburg*. Nevertheless, out of the approximately 1,400 troops and sailors on these two ships, 170 were lost and a further seventy-four hospitalised. More serious for the division was the loss of equipment, which included sixty-six guns, ninety-three tractors, fifteen armoured cars and 136 motor vehicles.[1]

Glossary

Ranks

British	German Army	Waffen SS
Private	Gemeiner/Landser	Schütze
		Oberschütze
Lance corporal	Grenadier	Sturmann
	Obergrenadier	
Corporal	Gefreiter	Rottenführer
	Obergefreiter	Unterscharführer
	Stabsgefreiter	
Sergeant	Unteroffizier	Scharführer
Colour sergeant	Unterfeldwebel	Oberscharführer
	Feldwebel	
Sergeant major	Oberfeldwebel	Hauptscharführer
	Stabsfeldwebel	Hauptbereitschaftsleiter
Warrant officer	Sturmscharführer	
Second lieutenant	Leutnant	Untersturmführer
First lieutenant	Oberleutnant	Obersturmführer
Captain	Hauptmann	Hauptsturmführer
Major	Major	Sturmbannführer
Lieutenant colonel	Oberstleutnant	Obersturmbannführer
Colonel	Oberst	Standartenführer
Brigadier	Oberführer	
Major general	Generalmajor	Brigadeführer
Lieutenant colonel	Generalleutnant	Gruppenführer
General	General	Obergruppenführer
	Generaloberst	Oberstgruppenführer
Field marshall	Generalfeldmarschall	Reichsführer-SS

German terminology

Aufklärungsabteilung	Reconnaissance battalion
Beiwagen-Krad	Motorcycle with sidecar
Fliegerabwehrkanone (Flak)	Anti-aircraft gun
Gebirgs-Division	Mountain Division
Kampfgruppe	Battle group
Kradschutzen-Bataillon	Motorcycle Battalion
Kompanie	Company
Panzerkampfwagen (PzKpfw)	Armoured fighting vehicle or tank
Sturmgeschütze (StuG)	Assault gun
Zug	Platoon

Notes

Chapter 1: The Road to War

1. Major General I.S.O. Playfair, *The Mediterranean and the Middle East. Volume I. Early Successes against Italy (to May 1941)*. London, Her Majesty's Stationery Office, 1954, p. 40.
2. Ibid. p. 24.
3. Ibid. p. 36.
4. Ibid. p. 36.
5. W.G. McClymont, *To Greece. Official History of New Zealand in the Second World War 1939-45*. War History Branch, Department of Internal Affairs, New Zealand, 1959, p. 2.
6. Ibid. p. 88.
7. Ibid, p. 109.
8. McClymont, p. 47.
9. Ibid, p. 21.
10. Playfair, p. 110.
11. Ibid, p. 163
12. Ibid. pp. 112-113.
13. Ibid. p. 118.
14. Ibid. pp. 169-176.
15. Ibid. p. 225; 'The German Campaigns in the Balkans (Spring 1941)', Department of the Army Pamphlet No. 20-260, November 1953, pp. 2-3.
16. Playfair. pp. 205-211.
17. Ibid. p. 226.
18. Ibid. pp. 228-230; McClymont, p. 89.
19. Playfair. p. 232.
20. Pamphlet No. 20-260, November 1953, pp. 4-5.
21. McClymont, p. 91; Wards I., *The Balkan Dilemma*. In *Kia Kaha. New Zealand in the Second World War*. (ed. Crawford, J.) Oxford University Press, Auckland, 2000, p. 22.
22. Playfair. pp. 231-232; McClymont, p. 89.
23. Playfair. pp. 233-234.
24. Ibid. pp. 235-237.

25. F.H. Hinsley *British Intelligence in the Second World War*. Her Majesty's Stationery Office, London, 1993, p. 66.
26. Playfair, p. 257.
27. Ibid. pp. 267-292.
28. Hinsley, p. 63.
29. Playfair, pp. 357-361.

Chapter 2: Political Machinations

1. Major-General I.S.O. Playfair *The Mediterranean and the Middle East. Volume II. The Germans Come to Help their Ally (1941)*. London, Her Majesty's Stationery Office, 1956, p. 14.
2. F.H. Hinsley *British Intelligence in the Second World War. Volume 1*, Her Majesty's Stationery Office, London, 1979, p. 386.
3. Ibid, pp. 347-348.
4. 'The German Campaigns in the Balkans (Spring 1941)', Department of the Army Pamphlet No. 20-260, November 1953, pp. 7-10.
5. Hinsley, pp. 351-354; Major-General I.S O. Playfair *The Mediterranean and the Middle East. Volume 1. The Early Successes Against Italy (to May 1941)*. Her Majesty's Stationery Office, London, 1954, p. 339.
6. Hinsley, p. 352.
7. Hinsley, p. 352; Pamphlet No. 20-260, p. 11.
8. Major-General I.S.O. Playfair, *The Mediterranean and the Middle East. Volume I. Early Successes against Italy (to May 1941)*. London, Her Majesty's Stationery Office, 1954, p. 347.
9. Ibid, p. 335.
10. J. Elworthy, *Greece Crete Stalag Dachau. A New Zealand Soldier's encounters with Hitler's army*. Awa Press, Wellington, 1994, p. 40.
11. Ibid, p. 340-344
12. Ibid, p. 347.
13. Ibid, p. 394.
14. Ibid, p. 1-3.
15. D.M. Horner, *High Command. Australia and Allied Strategy 1939-1945*. George Allen & Unwin Pity, Sydney, 1982, p. 54.
16. Ibid, pp. 78-79.
17. Ibid, pp. 66-67.
18. W.G. McClymont, *To Greece. Official History of New Zealand in the Second World War 1939-45*. War History Branch, Department of Internal Affairs, New Zealand, 1959, p. 99.

19. P. Freyberg, *Bernard Freyberg, VC: Soldier of Two Nations*. Hodder & Stoughton, London, 1991, pp. 238-9.
20. R.K. Mackie, *Freyberg's High-Command Relationships, 1939-1941*. Master of Philosophy Thesis, Centre for Defence and Strategic Studies, Massey University, Palmerston North, 2014, p. 29.
21. McClymont, p. 18.
22. Horner, p. 67.
23. Horner, p. 67; McClymont, p. 99.
24. Mackie, p. 104.
25. Horner, p. 77.
26. *Documents Relating to New Zealand's Participation in the Second World War 1939-45. Volume I*. War History Branch, Department of Internal Affairs, New Zealand, 1949, p. 239.
27. Wards, I., *The Balkan Dilemma*. In *Kia Kaha. New Zealand in the Second World War*. (ed. Crawford J.) Oxford University Press, Auckland, 2000, p. 24.
28. Ibid, p. 26.
29. Playfair, Vol I, pp. 372-378; Wards, pp. 25-26.
30. Horner, p. 69.
31. Long G. *Greece, Crete and Syria. Australia in the War of 1939-1945. Series One. Army. Volume II*, Australian War Memorial, Canberra, 1953, p. 21
32. Horner, p. 80.
33. *Documents I*, pp. 239-242.
34. Horner, p. 81.
35. Long, p. 12.
36. Wards, p. 26.
37. Long, p. 12.
38. Playfair, Vol I, pp. 381-384.
49. Wards, p. 27.
40. Long, p. 48; *Documents I*, pp. 246-249.
41. Wards, p. 30.
42. Ibid, p. 17.
43. Long, pp. 17-20; *Documents I*, pp. 246-249.

Chapter 3: Operation Lustre

1. P. Delaforce, *Taming the Panzers. Monty's Tank Battalions, 3 Royal Tanks at War*. Sutton Publishing, Phoenix Mill, 2000, p. 43.
2. Charrington, Brig Harold Vincent Harold Spencer (1986-1965), Charrington 5/1, Copy of a letter from Brigadier Charrington to his daughter, Tuesday 29 April 1941, p. 5. C.M. Wheeler, *Kalamera Kiwi!*

To Olympus with the New Zealand Engineers. A.H. and A.W. Reed, Wellington, 1946, pp.109-111.

3. WO 169/1386 HQ 4th Hussars 1941, 8 March.

4. WO 169/1141, 10 March.

5. Delaforce, p. 45.

6. F.H. Hinsley, *British Intelligence in the Second World War. Volume 1*, Her Majesty's Stationery Office, London, 1979, p. 364.

7. Major-General I.S.O. Playfair, *The Mediterranean and the Middle East. Volume II. The Germans Come to Help their Ally (1941).* London, Her Majesty's Stationery Office, 1956, p. 77.

8. R. Kay, *27 Machine Gun Battalion. Official History of New Zealand in the Second World War 1939-45.* War History Branch, Department of Internal Affairs, New Zealand, 1958, pp. 29-30.

9. G. Long, *Greece, Crete and Syria. Australia in the War of 1939-1945. Series One. Army. Volume II*, Australian War Memorial, Canberra, 1953, p. 7.

10. D.M. Horner, *High Command. Australia and Allied Strategy 1939-1945.* George Allen & Unwin Pity, Sydney, 1982, p. 71.

11. Playfair, p. 8.

12. Ibid, pp. 61-62

13. W.G. McClymont, *To Greece. Official History of New Zealand in the Second World War 1939-45.* War History Branch, Department of Internal Affairs, New Zealand, 1959, p. 120.

14. F.H. Hinsley, *British Intelligence in the Second World War. Volume 1*, Her Majesty's Stationery Office, London, 1979, p. 403.

15. Playfair, p. 65.

16. Ibid, p. 67.

17. Ibid, pp. 62-67.

18. C.M. Wheeler, *Kalamera Kiwi! To Olympus with the New Zealand Engineers.* A.H. and A.W. Reed, Wellington, 1946, pp. 110-111.

19. Ibid, p. 77.

20. McClymont, p. 122.

21. Long, pp. 33-34.

22. Ibid, p. 47.

23. McClymont, p. 123.

24. Long, pp. 34-35.

25. Thompson, p. 134.

26. Long, p. 34; Playfair, p. 78; WO 169/1386 HQ 4th Hussars 1941, 20-27 March.

27. McClymont, p. 128.

28. Long, p. 35

29. WO 169/1141, 16 March.
30. Delaforce, p. 47-48
31. Long, p. 36.
32. Ibid. p. 32.
33. Ibid. p. 65.
34. AWM52 8/3/4 2/4 Battalion, 3 April 1941.
35. Long, p. 36.
36. Playfair, p. 85.

Chapter 4: The Fall of Yugoslavia

1. 'The German Campaigns in the Balkans (Spring 1941)', Department of the Army Pamphlet No. 20-260, November 1953, pp. 20-21.
2. Major General I.S.O. Playfair, *The Mediterranean and the Middle East. Volume II. The Germans Come to Help their Ally (1941)*. London, Her Majesty's Stationery Office, 1956, p. 71.
3. Playfair, pp. 72-74.
4. Pamphlet No. 20-260, p. 21.
5. Playfair, pp. 72-74.
6. Pamphlet No. 20-260, p. 24.
7. Ibid, p. 21.
8. Ibid, p. 33.
9. Ibid, p. 22.
10. Ibid. pp. 30-31.
11. F.H. Hinsley, *British Intelligence in the Second World War*. Her Majesty's Stationery Office, London, 1993, p. 71.
12. Time-Life Books Inc., *Conquest of the Balkans*. Joseph L. Ward, 1990, p. 43.
13. Pamphlet No. 20-260, p. 49.
14. Ibid, pp. 57-60.
15. *Conquest of the Balkans*, Chapter 2, pp. 50-51.
16. Pamphlet No. 20-260, pp. 61-64.

Chapter 5: Breakthrough at Vevi

1. F.H. Hinsley, *British Intelligence in the Second World War*. Her Majesty's Stationery Office, London, 1993, p. 71.
2. F.H. Hinsley, *British Intelligence in the Second World War*. Her Majesty's Stationery Office, London, 1993, p. 71.
3. Major General I.S.O. Playfair, *The Mediterranean and the Middle East. Volume II. The Germans Come to Help their Ally (1941)*. London, Her Majesty's Stationery Office, 1956, p. 82.

4. Time-Life Books Inc., Conquest of the Balkans. Joseph L. Ward, 1990, Chapter 2, pp. 11-12.

5. D.M. Horner, *High Command. Australia and Allied Strategy 1939-1945*. George Allen & Unwin Pity, Sydney, 1982, p. 86.

6. P. Thompson, *Anzac Fury. The Bloody Battle of Crete 1941*. Random House, North Sydney, Australia, 2010, pp. 150-151.

7. G. Long, *Greece, Crete and Syria. Australia in the War of 1939-1945. Series One. Army. Volume II*, Australian War Memorial, Canberra, 1953, p. 40; McClymont W.G. *To Greece. Official History of New Zealand in the Second World War 1939-45*. War History Branch, Department of Internal Affairs, New Zealand, 1959, p. 161; AWM52 8/5/1 2/1 Machine Gun Battalion March-April 1941, 7 April.

8. Playfair, p. 85.

9. Pamphlet No. 20-260, pp. 86-87.

10. Long, p. 46.

11. Hinsley, p. 74.

12. Long, p. 46.

13. Playfair, p. 79.

14. R. Kay, *27 Machine Gun Battalion. Official History of New Zealand in the Second World War 1939-45*. War History Branch, Department of Internal Affairs, New Zealand, 1958, p. 33.

15. McClymont, pp. 160-167.

16. Ibid, p. 86.

17. McClymont, p. 160.

18. J.F. Cody, *21 Battalion. Official History of New Zealand in the Second World War 1939-45*. War History Branch, Department of Internal Affairs, New Zealand, 1953, p. 40.

19. R.J.M. Loughnan, *Divisional Cavalry. Official History of New Zealand in the Second World War 1939-45*. War History Branch, Department of Internal Affairs, New Zealand, 1963, p. 55.

20. McClymont, pp. 163-173; 181-182.

21. Jack Elliott interview, Ourwar Project, Richard Carstens.

22. Sir E. Puttick, *25 Battalion. Official History of New Zealand in the Second World War 1939-45*. War History Branch, Department of Internal Affairs, New Zealand, 1960, p. 42.

23. McClymont, p. 164; Long, pp. 43-44.

24. Charrington, Brig Harold Vincent Harold Spencer (1986-1965), Charrington 5/1, Copy of a letter from Brigadier Charrington to his daughter, Tuesday 29 April 1941, p. 5.

25. Long, p. 47.

26. *White over Green. The 2/4th Battalion and Reference to the 4th Battalion.* Edited by The Unit History Editorial Committee, Angus and Robertson. 1963, pp. 105-108.
27. Ibid. pp. 112.
28. R. Lehmann, *The Leibstandarte I. 1 SS Panzer Division Leibstandarte Adolf Hitler.* J. J. Fedorowicz Publishing, Winnipeg, 1987, p. 203.
29. Loughnan, p. 58.
30. H. Quassowski, Twelve Years with Hitler. A History of 1. Kompanie Leibstandarte SS Adolf Hitler 1933-1945. Schffer Military History, Atglen, USA, 1999, p. 124.
31. Loughnan, pp. 57-58.
32. Harry Spencer, interview, 2004.
33. *White over Green*, pp. 113-114.
34. Lehmann, p. 207.
35. *The 2/8th Battalion.* The 2/8th Battalion Association, Melbourne, 1984, pp. 49-53.
36. *White over Green.*, pp. 115.
37. *White over Green.*, pp. 114-115.
38. The 2/8th Battalion, pp. 55-57.
39. AWM 54, 534/2/27, German Army Documents on the Campaign in Greece, (Pz Div War Diary, p. 56).
40. AWM 54, 534/2/27, p. 157.
41. The 2/8th Battalion, pp. 55-57.
42. R. Crisp, *The Gods Were Neutral.* Frederick Muller Ltd, London, 1960, pp. 109-110.
43. The 2/8th Battalion, pp. 57-59.
44. AWM 54, 534/2/27, p. 56.
45. R. Lehmann, p. 213
46. Lehmann, pp. 213-214.
47. The 2/8th Battalion, pp. 59-63.
48. Long, pp. 58-63.
49. *White over Green.* P. 120.
50. D. M. Horner, *General Vasey's War*, Melbourne University Press, Melbourne, 1992, pp. 95-96.
51. Ibid, p. 118.
52. White over Green, pp. 116-124; Long, pp. 62-63.
53. R. Lehmann, pp. 214-215
54. Long, pp. 66-68.
55. Crisp, pp. 117-118
56. Ibid, pp. 121-122.

57. R. Lehmann, pp. 215-216.

58. R. Lehmann, p. 216

59. P. Delaforce, *Taming the Panzers. Monty's Tank Battalions, 3 RTR at War.* Sutton Publishing, Phoenix Mill, 2000, p. 50.

60. Delaforce, p. 50.

61. Crisp, p. 127.

62. Long, pp. 68-69.

63. AWM 54, 534/2/27, p. 61. 33 Pz Regt. Report on Engagement south of Kato Ptolemais 13 Apr 41.

64. Crisp, p. 133.

65. Ibid, p. 61; Crisp, p. 133.

66. AWM 54, 534/2/27, p. 56. Extracts from 9 Pz Div War Diary (Greek Campaign)

67. Crisp, 133-136; WO 169/1141 3rd R. Tank Regt Jan–April 1941, Appendix. Operations in Greece.

68. Charrington, Brig Harold Vincent Harold Spencer (1986-1965), Charrington 4/4, p. 2.

69. Long, p.; 104; p. 90.

Chapter 6: The Battle for Servia Pass

1. D.W. Sinclair, *19 Battalion and Armoured Regiment. Official History of New Zealand in the Second World War 1939-45.* War History Branch, Department of Internal Affairs, New Zealand, 1954, p. 70.

2. S. Wick, *Purple Over Green. The History of the 2/2 Australian Infantry Battalion 1939-1945.* 2/2 Australian Infantry Battalion Association, 1977, p. 92.

3. G. Long, *Greece, Crete and Syria. Australia in the War of 1939-1945. Series One. Army. Volume II*, Australian War Memorial, Canberra, 1953, p. 85.

4. Major-General I.S.O. Playfair, *The Mediterranean and the Middle East. Volume II. The Germans Come to Help their Ally (1941).* London, Her Majesty's Stationery Office, 1956, p. 89.

5. Ibid, p. 80.

6. Long, pp. 77-81.

7. Ibid, p. 74.

8. Ibid, p. 90.

9. Sinclair, pp. 74–75.

10. Sinclair, p. 74.

11. D.J.C. Pringle and W.A. Glue, *20 Battalion and Armoured Regiment. Official History of New Zealand in the Second World War 1939-45.* War History Branch, Department of Internal Affairs, New Zealand, 1957, p. 53.

12. W.G. McClymont, To Greece. Official History of New Zealand in the Second World War 1939-45. War History Branch, Department of Internal Affairs, New Zealand, 1959, pp. 273-274.
13. AWM 54, 534/2/27, German Army Documents on the Campaign in Greece, p. 57.
14. Sinclair, p. 77.
15. AWM 54, 534/2/27, p. 66.
16. McClymont, p. 273.
17. Sinclair, p. 78.
18. Sinclair, pp. 77-85.
19. Possibly 7,5cm leichtes Infanteriegeschütz 18 (7,5cm le.IG 18)
20. AWM 54, 534/2/27, pp. 66-67.
21. W.D. Dawson, *18 Battalion and Armoured Regiment. Official History of New Zealand in the Second World War 1939-45*. War History Branch, Department of Internal Affairs, New Zealand, 1961, p. 95.
22. AWM 54, 534/2/27, p. 66.
23. A.D. von Plato *Die Geschichte der 5. Panzerdivision 1938-1945*, Walhala und Praetoria Vergag KG Georg Zwickenpflug, Regensburg,1978, p. 115.
24. Long , p. 80.
25. AWM52 8/2/17/28 17 Infantry Brigade April 1941 Appendices.
26. Ibid.
27. Ibid.
28. S. Trigellis-Smith, *All the King's Enemies – A History of the 2/5th Australian Infantry Battalion.* 2/5 Battalion Association, 1988, pp. 88-91.
29. Trigellis-Smith, 91-92.
30. M.G. Comeau MM., *Operation Mercury. A First Hand Account of the Fall of Crete.* Patrick Stephens Ltd, Sparkford, 1991, pp. 39-40.
31. F.H. Hinsley, *British Intelligence in the Second World War.* Her Majesty's Stationery Office, London, 1993, p. 75.
32. Long, p. 82.
33. AWM52 8/3/2 2/2 Infantry Battalion February-April 1941, 15-16 April.
34. AWM52 8/3/3 2/3 Infantry Battalion December 1940-June 1941, 16 April.
35. D.M. Horner, *General Vasey's War*, Melbourne University Press, Melbourne, 1992, pp. 87-88.
36. AWM52 8/3/1 2/1 Infantry Battalion March-May 1941, 16-17 March.
37. Long, pp 87-88.
38. *White over Green. The 2/4th Battalion and Reference to the 4th Battalion.* Edited by The Unit History Editorial Committee, Angus and Robertson , 1963, pp. 129-132.

39. F. D. Norton, *26 Battalion. Official History of New Zealand in the Second World War 1939-45*. War History Branch, Department of Internal Affairs, New Zealand, 1952, pp 38-43.

40. Playfair, p. 89.

41. McClymont, p. 362.

42. Kippenberger Major-General Sir H. *Infantry Brigadier*. Oxford University Press, London, 1949, pp. 27-29.

43. Sinclair, p. 86.

44. von Plato, p. 115.

45. WO 169/1141 3rd R. Tank Regt Jan-April 1941, Appendix; Crisp R. *The Gods Were Neutral*. Frederick Muller Ltd, London, 1960, pp. 178-179.

46. R. Crisp, *The Gods Were Neutral*. Frederick Muller Ltd, London, 1960, pp. 178-179.

47. Long, p. 125.

48. AWM52 8/3/11 2/11 Infantry Battalion January-June 1941.

49. W. Olson, Battalion into Battle. The History of the 2/11th Australian Infantry Battalion. 1939-1945, Wesley John Olsonm, 2011, p. 115.

50. Trigellis-Smith, p. 94.

Chapter 7: Repulse at Olympus Pass

1. R.J.M. Loughnan, *Divisional Cavalry. Official History of New Zealand in the Second World War 1939-45*. War History Branch, Department of Internal Affairs, New Zealand, 1963, pp 54-62.

2. W.G. McClymont, *To Greece. Official History of New Zealand in the Second World War 1939-45*. War History Branch, Department of Internal Affairs, New Zealand, 1959, p. 235.

3. Loughnan, pp. 62-68.

4. McClymont, pp. 237-238.

5. See Chapter 4

6. Jack Elliott interview, Ourwar Project, Richard Carstens, Jan 2016.

7. McClymont, p. 261; Henderson, pp. 15-18.

8. J. Elworthy, *Greece Crete Stalag Dachau. A New Zealand Soldier's encounters with Hitler's army*. Awa Press, Wellington, 1994, pp. 42-43.

9. C.M. Wheeler, *Kalamera Kiwi! To Olympus with the New Zealand Engineers*. A.H. and A.W. Reed, Wellington, 1946, pp.126-127.

10. Henderson, pp. 19-21.

11. McClymont, pp. 263-265.

12. J.F. Cody, *28 (Maori) Battalion. Official History of New Zealand in the Second World War 1939-45*. War History Branch, Department of Internal Affairs, New Zealand, 1956, pp. 58-59.

13. McClymont, pp. 266-269.

14. AWM 54, 534/2/27, German Army Documents on the Campaign in Greece, p. 36; WAII 1/334 DA 438.21/4 Enemy documents, Report by 1 Coy 2 Inf Regt, p.12.

15. Elworthy, pp. 47-48.

16. Ibid, pp. 285-292.

17. Ibid, pp. 293-295.

18. Ibid, pp. 299-301; Loughnan, pp. 70-72.

19. Kippenberger Major-General Sir H. *Infantry Brigadier*. Oxford University Press, London, 1949, p. 30.

20. McClymont, pp. 296-297.

21. Loughnan, pp. 72-73; Hugh Robinson citation for Military Cross from Sam Robinson.

22. McClymont, pp. 302-303.

23. Long, pp. 123-124.

24. Ibid, p. 124.

25. Ibid, pp. 305-308.

26. Jack Elliott interview, Ourwar Project, Richard Carstens, Jan 2016.

27. F.D. Norton, *26 Battalion. Official History of New Zealand in the Second World War 1939-45*. War History Branch, Department of Internal Affairs, New Zealand, 1952, pp. 47-53.

Chapter 8: A Near Run Thing at Pineios Gorge

1. J.F. Cody, *21 Battalion. Official History of New Zealand in the Second World War 1939-45*. War History Branch, Department of Internal Affairs, New Zealand, 1953, pp. 44-47.

2. Ibid, pp. 49-52.

3. 1990.441. Papers: Brigadier Reginald Miles - WWII, Macky Account, Day 15, p.1.

4. Ibid, Macky Account, Day 15, p. 1.

5. Ibid, Macky Account, Day 15, pp. 1-2.

6. AWM 54, 534/2/27, German Army Documents on the Campaign in Greece, p. 36; WAII 1/334 DA 438.21/4 Enemy documents, Report by I/3 Pz Regt, p.7.

7. 1990.441. Macky Account, Day 15, p.3.

8. Ibid, Day 15, p.4.

9. AWM 54, 534/2/27, p. 37; WAII 1/334 DA 438.21/4, Report by I/3 Pz Regt, p.7.

10. Cody, p. 58.

11. AWM 54, 534/2/27, p. 37; WAII 1/334 DA 438.21/4, Report by I/3 Pz Regt, p.7.

12. WAII/334 DA 438.21/14 6 Mountain Division Intelligence Report, p. 5.

13. AWM 54, 534/2/27, p. 125; 112 Recce Unit Report on the Fighting in the Tempe Gorge 17-18 Apr 41, p. 2

14. D.M. Horner, *High Command. Australia and Allied Strategy 1939-1945.* George Allen & Unwin Pity, Sydney, 1982, pp. 87-88.

15. Cody, p. 61; W. L. Ormond *Aspects of the Greek Campaign, April 1941.* Master of Arts Thesis, Defence Studies, Massey University, Palmerston North, 2009, p. 60.

16. Cody, pp. 62-63.

17. Ibid, p. 60.

18. AWM52 8/3/2 2/2 Infantry Battalion February-April 1941, Chilton's Report p. 2.

19. Long, p. 107; DA32/10/14 L Troop, 33 Battery, 7 NZ Anti-Tank Regiment at the Peneos Gorge, 18 Apr 1941.

20. Ibid, pp. 60-65; W.G. McClymont, *To Greece. Official History of New Zealand in the Second World War 1939-45.* War History Branch, Department of Internal Affairs, New Zealand, 1959, pp. 317.

21. R.J.M. Loughnan, *Divisional Cavalry. Official History of New Zealand in the Second World War 1939-45.* War History Branch, Department of Internal Affairs, New Zealand, 1963, p. 70.

22. AWM 54, 534/2/27, pp. 37-38; WAII 1/334 DA 438.21/4, Report by I/3 Pz Regt, p. 7.

23. Cody, pp. 65-66; Wood P. W., *A Battle to Win: An Analysis of Combat Effectiveness through the Second World War Experience of the 21st (Auckland) Battalion.* Doctor of Philosophy Thesis, Centre for Defence and Strategic Studies, Massey University, Palmerston North, 2012. p. 123.

24. AWM 54, 534/2/27, German Army Documents on the Campaign in Greece, p. 36; WAII 1/334 DA 438.21/4 Enemy documents, Report by I/3 Pz Regt, p.2.

25. Bundesarchiv, Bild 101I-162-0294-03A - 11A; AWM 54, 534/2/27, p. 37.

26. WAII 1/334 DA 438.21/4 Enemy documents, 2 Pz Div reports to XVIII Korps, p. 1.

27. Cody, pp. 66-67.

28. AWM52 8/3/2 2/2 Infantry Battalion February-April 1941, Appendix 2; Cody, pp. 68-69; AWM 54, 534/2/27, I/143. Mtn Regt Report on attack over the Pinios 18 Apr 41, p 127.

29. S. Wick, *Purple Over Green. The History of the 2/2 Australian Infantry Battalion 1939-1945.* 2/2 Australian Infantry Battalion Association, 1977, p. 97.

30. AWM 54, 534/2/27, I/143. Mtn Regt Report on attack over the Pinios 18 Apr 41, p. 127.

31. AWM 54, 534/2/27, pp. 2-3; WAII 1/334 DA 438.21/4, Report by I/3 Pz Regt, p. 126.

32. According to Lieutenant Robert Finlayson from 21 Battalion at least 6 (McClymont, p. 325).

33. WAII3/1/7 Campaign in Greece 1941. Correspondence files 21 Battalion, C. O'Neil letter, p. 3.

34. AWM 54, 534/2/27, pp. 37-38; WAII 1/334 DA 438.21/4, Report by I/3 Pz Regt, p. 8.

35. McClymont, pp. 324-326. AWM 54, 534/2/27, pp. 38-39; Wood, pp. 127-128; WAII3/1/7, C. O'Neil letter.

36. DA32/10/14 L Troop, 33 Battery, 7 NZ Anti-Tank Regiment at the Peneos Gorge, 18 Apr 1941.

37. AWM 54, 534/2/27, p. 38; WAII 1/334 DA 438.21/4, Report by I/3 Pz Regt, p. 8.

38. *2nd New Zealand Divisional Artillery. Official History of New Zealand in the Second World War 1939-45.* War History Branch, Department of Internal Affairs, New Zealand, 1966, pp. 61-62.

39. Ibid.

40. AWM52 8/3/1 2/1 Infantry Battalion March–May 1941

41. Pugsley C. *A Bloody Road Home. World War Two and New Zealand's Heroic Second Division.* Penguin Books, Auckland, 2014, p. 98.

42. Balck H. *Order ü Chaos. The Memoirs of General of Panzer Troops Hermann Balck.* University Press of Kentucky, Lexington, 2015, p. 183.

43. WAII3/1/7, O'Neil letter, p. 3; WAII 1/334 DA 438.21/4, Extracts from 6 Mtn Div War Diary, p. 8

44. Cody, p. 69; McClymont, pp. 327-334; AWM52 8/3/2, Appendix 2; G.Long, *Greece, Crete and Syria. Australia in the War of 1939-1945. Series One. Army. Volume II*, Australian War Memorial, Canberra, 1953, p. 118.

45. Murphy, p. 63.

46. Wick, p. 98.

47. AWM 54, 534/2/27, I/143. Mtn Regt Report on attack over the Pinios 18 Apr 41, pp. 127-8.

48. AWM 54, 534/2/27, I/141. Mtn Regt Report on attack over the Pinios 18 Apr 41, p. 131.

49. AWM52 8/3/2/19 – 2/2 Battalion – April 1941, Report on Action at Evangelismos 18 April 1941 by O/C A Company.

50. AWM52 8/3/2/19 – 2/2 Battalion – April 1941, Report on Operations of 2/2 Aust. Inf. Bn at Pineios Gorge. p. 7; Murphy, p. 65.

51. Murphy, p. 65. Long, p. 117.
52. AWM52 8/3/2, Appendix 2.
53. Murphy, p. 65.
54. AWM52 8/3/2 2/2 Infantry Battalion February-April 1941, Chilton's Report p. 7.
55. McClymont, p. 336.
56. Ibid, p. 116.
57. AWM52 8/3/3 2/3 Infantry Battalion December 1940-June 1941, 18 April 1941.
58. Murphy, p. 65; McClymont, p. 335-338.
59. Ibid, p, 129.
60. Wick, p. 98, pp.98-99; McClymont, p. 339.
61. AWM52 8/2/16/7 16, Friday 18 May.
62. Long, pp. 120-121.
63. McClymont, p. 339.
64. Frank White interview, May 1999.
65. Wick; Loughnan, p. 75.
66. AWM 54, 534/2/27, p. 38.
67. Ibid, p, 129.
68. Long, p. 121.
69. Wick, p. 107.
70. Loughnan, p. 74.
71. AWM 54, 534/2/27, p. 39.
72. McClymont, p. 340; K.-H. Golla, *Der Fall Griechenlands* 1941. Mittler Verlag, Hamburg, 2007, p. 294 (according to the latter *3. Panzer-Regiment* started the Greek campaign with 45 PzKpfw II, 51, PzKpfw III and 20 PzKpfw IV).
73. AWM52 8/3/2/19 – 2/2 Battalion – April 1941, Report on Operations of 2/2 Aust. Inf. Bn at Pinios Gorge. p. 7.

Chapter 9: The Thermopylae Line

1. G. Long, *Greece, Crete and Syria. Australia in the War of 1939-1945. Series One. Army. Volume II*, Australian War Memorial, Canberra, 1953, p. 131; W.G. McClymont, *To Greece. Official History of New Zealand in the Second World War 1939-45*. War History Branch, Department of Internal Affairs, New Zealand, 1959, p. 402.
2. Ibid, p. 133.
3. Ibid, p. 134.
4. Long, p. 134.
5. Long p. 134; McClymont, p. 348.

6. W. Olson, *Battalion into Battle. The History of the 2/11th Australian Infantry Battalion. 1939-1945*, Wesley John Olsonm, 2011, p. 116.

7. Ibid, p. 116.

8. Long, p. 134.

9. Ibid, pp. 136-137.

10. M.G. Comeau, MM. *Operation Mercury. A First Hand Account of the Fall of Crete*. Patrick Stephens Ltd, Sparkford, 1991, pp. 45-47.

11. A. D. von Plato *Die Geschichte der 5. Panzerdivision 1938-1945*, Walhala und Praetoria Vergag KG Georg Zwickenpflug, Regensburg, 1978, p. 116.

12. Long, p. 137; McClymont, p. 349.

13. AWM52 8/3/6 2/6 Infantry Battalion February-June 1941; Long, pp. 137-138

14. Long, pp. 137-138; McClymont, pp. 350-351.

15. McClymont, p. 356; Tam Wallace, letter, 1983.

16. J. Henderson, *22 Battalion. Official History of New Zealand in the Second World War 1939-45*. War History Branch, Department of Internal Affairs, New Zealand, 1958, p. 29.

17. Long, p. 133.

18. A. D. von Plato, p 117.

19. Long, pp. 139-140; McClymont, pp. 355-537.

20. Long, pp. 143-145; McClymont, p. 372.

21. Major-General I. S. O. Playfair, *The Mediterranean and the Middle East. Volume II. The Germans Come to Help their Ally (1941)*. London, Her Majesty's Stationery Office, 1956, p. 95-96.

22. McClymont, pp. 359-361.

23. Ibid, p. 384.

24. Long, pp. 146-147.

25. AWM 54, 534/2/27, German Army Documents on the Campaign in Greece, 55 MC Bn Report, pp. 2-3.

26. Long, p. 148.

27. Comeau, p. 49.

28. McClymont, pp. 376-377.

29. McClymont, p. 378.

30. Long, p. 149.

31. McClymont, pp. 413-414.

32. R. Dahl, *Going Solo*. Puffin Books, London, 1988, pp. 162-163.

33. Ibid, p. 178.

34. Ibid, pp. 178-183.

35. AWM 54, 534/2/27, German Army Documents on the Campaign in Greece, 55 MC Bn Report, p. 4.

36. A. Ross, *23 Battalion. Official History of New Zealand in the Second World War 1939-45*. War History Branch, Department of Internal Affairs, New Zealand, 1959, p. 52.
37. McClymont, p. 381.
38. Long, p. 150.
39. Thompson P. *Anzac Fury. The Bloody Battle of Crete 1941*. Random House, North Sydney, Australia, 2010, pp. 193-194.
40. McClymont, p. 400.
41. Ibid, p. 151.
42. McClymont, pp. 413-414.
43. McClymont, pp. 385-387.
44. Sir E. Puttick, *25 Battalion. Official History of New Zealand in the Second World War 1939-45*. War History Branch, Department of Internal Affairs, New Zealand, 1960, p. 55.
45. McClymont, p. 387.
46. Puttick, pp. 51-61.
47. EA 1 18/19/3 1 The New Zealand Division in Greece. Report of Major General B. Freyberg, Commanding 2 NZEF, 28 August 1941, NZ Forces – Evacuation of Senior Officers.
48. Long, p. 152.
49. AWM 54, 534/2/27, German Army Documents on the Campaign in Greece, p. 32.
50. R. Kay, *27 Machine Gun Battalion. Official History of New Zealand in the Second World War 1939-45*. War History Branch, Department of Internal Affairs, New Zealand, 1958, p. 72.
51. W.E. Murphy, *2nd New Zealand Divisional Artillery. Official History of New Zealand in the Second World War 1939-45*. War History Branch, Department of Internal Affairs, New Zealand, 1966, p. 89.
52. AWM 54, 534/2/27, p143.
53. McClymont, p. 393.
54. AWM 54, 534/2/27, p. 52.
55. Puttick, pp. 51-59.
56. Murphy, p. 93.
57. AWM 54, 534/2/27, p. 144.
58. McClymont, p. 398-399.
59. AWM 54, 534/2/27, p. 144.
60. Olson, pp. 129-136.

Chapter 10: Evacuation

1. W.G. McClymont, *To Greece. Official History of New Zealand in the Second World War 1939-45*. War History Branch, Department of Internal Affairs,

New Zealand, 1959, pp. 402-405; G. Long, *Greece, Crete and Syria. Australia in the War of 1939-1945. Series One. Army. Volume II*, Australian War Memorial, Canberra, 1953, p. 160.

2. A. Ross, *23 Battalion. Official History of New Zealand in the Second World War 1939-45*. War History Branch, Department of Internal Affairs, New Zealand, 1959, p. 51.

3. McClymont, pp. 402-405; Long, p. 160.

4. S. Wick, *Purple Over Green. The History of the 2/2 Australian Infantry Battalion 1939-1945*. 2/2 Australian Infantry Battalion Association, 1977, p. 112.

5. Ibid, pp. 118-119.

6. McClymont, p. 406.

7. Long, pp. 161-162.

8. Sir E. Puttick, *25 Battalion. Official History of New Zealand in the Second World War 1939-45*. War History Branch, Department of Internal Affairs, New Zealand, 1960, p. 67.

9. J. Henderson, *Soldier Country*. Milwood Press Ltd, Wellington, 1978, p. 99.

10. McCymont, pp. 407-408.

11. Long, pp. 163-164.

12. Long, p. 164; McClymont, p. 409.

13. *White over Green. The 2/4th Battalion and Reference to the 4th Battalion*. Edited by The Unit History Editorial Committee, Angus and Robertson, 1963, p. 138.

14. McClymont, p. 409.

15. R.J.M. Loughnan, *Divisional Cavalry. Official History of New Zealand in the Second World War 1939-45*. War History Branch, Department of Internal Affairs, New Zealand, 1963, p 84.

16. R. Crisp, *The Gods Were Neutral*. Frederick Muller Ltd, London, 1960, p. 203.

17. Long, pp. 165-166; McClymont, p. 417.

18. Loughnan, pp. 84-85.

19. McClymont, pp. 417-419.

20. Long, pp. 166-167.

21. McClymont, pp. 422-426; 432-435.

22. Long, pp. 166-167.

23. Loughnan, pp. 85-86.

24. Crisp, p. 204.

25. McClymont, pp. 422.

26. Long, p. 169; McClymont, pp. 432-436.

27. McClymont, pp. 436-437

28. Murray Loughnan interview, 1998.

29. McClymont, pp. 426-429; Long, p. 170.

30. EA 1 18/19/3 1 The New Zealand Division in Greece. Report of Major General B. Freyberg, Commanding 2 NZEF, 28 August 1941, NZ Forces – Campaigns and Actions – Secret and confidential reports on the Greece and Crete Campaigns by the GOC 2nd NZEF.
31. McClymont, pp. 429-430; Long, pp. 171-172
32. McClymont, pp.438-439; Long, p. 176.
33. McClymont, pp.440-441.
34. Ibid, p. 443 & 449.35. McClymont, pp. 420-421.
36. Ibid, p. 443.
37. 'Snow'Nicholas, interview, 2002.
38. F.D. Norton *26 Battalion. Official History of New Zealand in the Second World War 1939-45*. War History Branch, Department of Internal Affairs, New Zealand, 1952, pp. 64-65.
39. McClymont, pp.442-447.
40. Dunn, C. *Permission to Speak. An Autobiography*. Plane Tree, 2001, pp 77-78.
41. Jack Hinton, Victoria Cross citation, London Gazette, No. 35311, 14 October 1941.
42. McClymont, pp. 458-459.
43. 181/32/6 War History – Author – McClymont. W. G., Part 2, The Reinforcement Battalion at Kalamata, pp. 11-12

Chapter 11: Operation Lustre in Retrospect

1. D.M. Horner High Command. Australia and Allied Strategy 1939-1945. George Allen & Unwin Pity, Sydney, 1982, p. 71.
2. AWM 54, 534/2/27, German Army Documents on the Campaign in Greece, p. 66.
3. EA 1 18/19/3 1 The New Zealand Division in Greece. Report of Major General B. Freyberg, Commanding 2 NZEF, 28 August 1941, NZ Forces – Evacuation of Senior Officers.
4. AWM 54, 534/2/27, German Army Documents on the Campaign in Greece, Notes on English Methods of Fighting, p. 2.
5. 181/32/6 War History – Author – McClymont. W. G. Part 2, Letter to Gavin Long, 2 February 1954.
6. W.G. McClymont, *To Greece. Official History of New Zealand in the Second World War 1939-45*. War History Branch, Department of Internal Affairs, New Zealand, 1959, p. 253.
7. S. Wick, *Purple Over Green. The History of the 2/2 Australian Infantry Battalion 1939-1945*. 2/2 Australian Infantry Battalion Association, 1977, p. 105.
8. 1990-441 Brigadier Miles Papers, Notes on Campaign in Greece Part 4, p. 1.

9. Charrington, Brig Harold Vincent Harold Spencer (1986-1965), Charrington 5/1, Copy of a letter from Brigadier Charrington to his daughter, Tuesday 29 April 1941, p. 5.
10. P. Brown, *British Cruiser Tanks A8 & A10*. Model Centrum Progres, Warsaw, 2017, p. 17.
11. Ibid, p. 5.

Appendix IV: British Tank Losses in Greece

1. R. Crisp, *The Gods Were Neutral*. Frederick Muller Ltd, London, 1960; WO 169/1141 3rd R. Tank Regt Jan-April 1941.

Appendix V: Embarkations from Greece

1. McClymont, W.G. *To Greece. Official History of New Zealand in the Second World War 1939-45*. War History Branch, Department of Internal Affairs, New Zealand, 1959, p. 486; Balck H. *Order ii Chaos. The Memoirs of General of Panzer Troops Hermann Balck*. University Press of Kentucky, Lexington, 2015, pp. 186-187; Axis History Forum, (http://forum.axishistory.com/viewtopic. php?f=50&t=117843&e=1&view=unread#unread)

Bibliography

Archives

Archives New Zealand

EA 1 18/19/3 1 The New Zealand Division in Greece. Report of Major General B. Freyberg, Commanding 2 NZEF, 28 August 1941, NZ Forces – Campaigns and Actions – Secret and confidential reports on the Greece and Crete Campaigns by the GOC 2nd NZEF.

WAII3/1/3 Campaign in Greece 1941. Correspondence files 4 and 5 Field Regiment.

WAII3/1/7 Campaign in Greece 1941. Correspondence files 21 Battalion.

WAII3/1/11 Campaign in Greece 1941. Correspondence files 27 Machine Gun Battalion.

WAII3/1/16b Campaign in Greece 1941. Correspondence files W. G. McClymont's correspondence while writing a history of the campaign in Greece.

WAII1/334 DA 438.21/4 Enemy documents.

DA32/10/14 L Troop, 33 Battery, 7 NZ Anti-Tank Regiment at the Peneos Gorge, 18 Apr 1941.

181/32/6 War History – Author – McClymont. W. G. Part 2.

1990.441. Papers: Brigadier Reginald Miles

Australian War Memorial

AWM 54, 534/2/27, German Army Documents on the Campaign in Greece

AWM52 8/2/16/7 16 Infantry Brigade March–April 1941

AWM52 8/2/17/28 17 Infantry Brigade April 1941 Appendices

AWM52 8/3/1 2/1 Infantry Battalion March–May 1941

AWM52 8/3/2 2/2 Infantry Battalion February–April 1941

AWM52 8/3/3 2/3 Infantry Battalion December 1940–June 1941

AWM52 8/3/4 2/4 Infantry Battalion March–May 1941

AWM52 8/3/5 2/5 Infantry Battalion January–June 1941

AWM52 8/3/6 2/6 Infantry Battalion February–June 1941

AWM52 8/3/7 2/7 Infantry Battalion February–July 1941
AWM52 8/3/11 2/11 Infantry Battalion January–June 1941

National Archives (UK)
WO 169/1141 3rd R. Tank Regt Jan–April 1941
WO 169/1268 HQ 1 Armoured Brigade 1941
WO 169/1386 HQ 4th Hussars 1941
WO 201/509 HQ Reports on Operations of 1 Armoured Brigade Greece April 1941

US National Archives
The German Campaigns in the Balkans (Spring 1941), Department of the Army Pamphlet No. 20-260, November 1953.

Liddell-Hart Military Archives, Kings College, London
Charrington, Brig Harold Vincent Harold Spencer (1986-1965)

Australian Unit and War Histories

White over Green. The 2/4th Battalion and Reference to the 4th Battalion. Edited by The Unit History Editorial Committee, Angus and Robertson. 1963.
Long, G. *Greece, Crete and Syria. Australia in the War of 1939-1945. Series One. Army. Volume II*, Australian War Memorial, Canberra, 1953.
Olson, W. Battalion into Battle. The History of the 2/11th Australian Infantry Battalion. 1939-1945, Wesley John Olsonm, 2011.
The 2/8th Battalion. The 2/8th Battalion Association, Melbourne, 1984.
Trigellis-Smith, S. *All the King's Enemies – A History of the 2/5th Australian Infantry Battalion.* 2/5 Battalion Association, 1988.
Wick, S. *Purple Over Green. The History of the 2/2 Australian Infantry Battalion 1939-1945.* 2/2 Australian Infantry Battalion Association, 1977.

British Official Histories

Hinsley, F.H. *British Intelligence in the Second World War. Volume 1*, Her Majesty's Stationery Office, London, 1979.
Hinsley, F.H. *British Intelligence in the Second World War.* Her Majesty's Stationery Office, London, 1993.

Playfair, Major-General I.S.O. *The Mediterranean and the Middle East. Volume 1. The Early Successes Against Italy (to May 1941).* Her Majesty's Stationery Office, London, 1954.

Playfair, Major-General I.S.O. *The Mediterranean and the Middle East. Volume 2. The Germans Come to Help their Ally (1941).* Her Majesty's Stationery Office, London, 1956.

New Zealand Official Histories

Burdon, R.M. *24 Battalion. Official History of New Zealand in the Second World War 1939-45.* War History Branch, Department of Internal Affairs, New Zealand, 1953.

Cody, J.F. *21 Battalion. Official History of New Zealand in the Second World War 1939-45.* War History Branch, Department of Internal Affairs, New Zealand, 1953.

Cody, J.F. *28 (Maori) Battalion. Official History of New Zealand in the Second World War 1939-45.* War History Branch, Department of Internal Affairs, New Zealand, 1956.

Dawson, W.D. *18 Battalion and Armoured Regiment. Official History of New Zealand in the Second World War 1939-45.* War History Branch, Department of Internal Affairs, New Zealand, 1961.

Documents Relating to New Zealand's Participation in the Second World War 1939-45. Volume I. War History Branch, Department of Internal Affairs, New Zealand, 1949.

Henderson, J. *22 Battalion. Official History of New Zealand in the Second World War 1939-45.* War History Branch, Department of Internal Affairs, New Zealand, 1958.

Kay, R. *27 Machine Gun Battalion. Official History of New Zealand in the Second World War 1939-45.* War History Branch, Department of Internal Affairs, New Zealand, 1958.

Loughnan, R.J.M. *Divisional Cavalry. Official History of New Zealand in the Second World War 1939-45.* War History Branch, Department of Internal Affairs, New Zealand, 1963.

McClymont, W.G. *To Greece. Official History of New Zealand in the Second World War 1939-45.* War History Branch, Department of Internal Affairs, New Zealand, 1959.

Murphy, W.E. *2nd New Zealand Divisional Artillery. Official History of New Zealand in the Second World War 1939-45.* War History Branch, Department of Internal Affairs, New Zealand, 1966.

Norton, F.D. *26 Battalion. Official History of New Zealand in the Second World War 1939-45*. War History Branch, Department of Internal Affairs, New Zealand, 1952.

Pringle, D.J.C. and Glue, W.A. *20 Battalion and Armoured Regiment. Official History of New Zealand in the Second World War 1939-45*. War History Branch, Department of Internal Affairs, New Zealand, 1957.

Puttick, Sir E. *25 Battalion. Official History of New Zealand in the Second World War 1939-45*. War History Branch, Department of Internal Affairs, New Zealand, 1960.

Ross, A. *23 Battalion. Official History of New Zealand in the Second World War 1939-45*. War History Branch, Department of Internal Affairs, New Zealand, 1959.

Sinclair, D.W. *19 Battalion and Armoured Regiment. Official History of New Zealand in the Second World War 1939-45*. War History Branch, Department of Internal Affairs, New Zealand, 1954.

Theses

Mackie, R.K. *Freyberg's High-Command Relationships, 1939-1941*. Master of Philosophy Thesis, Centre for Defence and Strategic Studies, Massey University, Palmerston North, 2014.

Ormond, W.L. *Aspects of the Greek Campaign, April 1941*. Master of Arts Thesis, Defence Studies, Massey University, Palmerston North, 2009.

Wood, P.W., *A Battle to Win: An Analysis of Combat Effectiveness through the Second World War Experience of the 21st (Auckland) Battalion*. Doctor of Philosophy Thesis, Centre for Defence and Strategic Studies, Massey University, Palmerston North, 2012.

Books

Balck, H. *Order in Chaos. The Memoirs of General of Panzer Troops Hermann Balck*. University Press of Kentucky, Lexington, 2015.

Brown, P., *British Cruiser Tanks A8 & A10*. Model Centrum Progres, Warsaw, 2017.

Comeau, M.G. MM. *Operation Mercury. A First Hand Account of the Fall of Crete*. Patrick Stephens Ltd, Sparkford, 1991.

Crisp, R. *The Gods Were Neutral*. Frederick Muller Ltd, London, 1960.

Dahl, R. *Going Solo*. Puffin Books, London, 1988.

Delaforce, P. *Taming the Panzers. Monty's Tank Battalions, 3 RTR at War*. Sutton Publishing, Phoenix Mill, 2000.

Dunn, C. *Permission to Speak*. An Autobiography. Plane Tree, 2001.

Elworthy, J. *Greece Crete Stalag Dachau. A New Zealand Soldier's encounters with Hitler's army*. Awa Press, Wellington, 1994.

Freyberg, P. *Bernard Freyberg, VC : Soldier of Two Nations*. Hodder & Stoughton, London, 1991.

Golla, K.-H. *Der Fall Griechenlands* 1941. Mittler Verlag, Hamburg, 2007.

Greentree, D. *Greece and Crete 1941. New Zealand Infantrymen versus German Motorcycle Soldier*. Osprey Publishing Ltd, Oxford, 2017

Harper, G. *Kippenberger. An Inspired New Zealand Commander*. Harper-Collins, Auckland, 1997.

Henderson, J. *Soldier Country*. Milwood Press Ltd, Wellington, 1978.

Hooton, E.R. *Prelude to the First World War. The Balkan Wars 1912-1913*. Fonthill Media Ltd, Oxford, England, 2014.

Horner, D.M. *High Command. Australia and Allied Strategy 1939-1945*. George Allen & Unwin Pity, Sydney, 1982.

Horner, D.M. *General Vasey's War*, Melbourne University Press, Melbourne, 1992.

Kippenberger, Major General Sir H. *Infantry Brigadier*. Oxford University Press, London, 1949.

Lehmann, R. *The Leibstandarte I. 1 SS Panzer Division Leibstandarte Adolf Hitler*. J.J Fedorowicz Publishing, Winnipeg, 1987.

McLeod, J. *Myth and Reality. The New Zealand Soldier in World War II*. Reed Methuen, Auckland, 1986.

Pugsley, C. *A Bloody Road Home. World War Two and New Zealand's Heroic Second Division*. Penguin Books, Auckland, 2014.

Quassowski, H. *Twelve Years with Hitler. A History of 1. Kompanie Leibstandarte SS Adolf Hitler 1933-1945*. Schffer Military History, Atglen, USA, 1999.

Shores, C., Cull, B. & Malizia, N. *Air War for Yugoslavia, Greece and Crete 1940-41*. Grub Street, London, 1987.

Thompson, P. *Anzac Fury. The Bloody Battle of Crete 1941*. Random House, North Sydney, Australia, 2010.

Time-Life Books Inc., *Conquest of the Balkans*. Joseph L. Ward, 1990.

von Plato, Anton Detlev *Die Geschichte der 5. Panzerdivision 1938-1945*, Walhala und Praetoria Vergag KG Georg Zwickenpflug, Regensburg, 1978.

Wards, I., *The Balkan Dilemma*. In *Kia Kaha. New Zealand in the Second World War*. (ed. Crawford J.) Oxford University Press, Auckland, 2000.

Wheeler, C.M. *Kalamera Kiwi! To Olympus with the New Zealand Engineers*. A.H. and A.W. Reed, Wellington, 1946.

Index

Names

Allen, Brigadier Arthur   46, 73, 104-105, 111, 116, 145, 174
Baillie-Grohman, Rear-Admiral Tom   78,
Balck, Oberstleutnant Hermann   97, 101-102, 105, 111-112, 118, 120-123, 165, 167-170
Bedalls, Lieutenant Jack   124
Blamey, Lieutenant-General Thomas   10-11, 13, 15-16, 18, 22, 24, 37, 60, 62, 65, 69, 74-75, 83, 128, 133, 163, 174, 177-178
Böhme, Generalleutnant Franz   34, 123, 175, 184
Cavanagh, Sergeant Daniel   110-111, 170
Chilton, Lieutenant-Colonel Henry   19, 104, 108, 111-115, 144, 166-167
Cincar-Marković, Foreign Minister Lazar   27-28
Charrington, Brigadier Harold   10, 17, 25, 38, 150, 154, 169, 173, 180
Churchill, Prime Minister Winston   10, 12-13, 15, 78, 140, 157, 176
Clowes, Brigadier Cyril   74, 102-103, 166
Cole, Lieutenant Darcy   41, 42
Comeau, Aircraftsman Marcel   72
Crisp, Lieutenant Robert   45, 53-54, 56 59, 80, 147, 149
Crystal, Lieutenant Cec   44
Cullen, Major   143, 144
Cunningham, Admiral Sir John   14, 19-22, 133
Cvetković, Premier Dragisha   27-28
Dahl, Pilot Officer Roald   131-132
Dale, Captain Richard   37, 83
Dean, Captain H. A.   145, 148
Dickinson, Lieutenant Allen   136
Dietrich, General Sepp   124, 175, 183

Dougherty, Lieutenant-Colonel Ivan   40, 50-51
Dunn, Clive   158
Eden, Foreign Secretary Anthony   12-14, 25, 27
Elliott Jack   38, 85, 94
Elworthy, Jack   9, 86, 90
Franklin, Sergeant John   114
Fraser, Prime Minister Peter   11, 36
Fend, Obersturmführer   52, 55
Freyberg, Major-General Bernard   10-11, 24, 73, 83, 89, 98, 111-112, 127, 134-135, 145, 149-150, 152, 157, 165-166, 173, 179-180
Guinn, Major Henry   70
Gunn, Sergeant Jeffrey   114
Harford, Captain Roy   147-148
Hargest, Brigadier James   83, 173
Hinton, Sergeant Jack   159
Hitler, Chancellor of Germany Adolf   1-9, 17, 27-29, 40
Iachino, Admiral Angelo   19-21
King, Lieutenant-Colonel Roy   81
Kippenberger, Lieutenant-Colonel Howard   78, 80, 92, 166
Koryzis, Prime Minister Alexander   10, 12
Lavarack, Lieutenant-General John   10, 163
List, Generalfeldmarschall Wilhelm   34, 123, 175, 181-182
Longmore, Air Chief Marshall Arthur   9, 14
McCarthy, Jack   62
Macky, Lieutenant-Colonel Neil   97-99, 101-106, 108, 111, 166-168
MacKay, Major-General Iven   6, 38, 40, 46, 59, 65, 136, 174, 178-179
Mitchell, Lieutenant-Colonel John   41, 46, 48-49

Metaxas, Prime Minister General
    Ioannis   4, 9-10, 62
Menzies, Prime Minister
    Robert   4, 9-10-13, 16
Mussolini, Prime Minister Beneto   xiv-xv,
    1-6, 27-28
O'Neill, Lieutenant Michael   109
Page, Lieutenant-Colonel James   77
Papagos, General Alexander   9, 12, 14, 24,
    36-37, 46, 65, 78, 123-124, 174, 181
Parkinson, Lieutenant-Colonel 'Ike'   104,
    111, 115, 167
Pfeffer, Karl   42
Pridham-Wippell, Rear-Admiral
    Henry   20-21, 128
Puttick, Brigadier
    Edward   150, 154-155, 173
Robinson, Lieutenant Hugh   83, 92-93
Rowell, Brigadier Sydney   24, 74-75, 102
Russell, Major John   104, 112, 116-117, 119
Sandover, Major Ray   138-139
Savige, Brigadier Stanley   65, 145, 174
Schörner, Generalmajor
    Ferdinand   102, 175, 185
Schulze, Hauptsturmführer   48
Spencer, Harry   42
Sturm, Colonel Alfred   147
Stumme, Generalleutnant Georg   34, 55,
    69, 123, 127, 135, 150, 164, 175, 182-183
Tsolakogou, General Georgios   123-124
von Hubkicki, Generalleutnant
    Alfred   69, 175, 183
von Ribbentrop, Foreign Minister
    Joachim   27, 29
von Sponeck, Colonel Graf   67-68
Vasey, Brigadier George   37, 48-50, 76-77,
    130, 138, 174
Wavell, General Archibald   3, 6, 8-13, 15,
    18-19, 35, 78, 123, 128, 133, 140, 170,
    176, 178
Weiser, Major   108, 110
Wheeler, Chas   22-23, 86
White, Frank   116
Wilson, General Henry Maitland   12-13
    18, 24, 36-37, 46, 64-65, 70, 73, 78,
    116, 123, 133, 139, 145-147, 152, 173,
    176-178

Places

Albania
    Epirus   4-5, 65, 123
    Kalamas River   5
    Pindus Range   5

Crete
    Maleme   4, 21
    Suda Bay   3-4, 19, 152-153, 157, 186

Greece
    Aliákmon River   23-24, 37-38, 49,
        57-59, 61-62, 65, 69, 76, 82-84, 163
    Aliákmon Line   12, 14, 22, 23, 37, 46,
        63, 71, 83
    Aliákmon-Venetikos Line   61, 81
    Ambelakia   103, 168
    Amyntaio   25, 37-38, 49, 54, 188
    Argos   131, 133, 136, 145-146, 148-149
    Athens   5, 9, 12, 14, 24, 34, 37, 41, 46,
        52, 64, 70, 73, 78, 81, 84, 97, 123, 127-
        128, 130, 133, 135, 145, 147, 150-151,
        154, 161, 164, 181
    Ay Dhimitrios   88-89
    Brallos   65, 124,127-128, 130, 133-134,
        138-139
    Corinth   131, 145, 147-149, 154-155
    Corinth Canal   1, 131, 133, 145-146,
        149-150
    Delphi   130-131
    Delphi Pass   65, 128, 131
    Domokos   70, 72-73, 76, 81, 94, 124-
        125, 139, 189
    Edessa   83
    Edessa Pass   24-25
    Elasson   24, 72-74, 77, 83, 85, 90, 93,
        112
    Eleusis   125, 131, 133, 145, 151
    Euboea   128, 130-131, 150
    Evangelismos   104, 110, 113-114, 143
    Florina   24-25, 34, 37, 40-41, 45-46, 65
    Glyphada   127
    Gonos   102, 106, 108
    Grevená   59, 61, 65, 69, 80, 82, 123,
        139, 164, 188
    Kalabaka   69, 74, 81-82, 123, 125-126,
        139, 164, 169, 189

Kalamata 133, 149, 152-153, 155, 157-161, 191-192
Katerini 24, 37-38, 66, 75, 84, 97, 106, 164-165, 169
Khalkis 36, 127, 150
Kleidi Pass 37, 40, 45, 54-55
Klisoura Pass 37, 65
Kozani 65-66, 69, 164, 188
Kriekouki 128, 133, 145, 149-150
Lamia 80, 90, 94, 96, 103, 120, 124-129, 133, 139, 165, 188-189
Larissa
Makrikhorion 25, 40-41, 65, 70, 72-74, 76, 79-81, 84, 89, 93-94, 96-97, 102, 104, 111-112, 115-121, 123-125, 139, 162, 164-165, 169-170, 188
Malaoi 157
Marathon 128, 133
Markopoulon 151, 154
Matapan 22, 163, 186
Megara 128, 131, 146, 150, 190
Menidi 125, 130
Metaxas Line 12, 29, 34-36, 185
Molos 96, 128, 130, 134-138 164
Monastir Gap 24-25, 29, 36, 61
Monemvasia 149, 152, 157, 192
Mount Olympus 9, 12, 23, 73, 82-83, 97, 102, 105
Moskhokori 64
Myloi 145, 147, 149, 152, 191-192
Navplion 143, 152, 155, 157, 190-191
Nestos River 34
Olympus Pass 23-24, 37, 61, 82-86, 89-90, 92, 96, 123, 164
Panteleimonas 98-101, 105
Patras 131, 149, 193
Phársala 73, 81, 126-127, 139
Peloponnese 24, 133, 145, 149
Lake Petron 40, 45, 49
Pineios River 69, 81, 101, 103-105, 107-108, 117, 120-121, 123, 166, 170
Pineios Gorge 74, 97-98, 102, 111, 120, 131, 143, 166-168
Pineios Valley 165, 167, 170
Piraeus 17, 19, 35-36, 65, 127, 141, 155, 163, 190

Platamon 37, 61, 74, 83, 96-98, 102, 120-121, 165-166
Porto Rafti 141, 145, 151, 154, 190-191
Ptolemais 41, 56, 57, 60-61, 69, 163, 188
Rafina 145, 151, 154-155, 191
Salonika 9, 12, 14, 24, 27, 34-36, 83, 164
Servia 61-62, 66-69, 73-75, 78, 85, 164
Servia Pass 25, 37-38, 61, 65, 69, 72-74, 82-83, 92-93, 96, 123, 141, 163
Sotir 38, 49, 51, 53-54, 59-61, 65, 163
Spercheios River 127, 129, 133-134
Struma River 12
Tirnavos 73, 90, 94
Thermopylae 65, 73, 78, 81-82, 89-90, 98, 111, 120, 124, 127, 133-134, 136
Thermopylae Line 91, 97, 123, 130, 132, 139, 164
Tolos 152, 155-156, 191
Trikkala 69, 73, 75, 104, 112, 169, 189
Tripolis 145, 149, 155-157
Vardar Valley 29, 38
Vale of Tempe 74, 97, 121, 123
Tempe 69, 90, 102-105, 108-109, 111-113, 117, 165
Lake Vegorritis 40, 45, 53
Venetikos River 37, 59, 65, 69-70, 169, 188
Veria Pass 37, 61-62
Veria 41, 62
Vevi 37, 41, 43, 45, 47, 62, 84
Vermion Range 12, 37, 62, 64, 82, 96
Volos 12, 36, 40, 73, 80, 89, 120, 124, 139, 143, 165
Xinon Neron 41, 44, 51-52

Yugoslavia
Belgrade 14, 27-33, 36, 78, 162
Sarajevo 31-32
Zagreb 31

Units

Allied

W-Force 12, 16-19, 24-25, 34-39, 59-61, 123, 128, 133, 139-140, 145, 149, 152, 161, 163, 172-173

Lustreforce   13
Allen Force   104, 111, 113, 115, 169
Savige Force   70, 73-74, 81, 111,
    120, 122, 164
MacKay Force   40, 45, 59, 62
Amyntaio Detachment   37
Anzac Corps   63-65, 74, 82-83, 97, 102,
    104, 123-124, 127, 133, 165-166, 178, 190
1 Armoured Brigade   10, 17-18, 24,
    Brigade Headquarters Squadron   37,
        150, 169, 189
    3 Royal Tank Regiment   17, 25, 37, 45,
        53, 55-56, 59, 80, 127, 147, 149, 152,
        157-158, 163-164, 169, 173, 186, 188
    4 Queen's Own Hussars   17, 25, 49, 53,
        57, 59, 127, 131, 134, 145, 149, 155,
        158, 173, 186
    102 Anti-Tank Regiment   45, 53, 127,
        173
    1 Rangers King's Rifle Corps   45-49,
        52-53, 57, 60, 127, 163, 173, 186
    2 Royal Horse Artillery   25, 49, 53, 127,
        173
64 Medium Regiment   37, 90, 93, 141,
    186, 190
6 Australian Division   6, 10, 18, 22, 25,
    38, 60, 73, 136, 163, 174, 186, 187
    2/1 Australian Machine Gun
        Battalion   36, 61, 126, 130, 174
    2/1 Anti-Tank Regiment   47, 52, 69,
        111, 174
    2/2 Australian Field Regiment   111,
        128, 130, 134, 138, 174
    2/3 Australian Field Regiment   76, 90,
        93, 174
    2/1 Australian Field Company   64, 76,
        104
    16 Australian Brigade   19, 25, 37,
        61-62, 73-75, 125, 174
        2/1 Australian Battalion   64, 75, 111,
            130, 139, 174
        2/2 Australian Battalion   62, 64, 69,
            104, 108, 111-116, 119, 121, 124,
            143-144, 166, 174
        2/3 Australian Battalion   62, 64, 74,
            104, 112, 114-115, 118, 130, 167,
            174

17 Australian Brigade   65, 69-70, 133,
    145, 149, 153
    2/5 Australian Battalion   69-70, 81,
        125, 131, 141, 174
    2/6 Australian Battalion   72, 125-
        126, 145, 148-149, 174
    2/7 Australian Battalion   72, 126, 174
19 Australian Brigade   25, 37, 16, 73,
    76-77, 146, 174
    2/4 Australian Battalion   19, 40, 43,
        49-50, 76, 138, 146, 174
    2/8 Australian Battalion   43-44,
        46-47, 49, 59, 127, 130, 139, 163, 174
    2/11 Australian Battalion   65, 69, 81,
        116, 124-125, 134, 138, 174
7 Australian Division   2, 10, 18, 22, 35,
    60, 163
2 New Zealand Division   10, 18, 24, 37,
    73, 83, 111, 127, 141, 173, 180, 190
    2 NZ Divisional Cavalry   18, 24, 37,
        40-41, 74, 78, 83-84, 89-90, 92-93,
        104, 116, 126, 128, 130-131, 146, 149,
        151-152, 155, 157, 173, 186
    4 NZ Field Regiment   104, 112, 115-
        116, 151, 157, 173, 186
    5 NZ Field Regiment   83-84, 87, 89-90,
        93, 97, 114, 127, 133, 138, 173, 186
    7 NZ Anti-Tank Regiment   83, 89, 104,
        127, 138, 173
        32 Anti-Tank Battery   61
    27 NZ MG Battalion   37, 52-53, 89,
        136, 173, 186
    4 NZ Brigade   18, 24, 37-38, 61-62, 73,
        78, 80, 82-83, 89, 127-128, 130, 133,
        145, 149-150, 153-154, 173
        18 NZ Battalion   18, 61, 68, 78, 173,
            186
        19 NZ Battalion   61, 66-69, 78, 128,
            130, 147, 173, 186
        20 NZ Battalion   61, 66, 78, 154, 173,
            186
    5 NZ Brigade   2, 19, 24, 61, 73, 82-83,
        85, 89-90, 127, 130, 135, 141, 173
        21 NZ Battalion   37, 73-74, 83, 97,
            100-102, 104-105, 108-109, 112,
            115-116, 120-121, 166-167, 170,
            173, 186

22 NZ Battalion   85, 87-88, 127-128, 146, 173, 186

23 NZ Battalion   83, 88-89, 133, 173, 186

28 (Maori) Battalion   83, 133, 146, 148, 173, 186

6 NZ Brigade   18, 22, 24, 37-38, 61, 64, 73, 83, 85, 90, 93, 111, 120, 122, 127-128, 138, 145, 149, 157, 173

24 NZ Battalion   38, 90, 93, 128-94, 149, 173

25 NZ Battalion   38, 85, 90, 93, 124, 128, 135, 137-138, 145, 156, 173, 186

26 NZ Battalion   38, 66, 76-77, 83, 90, 93-94, 128, 148-149, 156, 173, 186

RAF

33 Squadron   72

113 Squadron   72

80 Squadron   125

208 Squadron   125

Royal Navy ships

Battle of Matapan:

HMS *Formidable*   20-21

Warspite   20-22

Ajax   20-22, 128, 154, 157, 191-192

Orion   20-21, 128, 152, 191,

Greyhound   21

Barnham   20-21

Valiant   20-21

HMAS *Perth*   20, 128, 141, 152, 160, 190-192

Evacuation:

HMS *Glengyle*   128, 141, 151, 190-191

Ulster Prince   143, 152, 190

Glenearn   128, 143, 152, 190

Slamat   152-153, 191

Wryneck   153, 190

Diamond   153, 191

SS *Costa Rica*   152-153, 191

SS *Clan Fraser*   187

Greek Units:

19 Motorised Division   24, 174

12 Infantry Division   24-25, 37, 57, 64, 174

19 Greek Division   36

20 Infantry Division   64, 174

Greek Cavalry Regiment   40

Greek Cavalry Division   64

Cree Division   4

Axis

Centauro Division   5

Luftwaffe

Fliegerkorps VIII   26

LI. Corps   31

14. Panzer-Division   31-32

XLVI. Panzer-Corps   30-31

16. Motorisiert-Infanterie-Division   31

XLI. Panzer-Corps   31-32

8. Panzer-Division   31-32

XIV. Panzer-Korps   31

5. Panzer-Division   31, 69, 80, 123, 125-127, 139, 154-155, 158, 164, 175

9. Auflklarungs-Abteilung   150

I/31. Panzer-Regiment   134, 150

47. Panzerjäger-Abteilung   154

11. Panzer-Division   31

Panzer-Regiment 'Hermann Göring'   32

XII. Armee   30, 34, 123, 175

XL. Panzer-Korps   26, 31, 34-36, 80, 123, 168, 175

9. Panzer-Division   35, 45, 47, 54, 57, 66, 69, 175, 183

59. Kradschutzen-Bataillon   68

73. Infanterie-Division   35, 175

Leibstandarte SS Adolf Hitler (LSSAH)   40, 42-48, 52, 54-55, 124, 126, 139, 154, 164, 183

11. Infanterie-Regiment   67

XVIII. Gebirgs-Korps   26, 34-35, 83, 123, 150, 175

2. Panzer-Division   34-36, 84-85, 97-98, 106, 121, 123, 126-127, 139, 165, 170, 175, 184, 193

I/3. Panzer-Regiment   99, 102, 121, 168

II/3. Panzer-Regiment   84, 92

2. Kradschützen-Bataillon   99, 150, 154

72. Infanterie-Division   88, 135, 137-138, 175

5. Gebirgsjäger-Division   35, 175,
    185
6. Gebirgs-Division   35, 97, 102,
    105, 127, 175, 185
    Aufklärungs-Abteilung 112   102,
        105, 109, 112, 135
    II/143
        Gebirgsjäger-Regiment   108
    I/143. Gebirgsjäger-Regiment   106,
        108, 110, 113, 117
    I/141. Gebirgsjäger-
        Regiment   113-114
    II/141. Gebirgsjäger-
        Regiment   138-139
    8/800. Brandenberg-
        Regiment   108-109
    Infanterie-Regiment 120   127
55. Kradschützen-Bataillon   129-130,
    132, 134, 138
XXX. Infanterie-Korps   34, 175
Fallschirmjäger-Regiment 2   147

Italian Navy at Matapan:
    Vittorio Veneto   19, 21-22
    Zara   19, 21-22
    Fiume   19, 21-22
    Pola   19, 21-22

Operations

Ultra   6-7, 17, 19, 34, 82, 162
Operation Lustre   17, 34, 171
Operation Marita   8, 27, 29-30, 35
Operation Demon   78
Unternehmen Strafgericht   29